143

Concord Edition

THE COMPLETE WORKS OF RALPH WALDO EMERSON

WITH A BIOGRAPHICAL INTRODUCTION AND NOTES BY

EDWARD WALDO EMERSON AND A GENERAL INDEX

ILLUSTRATED WITH PHOTOGRAVURES

VOLUME II

1854

Ralph Waldo Emerson in 1854

ESSAYS

BY

RALPH WALDO EMERSON

FIRST SERIES

BOSTON AND NEW YORK
HOUGHTON, MIFFLIN AND COMPANY
The Riverside Press, Cambridge
1904

CONTENTS

LIST OF ILLUSTRATIONS

I

HISTORY

THERE is no great and no small
To the Soul that maketh all :
And where it cometh, all things are ;
And it cometh everywhere.

I am owner of the sphere,
Of the seven stars and the solar year,
Of Cæsar's hand, and Plato's brain,
Of Lord Christ's heart, and Shakspeare's strain.[1]

HISTORY

THERE is one mind common to all individual men. Every man is an inlet to
the same and to all of the same. He that is
once admitted to the right of reason is made a
freeman of the whole estate. What Plato has
thought, he may think ; what a saint has felt,
he may feel; what at any time has befallen any
man, he can understand. Who hath access to
this universal mind is a party to all that is or
can be done, for this is the only and sovereign
agent.

Of the works of this mind history is the
record. Its genius is illustrated by the entire
series of days. Man is explicable by nothing less
than all his history. Without hurry, without
rest, the human spirit goes forth from the beginning to embody every faculty, every thought,
every emotion which belongs to it, in appropriate events. But the thought is always prior
to the fact ; all the facts of history preexist in
the mind as laws. Each law in turn is made by
circumstances predominant, and the limits of
nature give power to but one at a time. A man
is the whole encyclopædia of facts. The creation

laws derive hence their ultimate reason; all
express more or less distinctly some command
of this supreme, illimitable essence. Property
also holds of the soul, covers great spiritual
facts, and instinctively we at first hold to it with
swords and laws and wide and complex com-
binations. The obscure consciousness of this
fact is the light of all our day, the claim of
claims; the plea for education, for justice, for
charity; the foundation of friendship and love
and of the heroism and grandeur which belong
to acts of self-reliance. It is remarkable that
involuntarily we always read as superior beings.
Universal history, the poets, the romancers, do
not in their stateliest pictures, — in the sacer-
dotal, the imperial palaces, in the triumphs of
will or of genius, — anywhere lose our ear, anywhere make us feel that we intrude, that this
is for better men; but rather is it true that in
their grandest strokes we feel most at home.
All that Shakspeare says of the king, yonder
slip of a boy that reads in the corner feels to
be true of himself.[1] We sympathize in the great
moments of history, in the great discoveries,
the great resistances, the great prosperities of
men; — because there law was enacted, the sea
was searched, the land was found, or the blow

was struck, *for us,* as we ourselves in that place would have done or applauded.

We have the same interest in condition and character. We honor the rich because they have externally the freedom, power, and grace which we feel to be proper to man, proper to us. So all that is said of the wise man by Stoic or Oriental or modern essayist, describes to each reader his own idea, describes his unattained but attainable self. All literature writes the character of the wise man. Books, monuments, pictures, conversation, are portraits in which he finds the lineaments he is forming. The silent and the eloquent praise him and accost him, and he is stimulated wherever he moves, as by personal allusions. A true aspirant therefore never needs look for allusions personal and laudatory in discourse. He hears the commendation, not of himself, but, more sweet, of that character he seeks, in every word that is said concerning character, yea further in every fact and circumstance, — in the running river and the rustling corn. Praise is looked, homage tendered, love flows, from mute nature, from the mountains and the lights of the firmament.[1]

These hints, dropped as it were from sleep and night, let us use in broad day. The student is to read history actively and not passively; to esteem his own life the text, and books the commentary. Thus compelled, the Muse of history will utter oracles, as never to those who do not respect themselves. I have no expectation that any man will read history aright who thinks that what was done in a remote age, by men whose names have resounded far, has any deeper sense than what he is doing to-day.[1]

The world exists for the education of each man. There is no age or state of society or mode of action in history to which there is not somewhat corresponding in his life. Every thing tends in a wonderful manner to abbreviate itself and yield its own virtue to him. He should see that he can live all history in his own person. He must sit solidly at home, and not suffer himself to be bullied by kings or empires, but know that he is greater than all the geography and all the government of the world; he must transfer the point of view from which history is commonly read, from Rome and Athens and London, to himself, and not deny his conviction that he is the court, and if England or Egypt have anything to say to him he will try the case; if not, let them forever be silent. He must attain and maintain that lofty sight where facts yield their secret sense, and poetry and annals are alike. The instinct of the mind, the purpose of nature, betrays itself in the use we make of the signal narrations of history. Time dissipates to shining ether the solid angularity of facts. No anchor, no cable, no fences avail to keep a fact a fact. Babylon, Troy, Tyre, Palestine, and even early Rome are passing already into fiction. The Garden of Eden, the sun standing still in Gibeon, is poetry thenceforward to all nations. Who cares what the fact was, when we have made a constellation of it to hang in heaven an immortal sign? London and Paris and New York must go the same way. "What is history," said Napoleon, "but a fable agreed upon?" This life of ours is stuck round with Egypt, Greece, Gaul, England, War, Colonization, Church, Court and Commerce, as with so many flowers and wild ornaments grave and gay. I will not make more account of them. I believe in Eternity.[1] I can find Greece, Asia, Italy, Spain and the Islands, — the genius and creative principle of each and of all eras, in my own mind.

We are always coming up with the emphatic facts of history in our private experience and

verifying them here. All history becomes subjective; in other words there is properly no
history, only biography. Every mind must
know the whole lesson for itself, — must go
over the whole ground. What it does not see,
what it does not live, it will not know. What
the former age has epitomized into a formula
or rule for manipular convenience, it will lose
all the good of verifying for itself, by means of
the wall of that rule. Somewhere, sometime,
it will demand and find compensation for that
loss, by doing the work itself. Ferguson discovered many things in astronomy which had
long been known. The better for him.

History must be this or it is nothing. Every
law which the state enacts indicates a fact in
human nature; that is all. We must in ourselves see the necessary reason of every fact, —
see how it could and must be. So stand before every public and private work; before an
oration of Burke, before a victory of Napoleon, before a martyrdom of Sir Thomas More,
of Sidney, of Marmaduke Robinson;[1] before a
French Reign of Terror, and a Salem hanging
of witches; before a fanatic Revival and the
Animal Magnetism in Paris, or in Providence.
We assume that we under like influence should

be alike affected, and should achieve the like;
and we aim to master intellectually the steps
and reach the same height or the same degradation that our fellow, our proxy has done.

All inquiry into antiquity, all curiosity re-
specting the Pyramids, the excavated cities,
Stonehenge, the Ohio Circles, Mexico, Mem-
phis, — is the desire to do away this wild,
savage, and preposterous There or Then, and
introduce in its place the Here and the Now.
Belzoni digs and measures in the mummy-pits
and pyramids of Thebes until he can see the
end of the difference between the monstrous
work and himself. When he has satisfied himself, in general and in detail, that it was made
by such a person as he, so armed and so mo-
tived, and to ends to which he himself should
also have worked, the problem is solved; his
thought lives along the whole line of temples
and sphinxes and catacombs, passes through
them all with satisfaction, and they live again
to the mind, or are *now*.

A Gothic cathedral affirms that it was done
by us and not done by us. Surely it was by
man, but we find it not in our man. But we
apply ourselves to the history of its production.
We put ourselves into the place and state of

the builder. We remember the forest-dwellers, the first temples, the adherence to the first type, and the decoration of it as the wealth of the nation increased ; the value which is given to wood by carving led to the carving over the whole mountain of stone of a cathedral. When we have gone through this process, and added thereto the Catholic Church, its cross, its music, its processions, its Saints' days and image-worship, we have as it were been the man that made the minster ; we have seen how it could and must be. We have the sufficient reason.[1]

The difference between men is in their principle of association. Some men classify objects by color and size and other accidents of appearance; others by intrinsic likeness, or by the relation of cause and effect. The progress of the intellect is to the clearer vision of causes, which neglects surface differences. To the poet, to the philosopher, to the saint, all things are friendly and sacred, all events profitable, all days holy, all men divine. For the eye is fastened on the life, and slights the circumstance. Every chemical substance, every plant, every animal in its growth, teaches the unity of cause, the variety of appearance.

Upborne and surrounded as we are by this

all-creating nature, soft and fluid as a cloud or
the air, why should we be such hard pedants,
and magnify a few forms? Why should we make
account of time, or of magnitude, or of figure?
The soul knows them not, and genius, obeying
its law, knows how to play with them as a young
child plays with graybeards and in churches.
Genius studies the causal thought, and far back
in the womb of things sees the rays parting from
one orb, that diverge, ere they fall, by infinite
diameters. Genius watches the monad through
all his masks as he performs the metempsychosis
of nature. Genius detects through the fly, through
the caterpillar, through the grub, through the
egg, the constant individual; through count-
less individuals the fixed species; through many
species the genus; through all genera the stead-
fast type; through all the kingdoms of organ-
ized life the eternal unity. Nature is a mutable
cloud which is always and never the same. She
casts the same thought into troops of forms, as
a poet makes twenty fables with one moral.
Through the bruteness and toughness of matter, a subtle spirit bends all things to its own
will. The adamant streams into soft but precise
form before it, and whilst I look at it its outline
and texture are changed again. Nothing is so

fleeting as form ; yet never does it quite deny
itself. In man we still trace the remains or hints
of all that we esteem badges of servitude in the
lower races ; yet in him they enhance his nobleness and grace ; as Io, in Æschylus, transformed
to a cow, offends the imagination; but how
changed when as Isis in Egypt she meets Osi-
ris-Jove, a beautiful woman with nothing of the
metamorphosis left but the lunar horns as the
splendid ornament of her brows !

The identity of history is equally intrinsic,
the diversity equally obvious. There is, at the
surface, infinite variety of things ; at the centre
there is simplicity of cause. How many are
the acts of one man in which we recognize the
same character ! Observe the sources of our information in respect to the Greek genius. We
have the *civil history* of that people, as Herodotus, Thucydides, Xenophon, and Plutarch have
given it ; a very sufficient account of what manner of persons they were and what they did.
We have the same national mind expressed for
us again in their *literature*, in epic and lyric
poems, drama, and philosophy ; a very complete
form. Then we have it once more in their
architecture, a beauty as of temperance itself,
limited to the straight line and the square, — a

builded geometry. Then we have it once again in *sculpture*, the "tongue on the balance of expression," a multitude of forms in the utmost freedom of action and never transgressing the ideal serenity; like votaries performing some religious dance before the gods, and, though in convulsive pain or mortal combat, never daring to break the figure and decorum of their dance. Thus of the genius of one remarkable people we have a fourfold representation: and to the senses what more unlike than an ode of Pindar, a marble centaur, the peristyle of the Parthenon, and the last actions of Phocion? [1]

Every one must have observed faces and forms which, without any resembling feature, make a like impression on the beholder. A particular picture or copy of verses, if it do not awaken the same train of images, will yet superinduce the same sentiment as some wild mountain walk, although the resemblance is nowise obvious to the senses, but is occult and out of the reach of the understanding. Nature is an endless combination and repetition of a very few laws. She hums the old well-known air through innumerable variations. [2]

Nature is full of a sublime family likeness throughout her works, and delights in startling

us with resemblances in the most unexpected
quarters. I have seen the head of an old sachem
of the forest which at once reminded the eye of
a bald mountain summit, and the furrows of the
brow suggested the strata of the rock. There
are men whose manners have the same essential
splendor as the simple and awful sculpture on
the friezes of the Parthenon and the remains of
the earliest Greek art. And there are compositions of the same strain to be found in the books
of all ages. What is Guido's Rospigliosi Aurora but a morning thought, as the horses in it
are only a morning cloud?¹ If any one will but
take pains to observe the variety of actions to
which he is equally inclined in certain moods
of mind, and those to which he is averse, he
will see how deep is the chain of affinity.

A painter told me that nobody could draw a
tree without in some sort becoming a tree; or
draw a child by studying the outlines of its form
merely, — but by watching for a time his motions and plays, the painter enters into his nature and can then draw him at will in every
attitude. So Roos "entered into the inmost
nature of a sheep." I knew a draughtsman em-
ployed in a public survey who found that he
could not sketch the rocks until their geological

structure was first explained to him. In a certain state of thought is the common origin of very diverse works. It is the spirit and not the fact that is identical. By a deeper apprehension, and not primarily by a painful acquisition of many manual skills, the artist attains the power of awakening other souls to a given activity.

It has been said that "common souls pay with what they do, nobler souls with that which they are." And why? Because a profound nature awakens in us by its actions and words, by its very looks and manners, the same power and beauty that a gallery of sculpture or of pictures addresses.

Civil and natural history, the history of art and of literature, must be explained from individual history, or must remain words. There is nothing but is related to us, nothing that does not interest us, — kingdom, college, tree, horse, or iron shoe, — the roots of all things are in man. Santa Croce and the Dome of St. Peter's are lame copies after a divine model.[1] Strasburg Cathedral is a material counterpart of the soul of Erwin of Steinbach. The true poem is the poet's mind; the true ship is the ship-builder. In the man, could we lay him open, we should see the reason for the last

II

flourish and tendril of his work; as every spine
and tint in the sea-shell preexists in the secreting
organs of the fish. The whole of heraldry and
of chivalry is in courtesy. A man of fine manners shall pronounce your name with all the
ornament that titles of nobility could ever add.

The trivial experience of every day is always
verifying some old prediction to us and converting into things the words and signs which
we had heard and seen without heed. A lady
with whom I was riding in the forest said to me
that the woods always seemed to her *to wait*, as
if the genii who inhabit them suspended their
deeds until the wayfarer had passed onward;
a thought which poetry has celebrated in the
dance of the fairies, which breaks off on the approach of human feet. The man who has seen
the rising moon break out of the clouds at midnight, has been present like an archangel at the
creation of light and of the world. I remember
one summer day in the fields my companion
pointed out to me a broad cloud, which might
extend a quarter of a mile parallel to the horizon, quite accurately in the form of a cherub as
painted over churches, — a round block in the
centre, which it was easy to animate with eyes
and mouth, supported on either side by wide-

stretched symmetrical wings. What appears
once in the atmosphere may appear often, and
it was undoubtedly the archetype of that familiar ornament. I have seen in the sky a chain
of summer lightning which at once showed to
me that the Greeks drew from nature when
they painted the thunderbolt in the hand of
Jove. I have seen a snow-drift along the sides
of the stone wall which obviously gave the idea
of the common architectural scroll to abut a
tower.[1]

By surrounding ourselves with the original
circumstances we invent anew the orders and
the ornaments of architecture, as we see how
each people merely decorated its primitive
abodes. The Doric temple preserves the semblance of the wooden cabin in which the Dorian
dwelt. The Chinese pagoda is plainly a Tartar
tent. The Indian and Egyptian temples still
betray the mounds and subterranean houses
of their forefathers. " The custom of making
houses and tombs in the living rock," says
Heeren in his Researches on the Ethiopians,
" determined very naturally the principal character of the Nubian Egyptian architecture to
the colossal form which it assumed. In these
caverns, already prepared by nature, the eye

was accustomed to dwell on huge shapes and masses, so that when art came to the assistance of nature it could not move on a small scale without degrading itself. What would statues of the usual size, or neat porches and wings have been, associated with those gigantic halls before which only Colossi could sit as watchmen or lean on the pillars of the interior?"

The Gothic church plainly originated in a rude adaptation of the forest trees, with all their boughs, to a festal or solemn arcade; as the bands about the cleft pillars still indicate the green withes that tied them. No one can walk in a road cut through pine woods, without being struck with the architectural appearance of the grove, especially in winter, when the barrenness of all other trees shows the low arch of the Saxons. In the woods in a winter afternoon one will see as readily the origin of the stained glass window, with which the Gothic cathedrals are adorned, in the colors of the western sky seen through the bare and crossing branches of the forest. Nor can any lover of nature enter the old piles of Oxford and the English cathedrals, without feeling that the forest overpowered the mind of the builder, and that his chisel, his saw and plane still reproduced its ferns, its

spikes of flowers, its locust, elm, oak, pine, fir
and spruce.[1]

The Gothic cathedral is a blossoming in stone
subdued by the insatiable demand of harmony
in man. The mountain of granite blooms into
an eternal flower, with the lightness and delicate
finish as well as the aerial proportions and per-
spective of vegetable beauty.

In like manner all public facts are to be indi-
vidualized, all private facts are to be general-
ized. Then at once History becomes fluid and
true, and Biography deep and sublime. As the
Persian imitated in the slender shafts and capi-
tals of his architecture the stem and flower of
the lotus and palm, so the Persian court in its
magnificent era never gave over the nomadism
of its barbarous tribes, but travelled from Ec-
batana, where the spring was spent, to Susa in
summer and to Babylon for the winter.

In the early history of Asia and Africa, No·
madism and Agriculture are the two antagonist facts. The geography of Asia and of Africa
necessitated a nomadic life. But the nomads
were the terror of all those whom the soil or the
advantages of a market had induced to build
towns. Agriculture therefore was a religious
injunction, because of the perils of the state

from nomadism. And in these late and civil
countries of England and America these pro-
pensities still fight out the old battle, in the
nation and in the individual. The nomads of
Africa were constrained to wander, by the attacks of the gad-fly, which drives the cattle mad,
and so compels the tribe to emigrate in the
rainy season and to drive off the cattle to the
higher sandy regions. The nomads of Asia follow the pasturage from month to month. In
America and Europe the nomadism is of trade
and curiosity ; a progress, certainly, from the
gad-fly of Astaboras[1] to the Anglo and Italo-
mania of Boston Bay.[2] Sacred cities, to which
a periodical religious pilgrimage was enjoined,
or stringent laws and customs tending to invigorate the national bond, were the check on the
old rovers ; and the cumulative values of long
residence are the restraints on the itinerancy of
the present day. The antagonism of the two
tendencies is not less active in individuals, as
the love of adventure or the love of repose happens to predominate. A man of rude health and
flowing spirits has the faculty of rapid domestication, lives in his wagon and roams through all latitudes as easily as a Calmuc.[3] At sea, or in the
forest, or in the snow, he sleeps as warm, dines

with as good appetite, and associates as happily
as beside his own chimneys. Or perhaps his
facility is deeper seated, in the increased range
of his faculties of observation, which yield him
points of interest wherever fresh objects meet
his eyes. The pastoral nations were needy and
hungry to desperation; and this intellectual
nomadism, in its excess, bankrupts the mind
through the dissipation of power on a miscellany
of objects. The home-keeping wit, on the other
hand, is that continence or content which finds
all the elements of life in its own soil; and
which has its own perils of monotony and de-
terioration, if not stimulated by foreign infu-
sions.'

Every thing the individual sees without him
corresponds to his states of mind, and every
thing is in turn intelligible to him, as his onward
thinking leads him into the truth to which that
fact or series belongs.

The primeval world, — the Fore-World, as
the Germans say, — I can dive to it in myself
as well as grope for it with researching fingers
in catacombs, libraries, and the broken reliefs
and torsos of ruined villas.

What is the foundation of that interest all
men feel in Greek history, letters, art and poetry,

in all its periods from the Heroic or Homeric
age down to the domestic life of the Atheni-
ans and Spartans, four or five centuries later?
What but this, that every man passes personally
through a Grecian period. The Grecian state is
the era of the bodily nature, the perfection of
the senses, — of the spiritual nature unfolded
in strict unity with the body. In it existed those
human forms which supplied the sculptor with
his models of Hercules, Phœbus, and Jove;
not like the forms abounding in the streets of
modern cities, wherein the face is a confused
blur of features, but composed of incorrupt,
sharply defined and symmetrical features, whose
eye-sockets are so formed that it would be impossible for such eyes to squint and take fur-
tive glances on this side and on that, but they
must turn the whole head. The manners of
that period are plain and fierce. The reverence
exhibited is for personal qualities; courage, address, self-command, justice, strength, swiftness,
a loud voice, a broad chest. Luxury and ele-
gance are not known. A sparse population and
want make every man his own valet, cook,
butcher and soldier, and the habit of supplying
his own needs educates the body to wonderful
performances. Such are the Agamemnon and

Diomed of Homer, and not far different is the
picture Xenophon gives of himself and his com-
patriots in the Retreat of the Ten Thousand.
"After the army had crossed the river Teleboas
in Armenia, there fell much snow, and the troops
lay miserably on the ground covered with it.
But Xenophon arose naked, and taking an axe,
began to split wood; whereupon others rose
and did the like." [1] Throughout his army exists
a boundless liberty of speech. They quarrel for
plunder, they wrangle with the generals on each
new order, and Xenophon is as sharp-tongued
as any and sharper-tongued than most, and so
gives as good as he gets. Who does not see
that this is a gang of great boys, with such a
code of honor and such lax discipline as great
boys have?

The costly charm of the ancient tragedy, and
indeed of all the old literature, is that the persons speak simply, — speak as persons who
have great good sense without knowing it, before yet the reflective habit has become the predominant habit of the mind. Our admiration
of the antique is not admiration of the old, but
of the natural. The Greeks are not reflective,
but perfect in their senses and in their health,
· with the finest physical organization in the

world. Adults acted with the simplicity and
grace of children. They made vases, tragedies
and statues, such as healthy senses should, —
that is, in good taste. Such things have continued to be made in all ages, and are now,
wherever a healthy physique exists ; but, as a
class, from their superior organization, they have
surpassed all. They combine the energy of
manhood with the engaging unconsciousness of
childhood. The attraction of these manners is
that they belong to man, and are known to
every man in virtue of his being once a child ;
besides that there are always individuals who
retain these characteristics. A person of childlike genius and inborn energy is still a Greek,
and revives our love of the Muse of Hellas. I
admire the love of nature in the Philoctetes. In
reading those fine apostrophes to sleep, to the
stars, rocks, mountains and waves, I feel time
passing away as an ebbing sea. I feel the eternity of man, the identity of his thought. The
Greek had, it seems, the same fellow-beings as I.
The sun and moon, water and fire, met his heart
precisely as they meet mine. Then the vaunted
distinction between Greek and English, between
Classic and Romantic schools, seems superficial
and pedantic. When a thought of Plato be-

comes a thought to me, — when a truth that fired
the soul of Pindar fires mine, time is no more.
When I feel that we two meet in a perception,
that our two souls are tinged with the same
hue, and do as it were run into one, why should
I measure degrees of latitude, why should I
count Egyptian years?

The student interprets the age of chivalry by
his own age of chivalry, and the days of mari-
time adventure and circumnavigation by quite
parallel miniature experiences of his own. To
the sacred history of the world he has the same
key. When the voice of a prophet out of the
deeps of antiquity merely echoes to him a sentiment of his infancy, a prayer of his youth, he
then pierces to the truth through all the confusion of tradition and the caricature of institutions.

Rare, extravagant spirits come by us at intervals, who disclose to us new facts in nature. I
see that men of God have from time to time
walked among men and made their commission
felt in the heart and soul of the commonest
hearer. Hence evidently the tripod, the priest,
the priestess inspired by the divine afflatus.

Jesus astonishes and overpowers sensual people. They cannot unite him to history, or re-

concile him with themselves. As they come to
revere their intuitions and aspire to live holily,
their own piety explains every fact, every word.

How easily these old worships of Moses, of
Zoroaster, of Menu, of Socrates, domesticate
themselves in the mind. I cannot find any antiquity in them. They are mine as much as
theirs.

I have seen the first monks and anchorets,
without crossing seas or centuries. More than
once some individual has appeared to me with
such negligence of labor and such commanding
contemplation, a haughty beneficiary begging in
the name of God, as made good to the nineteenth century Simeon the Stylite, the Thebais,
and the first Capuchins.[1]

The priestcraft of the East and West, of the
Magian, Brahmin, Druid, and Inca, is expounded
in the individual's private life. The cramping
influence of a hard formalist on a young child,
in repressing his spirits and courage, paralyzing
the understanding, and that without producing
indignation, but only fear and obedience, and
even much sympathy with the tyranny, — is a
familiar fact, explained to the child when he becomes a man, only by seeing that the oppressor
of his youth is himself a child tyrannized over

by those names and words and forms of whose
influence he was merely the organ to the youth.
The fact teaches him how Belus was worshipped
and how the Pyramids were built, better than
the discovery by Champollion of the names of
all the workmen and the cost of every tile. He
finds Assyria and the Mounds of Cholula at
his door, and himself has laid the courses.

Again, in that protest which each considerate
person makes against the superstition of his
times, he repeats step for step the part of old
reformers, and in the search after truth finds,
like them, new perils to virtue. He learns again
what moral vigor is needed to supply the girdle
of a superstition. A great licentiousness treads
on the heels of a reformation. How many times
in the history of the world has the Luther of
the day had to lament the decay of piety in his
own household! "Doctor," said his wife to
Martin Luther, one day, "how is it that whilst
subject to papacy we prayed so often and with
such fervor, whilst now we pray with the utmost
coldness and very seldom?"[1]

The advancing man discovers how deep a
property he has in literature, — in all fable as
well as in all history. He finds that the poet
was no odd fellow who described strange and

impossible situations, but that universal man wrote by his pen a confession true for one and true for all. His own secret biography he finds in lines wonderfully intelligible to him, dotted down before he was born. One after another he comes up in his private adventures with every fable of Æsop, of Homer, of Hafiz, of Ariosto, of Chaucer, of Scott, and verifies them with his own head and hands.

The beautiful fables of the Greeks, being proper creations of the imagination and not of the fancy, are universal verities. What a range of meanings and what perpetual pertinence has the story of Prometheus! Beside its primary value as the first chapter of the history of Europe, (the mythology thinly veiling authentic facts, the invention of the mechanic arts and the migration of colonies,) it gives the history of religion, with some closeness to the faith of later ages. Prometheus is the Jesus of the old mythology. He is the friend of man; stands between the unjust "justice" of the Eternal Father and the race of mortals, and readily suffers all things on their account.[1] But where it departs from the Calvinistic Christianity and exhibits him as the defier of Jove, it represents a state of mind which readily appears wherever

the doctrine of Theism is taught in a crude,
objective form, and which seems the self-defence
of man against this untruth, namely a discontent with the believed fact that a God exists,
and a feeling that the obligation of reverence is
onerous. It would steal if it could the fire of
the Creator, and live apart from him and independent of him. The Prometheus Vinctus is
the romance of skepticism. Not less true to all
time are the details of that stately apologue.
Apollo kept the flocks of Admetus, said the
poets. When the gods come among men, they
are not known. Jesus was not; Socrates and
Shakspeare were not. Antæus was suffocated
by the gripe of Hercules, but every time he
touched his mother-earth his strength was re-
newed. Man is the broken giant, and in all his
weakness both his body and his mind are invig-
orated by habits of conversation with nature.
The power of music, the power of poetry, to
unfix and as it were clap wings to solid nature,
interprets the riddle of Orpheus.¹ The philosophical perception of identity through endless
mutations of form makes him know the Pro-
teus. What else am I who laughed or wept yesterday, who slept last night like a corpse, and
this morning stood and ran? And what see I

on any side but the transmigrations of Pro-
teus? I can symbolize my thought by using
the name of any creature, of any fact, because
every creature is man agent or patient. Tantalus is but a name for you and me. Tantalus
means the impossibility of drinking the waters
of thought which are always gleaming and waving within sight of the soul.ʹ The transmigra-
tion of souls is no fable. I would it were; but
men and women are only half human. Every
animal of the barn-yard, the field and the forest, of the earth and of the waters that are
under the earth, has contrived to get a footing
and to leave the print of its features and form
in some one or other of these upright, heaven-
facing speakers. Ah! brother, stop the ebb of
thy soul, — ebbing downward into the forms
into whose habits thou hast now for many years
slid.ᶻ As near and proper to us is also that old
fable of the Sphinx, who was said to sit in the
road-side and put riddles to every passenger.
If the man could not answer, she swallowed him
alive. If he could solve the riddle, the Sphinx
was slain. What is our life but an endless flight
of winged facts or events? In splendid variety
these changes come, all putting questions to the
human spirit. Those men who cannot answer

by a superior wisdom these facts or questions
of time, serve them. Facts encumber them,
tyrannize over them, and make the men of
routine, the men of *sense*, in whom a literal obedience to facts has extinguished every spark of
that light by which man is truly man. But if
the man is true to his better instincts or sentiments, and refuses the dominion of facts, as one
that comes of a higher race; remains fast by the
soul and sees the principle, then the facts fall
aptly and supple into their places; they know
their master, and the meanest of them glorifies
him.[1]

See in Goethe's Helena the same desire that
every word should be a thing. These figures,
he would say, these Chirons, Griffins, Phorkyas,
Helen and Leda, are somewhat, and do exert a
specific influence on the mind. So far then are
they eternal entities, as real to-day as in the
first Olympiad. Much revolving them he writes
out freely his humor, and gives them body to
his own imagination. And although that poem
be as vague and fantastic as a dream, yet is it
much more attractive than the more regular
dramatic pieces of the same author, for the reason that it operates a wonderful relief to the
mind from the routine of customary images, —

awakens the reader's invention and fancy by
the wild freedom of the design, and by the un-
ceasing succession of brisk shocks of surprise.

The universal nature, too strong for the petty
nature of the bard, sits on his neck and writes
through his hand; so that when he seems to
vent a mere caprice and wild romance, the issue
is an exact allegory.   Hence Plato said that
"poets utter great and wise things which they
do not themselves understand."[1] All the fic-
tions of the Middle Age explain themselves as
a masked or frolic expression of that which in
grave earnest the mind of that period toiled to
achieve.   Magic and all that is ascribed to it is
a deep presentiment of the powers of science.
The shoes of swiftness, the sword of sharpness,
the power of subduing the elements, of using
the secret virtues of minerals, of understanding the voices of birds, are the obscure efforts
of the mind in a right direction. The preternat-
ural prowess of the hero, the gift of perpetual
youth, and the like, are alike the endeavor of
the human spirit " to bend the shows of things
to the desires of the mind."

In Perceforest and Amadis de Gaul a garland
and a rose bloom on the head of her who is
faithful, and fade on the brow of the inconstant.

In the story of the Boy and the Mantle [1] even a mature reader may be surprised with a glow of virtuous pleasure at the triumph of the gentle Genelas; and indeed all the postulates of elfin annals, — that the fairies do not like to be named; that their gifts are capricious and not to be trusted; that who seeks a treasure must not speak; and the like, — I find true in Concord, however they might be in Cornwall or Bretagne.

Is it otherwise in the newest romance? I read the Bride of Lammermoor. Sir William Ashton is a mask for a vulgar temptation, Ravenswood Castle a fine name for proud poverty, and the foreign mission of state only a Bunyan disguise for honest industry. We may all shoot a wild bull that would toss the good and beautiful, by fighting down the unjust and sensual. Lucy Ashton is another name for fidelity, which is always beautiful and always liable to calamity in this world.

But along with the civil and metaphysical history of man, another history goes daily forward, — that of the external world, — in which he is not less strictly implicated. He is the compend of time; he is also the correlative of nature. His power consists in the multitude of his affinities, in the fact that his life is intertwined with the whole chain of organic and inorganic being. In old Rome the public roads beginning at the Forum proceeded north, south, east, west, to the centre of every province of the empire, making each market - town of Persia, Spain and Britain pervious to the soldiers of the capital : so out of the human heart go as it were highways to the heart of every object in nature, to reduce it under the dominion of man. A man is a bundle of relations, a knot of roots, whose flower and fruitage is the world. His faculties refer to natures out of him and predict the world he is to inhabit, as the fins of the fish foreshow that water exists, or the wings of an eagle in the egg presuppose air. He cannot live without a world.' Put Napoleon in an island prison, let his faculties find no men to act on, no Alps to climb, no stake to play for, and he would beat the air, and appear stupid. Transport him to large countries, dense population, complex interests and antagonist power, and you shall see that the man Napoleon, bounded that is by such a profile and outline, is not the virtual Napoleon. This is but Talbot's shadow ; —

"His substance is not here.
For what you see is but the smallest part
And least proportion of humanity;
But were the whole frame here,
It is of such a spacious, lofty pitch,
Your roof were not sufficient to contain it."[1]

Columbus needs a planet to shape his course
upon. Newton and Laplace need myriads of
age and thick-strewn celestial areas. One may
say a gravitating solar system is already pro-
phesied in the nature of Newton's mind. Not
less does the brain of Davy or of Gay-Lussac,
from childhood exploring the affinities and
repulsions of particles, anticipate the laws of
organization. Does not the eye of the human
embryo predict the light? the ear of Handel
predict the witchcraft of harmonic sound? Do
not the constructive fingers of Watt, Fulton,
Whittemore, Arkwright, predict the fusible,
hard, and temperable texture of metals, the
properties of stone, water, and wood? Do not
the lovely attributes of the maiden child predict
the refinements and decorations of civil society? Here also we are reminded of the action
of man on man. A mind might ponder its
thoughts for ages and not gain so much self-
knowledge as the passion of love shall teach it

in a day. Who knows himself before he has
been thrilled with indignation at an outrage, or
has heard an eloquent tongue, or has shared the
throb of thousands in a national exultation or
alarm? No man can antedate his experience, or
guess what faculty or feeling a new object shall
unlock, any more than he can draw to-day the
face of a person whom he shall see to-morrow
for the first time.

I will not now go behind the general statement to explore the reason of this correspon-
dency. Let it suffice that in the light of these
two facts, namely, that the mind is One, and
that nature is its correlative, history is to be
read and written.

Thus in all ways does the soul concentrate
and reproduce its treasures for each pupil. He
too shall pass through the whole cycle of experience. He shall collect into a focus the rays
of nature. History no longer shall be a dull
book. It shall walk incarnate in every just and
wise man. You shall not tell me by languages
and titles a catalogue of the volumes you have
read. You shall make me feel what periods you
have lived. A man shall be the Temple of
Fame. He shall walk, as the poets have described that goddess, in a robe painted all over

with wonderful events and experiences; — his
own form and features by their exalted intelligence shall be that variegated vest. I shall find
in him the Foreworld; in his childhood the
Age of Gold, the Apples of Knowledge, the
Argonautic Expedition, the calling of Abraham, the building of the Temple, the Advent
of Christ, Dark Ages, the Revival of Letters,
the Reformation, the discovery of new lands,
the opening of new sciences and new regions in
man. He shall be the priest of Pan, and bring
with him into humble cottages the blessing of
the morning stars, and all the recorded benefits
of heaven and earth.

Is there somewhat overweening in this claim?
Then I reject all I have written, for what is the
use of pretending to know what we know not?
But it is the fault of our rhetoric that we cannot strongly state one fact without seeming to
belie some other. I hold our actual knowledge
very cheap. Hear the rats in the wall, see the
lizard on the fence, the fungus under foot, the
lichen on the log. What do I know sympa-
thetically, morally, of either of these worlds of
life? As old as the Caucasian man, — perhaps
older, — these creatures have kept their counsel
beside him, and there is no record of any word

or sign that has passed from one to the other.[1]
What connection do the books show between
the fifty or sixty chemical elements and the historical eras? Nay, what does history yet record of the metaphysical annals of man? What
light does it shed on those mysteries which we
hide under the names Death and Immortality?
Yet every history should be written in a wisdom which divined the range of our affinities
and looked at facts as symbols. I am ashamed
to see what a shallow village tale our so-called
History is. How many times we must say
Rome, and Paris, and Constantinople! What
does Rome know of rat and lizard? What are
Olympiads and Consulates to these neighboring systems of being? Nay, what food or experience or succor have they for the Esquimaux
seal-hunter, for the Kanàka in his canoe, for
the fisherman, the stevedore, the porter?

Broader and deeper we must write our annals,
— from an ethical reformation, from an influx
of the ever new, ever sanative conscience, — if
we would trulier express our central and wide-
related nature, instead of this old chronology
of selfishness and pride to which we have too
long lent our eyes. Already that day exists for
us, shines in on us at unawares, but the path of

science and of letters is not the way into nature.
The idiot, the Indian, the child and unschooled
farmer's boy stand nearer to the light by which
nature is to be read, than the dissector or the
antiquary.[1]

II

SELF–RELIANCE

"Ne te quæsiveris extra."

Man is his own star; and the soul that can
Render an honest and a perfect man,
Commands all light, all influence, all fate;
Nothing to him falls early or too late.
Our acts our angels are, or good or ill,
Our fatal shadows that walk by us still.

Epilogue to Beaumont and Fletcher's Honest Man's Fortune

Cast the bantling on the rocks,
Suckle him with the she-wolf's teat,
Wintered with the hawk and fox,
Power and speed be hands and feet.

SELF-RELIANCE

I READ the other day some verses written by an eminent painter which were original and not conventional.[1] The soul always hears an admonition in such lines, let the subject be what it may. The sentiment they instil is of more value than any thought they may contain. To believe your own thought, to believe that what is true for you in your private heart is true for all men, — that is genius. Speak your latent conviction, and it shall be the universal sense; for the inmost in due time becomes the outmost, and our first thought is rendered back to us by the trumpets of the Last Judgment. Familiar as the voice of·the mind is to each, the highest merit we ascribe to Moses, Plato and Milton is that they set at naught books and traditions, and spoke not what men, but what *they* thought. A man should learn to detect and watch that gleam of light which flashes across his mind from within, more than the lustre of the firmament of bards and sages. Yet he dismisses without notice his thought, because it is his. In every work of genius we recognize our own rejected thoughts; they come back to us with a certain alienated majesty.[1] Great works of art have no more affecting lesson for us than this. They teach us to abide by our spontaneous impression with good-humored inflexibility then most when the whole cry of voices is on the other side. Else to-morrow a stranger will say with masterly good sense precisely what we have thought and felt all the time, and we shall be forced to take with shame our own opinion from another.

There is a time in every man's education when he arrives at the conviction that envy is ignorance; that imitation is suicide; that he must take himself for better for worse as his portion; that though the wide universe is full of good, no kernel of nourishing corn can come to him but through his toil bestowed on that plot of ground which is given to him to till. The power which resides in him is new in nature, and none but he knows what that is which he can do, nor does he know until he has tried. Not for nothing one face, one character, one fact, makes much impression on him, and another none. This sculpture in the memory is not without preëstablished harmony. The eye was placed where one ray should fall, that it might testify of that particular ray. We but half express ourselves, and are ashamed of that divine idea which each of us represents.[1] It may be safely trusted as proportionate and of good issues, so it be faithfully imparted, but God will not have his work made manifest by cowards. A man is relieved and gay when he has put his heart into his work and done his best; but what he has said or done otherwise shall give him no peace. It is a deliverance which does not deliver. In the attempt his genius deserts him; no muse befriends; no invention, no hope.

Trust thyself: every heart vibrates to that iron string. Accept the place the divine providence has found for you, the society of your contemporaries, the connection of events. Great men have always done so, and confided themselves childlike to the genius of their age, betraying their perception that the absolutely trustworthy was seated at their heart, working through their hands, predominating in all their being. And we are now men, and must accept in the highest mind the same transcendent destiny; and not minors and invalids in a protected corner, not cowards fleeing before a revolution, but guides, redeemers and benefactors, obeying the Almighty effort and advancing on Chaos and the Dark.

What pretty oracles nature yields us on this text in the face and behavior of children, babes, and even brutes! That divided and rebel mind, that distrust of a sentiment because our arithmetic has computed the strength and means opposed to our purpose, these have not. Their mind being whole, their eye is as yet unconquered, and when we look in their faces we are disconcerted. Infancy conforms to nobody ; all conform to it ; so that one babe commonly makes four or five out of the adults who prattle and play to it. So God has armed youth and puberty and manhood no less with its own piquancy and charm, and made it enviable and gracious and its claims not to be put by, if it will stand by itself. Do not think the youth has no force, because he cannot speak to you and me. Hark! in the next room his voice is sufficiently clear and emphatic. It seems he knows how to speak to his contemporaries. Bashful or bold then, he will know how to make us seniors very unnecessary.'

The nonchalance of boys who are sure of a dinner, and would disdain as much as a lord to do or say aught to conciliate one, is the healthy attitude of human nature. A boy is in the parlor what the pit is in the playhouse; indepen-

dent, irresponsible, looking out from his corner
on such people and facts as pass by, he tries and
sentences them on their merits, in the swift,
summary way of boys, as good, bad, interesting,
silly, eloquent, troublesome. He cumbers himself never about consequences, about interests ;
he gives an independent, genuine verdict. You
must court him ; he does not court you. But
the man is as it were clapped into jail by his
consciousness. As soon as he has once acted
or spoken with *éclat* he is a committed person,
watched by the sympathy or the hatred of hun-
dreds, whose affections must now enter into his
account. There is no Lethe for this. Ah, that he
could pass again into his neutrality! Who can
thus avoid all pledges and, having observed, observe again from the same unaffected, unbiased,
unbribable, unaffrighted innocence, — must always be formidable. He would utter opinions
on all passing affairs, which being seen to be not
private but necessary, would sink like darts into
the ear of men and put them in fear.[1]

These are the voices which we hear in solitude, but they grow faint and inaudible as we
enter into the world. Society everywhere is in
conspiracy against the manhood of every one
of its members. Society is a joint-stock com-

pany, in which the members agree, for the better securing of his bread to each shareholder, to surrender the liberty and culture of the eater. The virtue in most request is conformity. Self-reliance is its aversion. It loves not realities and creators, but names and customs.

Whoso would be a man, must be a nonconformist. He who would gather immortal palms must not be hindered by the name of goodness, but must explore if it be goodness. Nothing is at last sacred but the integrity of your own mind. Absolve you to yourself, and you shall have the suffrage of the world. I remember an answer which when quite young I was prompted to make to a valued adviser who was wont to importune me with the dear old doctrines of the church. On my saying, "What have I to do with the sacredness of traditions, if I live wholly from within?" my friend suggested, — "But these impulses may be from below, not from above." I replied, "They do not seem to me to be such; but if I am the Devil's child, I will live then from the Devil." No law can be sacred to me but that of my nature. Good and bad are but names very readily transferable to that or this; the only right is what is after my constitution; the only wrong what is against it.

A man is to carry himself in the presence of all opposition as if every thing were titular and ephemeral but he. I am ashamed to think how easily we capitulate to badges and names, to large societies and dead institutions. Every decent and well-spoken individual affects and sways me more than is right. I ought to go upright and vital, and speak the rude truth in all ways. If malice and vanity wear the coat of philanthropy, shall that pass? If an angry bigot assumes this bountiful cause of Abolition, and comes to me with his last news from Barbadoes, why should I not say to him, 'Go love thy infant; love thy wood-chopper; be good-natured and modest; have that grace; and never varnish your hard, uncharitable ambition with this incredible tenderness for black folk a thousand miles off. Thy love afar is spite at home.' Rough and graceless would be such greeting, but truth is handsomer than the affectation of love. Your goodness must have some edge to it, — else it is none. The doctrine of hatred must be preached, as the counteraction of the doctrine of love, when that pules and whines. I shun father and mother and wife and brother when my genius calls me. I would write on the lintels of the door - post, *Whim*. I hope it is somewhat better than whim at last, but we cannot spend the day in explanation.¹ Expect me ·not to show cause why I seek or why I exclude company. Then again, do not tell me, as a good man did to-day, of my obligation to put all poor men in good situations. Are they *my* poor? I tell thee, thou foolish philanthropist, that I grudge the dollar, the dime, the cent I give to such men as do not belong to me and to whom I do not belong. There is a class of persons to whom by all spiritual affinity I am bought and sold; for them I will go to prison if need be; but your miscellaneous popular charities; the education at college of fools; the building of meeting-houses to the vain end to which many now stand; alms to sots, and the thousand-fold Relief Societies; — though I confess with shame I sometimes succumb and give the dollar, it is a wicked dollar, which by and by I shall have the manhood to withhold.²

Virtues are, in the popular estimate, rather the exception than the rule. There is the man *and* his virtues. Men do what is called a good action, as some piece of courage or charity, much as they would pay a fine in expiation of daily non-appearance on parade. Their works are done as an apology or extenuation of their living in the world, — as invalids and the insane pay a high board. Their virtues are penances. I do not wish to expiate, but to live. My life is for itself and not for a spectacle. I much prefer that it should be of a lower strain, so it be genuine and equal, than that it should be glittering and unsteady. I wish it to be sound and sweet, and not to need diet and bleeding. I ask primary evidence that you are a man, and refuse this appeal from the man to his actions. I know that for myself it makes no difference whether I do or forbear those actions which are reckoned excellent. I cannot consent to pay for a privilege where I have intrinsic right. Few and mean as my gifts may be, I actually am, and do not need for my own assurance or the assurance of my fellows any secondary testimony.

What I must do is all that concerns me, not what the people think. This rule, equally arduous in actual and in intellectual life, may serve for the whole distinction between greatness and meanness. It is the harder because you will always find those who think they know what is your duty better than you know it. It is easy in the world to live after the world's opinion;

it is easy in solitude to live after our own ; but the great man is he who in the midst of the crowd keeps with perfect sweetness the independence of solitude.

The objection to conforming to usages that have become dead to you is that it scatters your force. It loses your time and blurs the impression of your character. If you maintain a dead church, contribute to a dead Bible-society, vote with a great party either for the government or against it,¹ spread your table like base housekeepers, — under all these screens I have difficulty to detect the precise man you are : and of course so much force is withdrawn from your proper life. But do your work, and I shall know you. Do your work, and you shall reinforce yourself. A man must consider what a blindman's-buff is this game of conformity. If I know your sect I anticipate your argument. I hear a preacher announce for his text and topic the expediency of one of the institutions of his church. Do I not know beforehand that not possibly can he say a new and spontaneous word ? Do I not know that with all this ostentation of examining the grounds of the institution he will do no such thing ? Do I not know that he is pledged to himself not to look but at one side, the

permitted side, not as a man, but as a parish
minister? He is a retained attorney, and these
airs of the bench are the emptiest affectation.
Well, most men have bound their eyes with one
or another handkerchief, and attached themselves to some one of these communities of
opinion. This conformity makes them not false
in a few particulars, authors of a few lies, but
false in all particulars. Their every truth is
not quite true. Their two is not the real two,
their four not the real four; so that every word
they say chagrins us and we know not where to
begin to set them right. Meantime nature is
not slow to equip us in the prison-uniform of
the party to which we adhere. We come to wear
one cut of face and figure, and acquire by degrees the gentlest asinine expression. There is
a mortifying experience in particular, which does
not fail to wreak itself also in the general history; I mean " the foolish face of praise," the
forced smile which we put on in company where
we do not feel at ease, in answer to conversation
which does not interest us. The muscles, not
spontaneously moved but moved by a low usurp-
ing wilfulness, grow tight about the outline of
the face, with the most disagreeable sensation.

For nonconformity the world whips you with

its displeasure. And therefore a man must know how to estimate a sour face. The by-standers look askance on him in the public street or in the friend's parlor. If this aversion had its origin in contempt and resistance like his own, he might well go home with a sad countenance ; but the sour faces of the multitude, like their sweet faces, have no deep cause, but are put on and off as the wind blows and a newspaper directs. Yet is the discontent of the multitude more formidable than that of the senate and the college. It is easy enough for a firm man who knows the world to brook the rage of the cultivated classes. Their rage is decorous and prudent, for they are timid, as being very vulnerable themselves. But when to their feminine rage the indignation of the people is added, when the ignorant and the poor are aroused, when the unintelligent brute force that lies at the bottom of society is made to growl and mow, it needs the habit of magnanimity and religion to treat it godlike as a trifle of no concernment.

The other terror that scares us from self-trust is our consistency ; a reverence for our past act or word because the eyes of others have no other data for computing our orbit than our past acts, and we are loth to disappoint them.

But why should you keep your head over your shoulder? Why drag about this corpse of your memory, lest you contradict somewhat you have stated in this or that public place? Suppose you should contradict yourself; what then? It seems to be a rule of wisdom never to rely on your memory alone, scarcely even in acts of pure memory, but to bring the past for judgment into the thousand-eyed present, and live ever in a new day. In your metaphysics you have denied personality to the Deity, yet when the devout motions of the soul come, yield to them heart and life, though they should clothe God with shape and color.' Leave your theory, as Joseph his coat in the hand of the harlot, and flee.

A foolish consistency is the hobgoblin of little minds, adored by little statesmen and philosophers and divines. With consistency a great soul has simply nothing to do. He may as well concern himself with his shadow on the wall. Speak what you think now in hard words and to-morrow speak what to-morrow thinks in hard words again, though it contradict every thing you said to-day. — 'Ah, so you shall be sure to be misunderstood.' — Is it so bad then to be misunderstood? Pythagoras was misunderstood,

and Socrates, and Jesus, and Luther, and Coper
nicus, and Galileo, and Newton, and every pure
and wise spirit that ever took flesh. To be great
is to be misunderstood.

I suppose no man can violate his nature. All
the sallies of his will are rounded in by the law
of his being, as the inequalities of Andes and
Himmaleh are insignificant in the curve of the
sphere. Nor does it matter how you gauge and
try him. A character is like an acrostic or Alex-
andrian stanza ; — read it forward, backward, or
across, it still spells the same thing. In this
pleasing contrite wood-life which God allows me,
let me record day by day my honest thought
without prospect or retrospect, and, I cannot
doubt, it will be found symmetrical, though I
mean it not and see it not. My book should
smell of pines and resound with the hum of
insects. The swallow over my window should
interweave that thread or straw he carries in his
bill into my web also. We pass for what we
are. Character teaches above our wills. Men
imagine that they communicate their virtue or
vice only by overt actions, and do not see that
virtue or vice emit a breath every moment.

There will be an agreement in whatever variety of actions, so they be each honest and natu-

ral in their hour. For of one will, the actions
will be harmonious, however unlike they seem.
These varieties are lost sight of at a little distance, at a little height of thought. One tendency unites them all. The voyage of the best
ship is a zigzag line of a hundred tacks. See the
line from a sufficient distance, and it straightens
itself to the average tendency. Your genuine
action will explain itself and will explain your
other genuine actions. Your conformity explains
nothing. Act singly, and what you have already
done singly will justify you now. Greatness
appeals to the future. If I can be firm enough
to-day to do right and scorn eyes, I must have
done so much right before as to defend me
now. Be it how it will, do right now. Always
scorn appearances and you always may. The
force of character is cumulative. All the fore-
gone days of virtue work their health into this.
What makes the majesty of the heroes of the
senate and the field, which so fills the imagination? The consciousness of a train of great
days and victories behind. They shed a united
light on the advancing actor. He is attended
as by a visible escort of angels. That is it which
throws thunder into Chatham's voice, and dignity into Washington's port, and America into

Adams's eye. Honor is venerable to us because it is no ephemera. It is always ancient virtue. We worship it to-day because it is not of to-day. We love it and pay it homage because it is not a trap for our love and homage, but is self-dependent, self-derived, and therefore of an old immaculate pedigree, even if shown in a young person.

I hope in these days we have heard the last of conformity and consistency. Let the words be gazetted and ridiculous henceforward. Instead of the gong for dinner, let us hear a whistle from the Spartan fife. Let us never bow and apologize more. A great man is coming to eat at my house. I do not wish to please him; I wish that he should wish to please me. I will stand here for humanity, and though I would make it kind, I would make it true. Let us affront and reprimand the smooth mediocrity and squalid contentment of the times, and hurl in the face of custom and trade and office, the fact which is the upshot of all history, that there is a great responsible Thinker and Actor working wherever a man works; that a true man belongs to no other time or place, but is the centre of things. Where he is, there is nature. He measures you and all men and all events. Ordinarily, every body in society reminds us of somewhat else, or of some other person. Character, reality, reminds you of nothing else; it takes place of the whole creation. The man must be so much that he must make all circumstances indifferent. Every true man is a cause, a country, and an age; requires infinite spaces and numbers and time fully to accomplish his design;—and posterity seem to follow his steps as a train of clients. A man Cæsar is born, and for ages after we have a Roman Empire. Christ is born, and millions of minds so grow and cleave to his genius that he is confounded with virtue and the possible of man. An institution is the lengthened shadow of one man; as, Monachism, of the Hermit Antony; the Reformation, of Luther; Quakerism, of Fox; Methodism, of Wesley; Abolition, of Clarkson. Scipio, Milton called "the height of Rome;" and all history resolves itself very easily into the biography of a few stout and earnest persons.[1]

Let a man then know his worth, and keep things under his feet. Let him not peep or steal, or skulk up and down with the air of a charity-boy, a bastard, or an interloper in the world which exists for him. But the man in the

street, finding no worth in himself which corresponds to the force which built a tower or sculp-
tured a marble god, feels poor when he looks
on these. To him a palace, a statue, or a costly
book have an alien and forbidding air, much
like a gay equipage, and seem to say like that,
"Who are you, Sir?" Yet they all are his, suit-
ors for his notice, petitioners to his faculties that
they will come out and take possession. The
picture waits for my verdict; it is not to command me, but I am to settle its claims to praise.
That popular fable of the sot who was picked
up dead - drunk in the street, carried to the
duke's house, washed and dressed and laid in
the duke's bed, and, on his waking, treated with
all obsequious ceremony like the duke, and assured that he had been insane, owes its popu-
larity to the fact that it symbolizes so well the
state of man, who is in the world a sort of sot,
but now and then wakes up, exercises his reason
and finds himself a true prince.[1]

Our reading is mendicant and sycophantic.
In history our imagination plays us false. Kingdom and lordship, power and estate, are a gau-
dier vocabulary than private John and Edward
in a small house and common day's work; but
the things of life are the same to both; the sum

total of both is the same. Why all this deference to Alfred and Scanderbeg and Gustavus?
Suppose they were virtuous; did they wear out
virtue? As great a stake depends on your private act to-day as followed their public and
renowned steps. When private men shall act
with original views, the lustre will be transferred
from the actions of kings to those of gentlemen.

The world has been instructed by its kings,
who have so magnetized the eyes of nations.
It has been taught by this colossal symbol the
mutual reverence that is due from man to man.
The joyful loyalty with which men have everywhere suffered the king, the noble, or the great
proprietor to walk among them by a law of his
own, make his own scale of men and things and
reverse theirs, pay for benefits not with money
but with honor, and represent the law in his
person, was the hieroglyphic by which they ob-
scurely signified their consciousness of their own
right and comeliness, the right of every man.

The magnetism which all original action exerts is explained when we inquire the reason of
self-trust. Who is the Trustee? What is the
aboriginal Self, on which a universal reliance
may be grounded? What is the nature and
power of that science-baffling star, without par-

allax, without calculable elements, which shoots
a ray of beauty even into trivial and impure
actions, if the least mark of independence appear? The inquiry leads us to that source, at
once the essence of genius, of virtue, and of
life, which we call Spontaneity or Instinct. We
denote this primary wisdom as Intuition, whilst
all later teachings are tuitions.[1] In that deep
force, the last fact behind which analysis cannot
go, all things find their common origin. For
the sense of being which in calm hours rises, we
know not how, in the soul, is not diverse from
things, from space, from light, from time, from
man, but one with them and proceeds obviously
from the same source whence their life and being
also proceed. We first share the life by which
things exist and afterwards see them as appearances in nature and forget that we have shared
their cause. Here is the fountain of action and
of thought. Here are the lungs of that inspiration which giveth man wisdom and which
cannot be denied without impiety and atheism.
We lie in the lap of immense intelligence, which
makes us receivers of its truth and organs of
its activity. When we discern justice, when we
discern truth, we do nothing of ourselves, but
allow a passage to its beams. If we ask whence

this comes, if we seek to pry into the soul that causes, all philosophy is at fault. Its presence or its absence is all we can affirm. Every man discriminates between the voluntary acts of his mind and his involuntary perceptions, and knows that to his involuntary perceptions a perfect faith is due. He may err in the expression of them, but he knows that these things are so, like day and night, not to be disputed. My wilful actions and acquisitions are but roving; — the idlest reverie, the faintest native emotion, command my curiosity and respect. Thoughtless people contradict as readily the statement of perceptions as of opinions, or rather much more readily; for they do not distinguish between perception and notion. They fancy that I choose to see this or that thing. But perception is not whimsical, but fatal. If I see a trait, my children will see it after me, and in course of time all mankind, — although it may chance that no one has seen it before me. For my perception of it is as much a fact as the sun.[1]

The relations of the soul to the divine spirit are so pure that it is profane to seek to interpose helps. It must be that when God speaketh he should communicate, not one thing, but

all things; should fill the world with his voice;
should scatter forth light, nature, time, souls,
from the centre of the present thought; and
new date and new create the whole. Whenever
a mind is simple and receives a divine wisdom,
old things pass away, — means, teachers, texts,
temples fall; it lives now, and absorbs past and
future into the present hour. All things are
made sacred by relation to it, — one as much as
another. All things are dissolved to their centre
by their cause, and in the universal miracle petty
and particular miracles disappear. If therefore
a man claims to know and speak of God and
carries you backward to the phraseology of some
old mouldered nation in another country, in
another world, believe him not. Is the acorn
better than the oak which is its fulness and com-
pletion? Is the parent better than the child into
whom he has cast his ripened being? Whence
then this worship of the past? The centuries
are conspirators against the sanity and authority
of the soul. Time and space are but physiolo-
gical colors which the eye makes, but the soul is
light: where it is, is day; where it was, is night;
and history is an impertinence and an injury if
it be any thing more than a cheerful apologue
or parable of my being and becoming.

Man is timid and apologetic; he is no longer
upright; he dares not say 'I think,' 'I am,' but
quotes some saint or sage.' He is ashamed before the blade of grass or the blowing rose.
These roses under my window make no reference to former roses or to better ones; they are
for what they are; they exist with God to-day.
There is no time to them. There is simply the
rose; it is perfect in every moment of its existence. Before a leaf-bud has burst, its whole life
acts; in the full-blown flower there is no more;
in the leafless root there is no less. Its nature
is satisfied and it satisfies nature in all moments
alike. But man postpones or remembers; he
does not live in the present, but with reverted
eye laments the past, or, heedless of the riches
that surround him, stands on tiptoe to foresee
the future. He cannot be happy and strong
until he too lives with nature in the present,
above time.

This should be plain enough. Yet see what
strong intellects dare not yet hear God himself
unless he speak the phraseology of I know not
what David, or Jeremiah, or Paul. We shall not
always set so great a price on a few texts, on a
few lives. We are like children who repeat by
rote the sentences of grandames and tutors, and,

as they grow older, of the men of talents and character they chance to see, — painfully recollecting the exact words they spoke; afterwards, when they come into the point of view which those had who uttered these sayings, they understand them and are willing to let the words go; for at any time they can use words as good when occasion comes. If we live truly, we shall see truly. It is as easy for the strong man to be strong, as it is for the weak to be weak. When we have new perception, we shall gladly disburden the memory of its hoarded treasures as old rubbish. When a man lives with God, his voice shall be as sweet as the murmur of the brook and the rustle of the corn.

And now at last the highest truth on this subject remains unsaid; probably cannot be said; for all that we say is the far-off remembering of the intuition. That thought by what I can now nearest approach to say it, is this. When good is near you, when you have life in yourself, it is not by any known or accustomed way; you shall not discern the footprints of any other; you shall not see the face of man; you shall not hear any name;—the way, the thought, the good, shall be wholly strange and new. It shall exclude example and experience. You take the

way from man, not to man. All persons that
ever existed are its forgotten ministers. Fear
and hope are alike beneath it. There is somewhat low even in hope. In the hour of vision
there is nothing that can be called gratitude, nor
properly joy. The soul raised over passion beholds identity and eternal causation, perceives
the self-existence of Truth and Right, and calms
itself with knowing that all things go well. Vast
spaces of nature, the Atlantic Ocean, the South
Sea; long intervals of time, years, centuries, are
of no account. This which I think and feel un-
derlay every former state of life and circumstances, as it does underlie my present, and what
is called life and what is called death.

Life only avails, not the having lived. Power
ceases in the instant of repose; it resides in the
moment of transition from a past to a new state,
in the shooting of the gulf, in the darting to an
aim. This óne fact the world hates; that the
soul *becomes*; for that forever degrades the past,
turns all riches to poverty, all reputation to a
shame, confounds the saint with the rogue, shoves
Jesus and Judas equally aside. Why then do we
prate of self-reliance? Inasmuch as the soul is
present there will be power not confident but
agent.[1] To talk of reliance is a poor external

way of speaking. Speak rather of that which relies because it works and is. Who has more obedience than I masters me, though he should not raise his finger. Round him I must revolve by the gravitation of spirits. We fancy it rhetoric when we speak of eminent virtue. We do not yet see that virtue is Height, and that a man or a company of men, plastic and permeable to principles, by the law of nature must overpower and ride all cities, nations, kings, rich men, poets, who are not.

This is the ultimate fact which we so quickly reach on this, as on every topic, the resolution of all into the ever-blessed ONE. Self-existence is the attribute of the Supreme Cause, and it constitutes the measure of good by the degree in which it enters into all lower forms. All things real are so by so much virtue as they contain. Commerce, husbandry, hunting, whaling, war, eloquence, personal weight, are somewhat, and engage my respect as examples of its presence and impure action. I see the same law working in nature for conservation and growth. Power is, in nature, the essential measure of right. Nature suffers nothing to remain in her kingdoms which cannot help itself. The genesis and maturation of a planet, its poise and orbit, the bended tree recovering itself from the strong wind, the vital resources of every animal and vegetable, are demonstrations of the self-sufficing and therefore self-relying soul.

Thus all concentrates: let us not rove; let us sit at home with the cause.[1] Let us stun and astonish the intruding rabble of men and books and institutions by a simple declaration of the divine fact. Bid the invaders take the shoes from off their feet, for God is here within. Let our simplicity judge them, and our docility to our own law demonstrate the poverty of nature and fortune beside our native riches.

But now we are a mob. Man does not stand in awe of man, nor is his genius admonished to stay at home, to put itself in communication with the internal ocean, but it goes abroad to beg a cup of water of the urns of other men. We must go alone. I like the silent church before the service begins, better than any preaching. How far off, how cool, how chaste the persons look, begirt each one with a precinct or sanctuary! So let us always sit. Why should we assume the faults of our friend, or wife, or father, or child, because they sit around our hearth, or are said to have the same blood? All men have my blood and I all men's. Not for

that will I adopt their petulance or folly, even
to the extent of being ashamed of it.' But your
isolation must not be mechanical, but spiritual, that is, must be elevation. At times the
whole world seems to be in conspiracy to importune you with emphatic trifles. Friend, client, child, sickness, fear, want, charity, all knock
at once at thy closet door and say, — ' Come
out unto us.' But keep thy state ; come not
into their confusion. The power men possess
to annoy me I give them by a weak curiosity.
No man can come near me but through my act.
" What we love that we have, but by desire we
bereave ourselves of the love."

If we cannot at once rise to the sanctities of
obedience and faith, let us at least resist our
temptations; let us enter into the state of war
and wake Thor and Woden, courage and con-
stancy, in our Saxon breasts. This is to be done
in our smooth times by speaking the truth.
Check this lying hospitality and lying affection. Live no longer to the expectation of these
deceived and deceiving people with whom we
converse. Say to them, ' O father, O mother,
O wife, O brother, O friend, I have lived with
you after appearances hitherto. Henceforward
I am the truth's. Be it known unto you that

henceforward I obey no law less than the eternal law. I will have no covenants but proximities. I shall endeavor to nourish my parents, to support my family, to be the chaste husband of one wife, — but these relations I must fill after a new and unprecedented way. I appeal from your customs. I must be myself. I cannot break myself any longer for you, or you. If you can love me for what I am, we shall be the happier. If you cannot, I will still seek to deserve that you should. I will not hide my tastes or aversions. I will so trust that what is deep is holy, that I will do strongly before the sun and moon whatever inly rejoices me and the heart appoints. If you are noble, I will love you; if you are not, I will not hurt you and myself by hypocritical attentions. If you are true, but not in the same truth with me, cleave to your companions; I will seek my own. I do this not selfishly but humbly and truly. It is alike your interest, and mine, and all men's, however long we have dwelt in lies, to live in truth. Does this sound harsh to-day? You will soon love what is dictated by your nature as well as mine, and if we follow the truth it will bring us out safe at last.' — But so may you give these friends pain. Yes, but I cannot

sell my liberty and my power, to save their
sensibility. Besides, all persons have their moments of reason, when they look out into the
region of absolute truth ; then will they justify
me and do the same thing.

The populace think that your rejection of
popular standards is a rejection of all standard,
and mere antinomianism ; and the bold sensu-
alist will use the name of philosophy to gild
his crimes. But the law of consciousness abides.
There are two confessionals, in one or the other
of which we must be shriven. You may fulfil
your round of duties by clearing yourself in the
direct, or in the *reflex* way. Consider whether
you have satisfied your relations to father, mother, cousin, neighbor, town, cat and dog —
whether any of these can upbraid you. But I
may also neglect this reflex standard and absolve
me to myself. I have my own stern claims and
perfect circle. It denies the name of duty to
many offices that are called duties. But if I can
discharge its debts it enables me to dispense
with the popular code. If any one imagines
that this law is lax, let him keep its command-
ment one day.[1]

And truly it demands something godlike in
him who has cast off the common motives of

humanity and has ventured to trust himself for
a taskmaster. High be his heart, faithful his
will, clear his sight, that he may in good earnest
be doctrine, society, law, to himself, that a simple
purpose may be to him as strong as iron necessity is to others !

If any man consider the present aspects of
what is called by distinction *society*, he will see
the need of these ethics. The sinew and heart
of man seem to be drawn out, and we are become timorous, desponding whimperers. We
are afraid of truth, afraid of fortune, afraid of
death, and afraid of each other. Our age yields
no great and perfect persons. We want men and
women who shall renovate life and our social
state, but we see that most natures are insol-
vent, cannot satisfy their own wants, have an
ambition out of all proportion to their practical
force and do lean and beg day and night continually. Our housekeeping is mendicant, our
arts, our occupations, our marriages, our religion
we have not chosen, but society has chosen for
us. We are parlor soldiers. We shun the rugged
battle of fate, where strength is born.

If our young men miscarry in their first en-
terprises they lose all heart. If the young merchant fails, men say he is *ruined*. If the finest

genius studies at one of our colleges and is not
installed in an office within one year afterwards
in the cities or suburbs of Boston or New York,
it seems to his friends and to himself that he is
right in being disheartened and in complaining
the rest of his life. A sturdy lad from New
Hampshire or Vermont, who in turn tries all
the professions, who *teams it, farms it, peddles*,
keeps a school, preaches, edits a newspaper,
goes to Congress, buys a township, and so forth,
in successive years, and always like a cat falls on
his feet, is worth a hundred of these city dolls.'
He walks abreast with his days and feels no
shame in not 'studying a profession,' for he
does not postpone his life, but lives already.
He has not one chance, but a hundred chances.
Let a Stoic open the resources of man and tell
men they are not leaning willows, but can and
must detach themselves ; that with the exercise
of self-trust, new powers shall appear ; that a
man is the word made flesh, born to shed heal-
ing to the nations ; that he should be ashamed
of our compassion, and that the moment he
acts from himself, tossing the laws, the books,
idolatries and customs out of the window, we
pity him no more but thank and revere him ;—
and that teacher shall restore the life of man

to splendor and make his name dear to all history.

It is easy to see that a greater self-reliance must work a revolution in all the offices and relations of men ; in their religion ; in their education ; in their pursuits ; their modes of living ; their association ; in their property ; in their speculative views.

1. In what prayers do men allow themselves ! That which they call a holy office is not so much as brave and manly. Prayer looks abroad and asks for some foreign addition to come through some foreign virtue, and loses itself in endless mazes of natural and supernatural, and mediatorial and miraculous. Prayer that craves a particular commodity, anything less than all good, is vicious. Prayer is the contemplation of the facts of life from the highest point of view. It is the soliloquy of a beholding and jubilant soul. It is the spirit of God pronouncing his works good. But prayer as a means to effect a private end is meanness and theft. It supposes dualism and not unity in nature and conscious-ness. As soon as the man is at one with God, he will not beg. He will then see prayer in all action. The prayer of the farmer kneeling in his field to weed it, the prayer of the rower

kneeling with the stroke of his oar, are true prayers heard throughout nature, though for cheap ends.¹ Caratach, in Fletcher's "Bonduca," when admonished to inquire the mind of the god Audate, replies, —

> His hidden meaning lies in our endeavors;
> Our valors are our best gods.

Another sort of false prayers are our regrets. Discontent is the want of self-reliance: it is infirmity of will. Regret calamities if you can thereby help the sufferer; if not, attend your own work and already the evil begins to be repaired. Our sympathy is just as base. We come to them who weep foolishly and sit down and cry for company, instead of imparting to them truth and health in rough electric shocks, putting them once more in communication with their own reason. The secret of fortune is joy in our hands. Welcome evermore to gods and men is the self-helping man. For him all doors are flung wide; him all tongues greet, all honors crown, all eyes follow with desire. Our love goes out to him and embraces him because he did not need it. We solicitously and apologetically caress and celebrate him because he held on his way and scorned our disapprobation. The gods love him because men hated him.

" To the persevering mortal," said Zoroaster,
" the blessed Immortals are swift."

As men's prayers are a disease of the will, so
are their creeds a disease of the intellect. They
say with those foolish Israelites, ' Let not God
speak to us, lest we die. Speak thou, speak any
man with us, and we will obey.' Everywhere
I am hindered of meeting God in my brother,
because he has shut his own temple doors and
recites fables merely of his brother's, or his
brother's brother's God. Every new mind is a
new classification. If it prove a mind of uncommon activity and power, a Locke, a Lavoisier,
a Hutton, a Bentham, a Fourier, it imposes its
classification on other men, and lo ! a new system. In proportion to the depth of the thought,
and so to the number of the objects it touches
and brings within reach of the pupil, is his
complacency. But chiefly is this apparent in
creeds and churches, which are also classifications
of some powerful mind acting on the elemental thought of duty and man's relation to the
Highest. Such is Calvinism, Quakerism, Swe-
denborgism. The pupil takes the same delight
in subordinating every thing to the new termi-
nology as a girl who has just learned botany in
seeing a new earth and new seasons thereby.

It will happen for a time that the pupil will find his intellectual power has grown by the study of his master's mind. But in all unbalanced minds the classification is idolized, passes for the end and not for a speedily exhaustible means, so that the walls of the system blend to their eye in the remote horizon with the walls of the universe; the luminaries of heaven seem to them hung on the arch their master built. They cannot imagine how you aliens have any right to see, — how you can see; 'It must be somehow that you stole the light from us.' They do not yet perceive that light, unsystematic, indomitable, will break into any cabin, even into theirs.¹ Let them chirp awhile and call it their own. If they are honest and do well, presently their neat new pinfold will be too strait and low, will crack, will lean, will rot and vanish, and the immortal light, all young and joyful, million-orbed, million-colored, will beam over the universe as on the first morning.

2. It is for want of self-culture that the superstition of Travelling, whose idols are Italy, England, Egypt, retains its fascination for all educated Americans. They who made England, Italy, or Greece venerable in the imagination, did so by sticking fast where they were,

like an axis of the earth. In manly hours we feel that duty is our place. The soul is no traveller; the wise man stays at home, and when his necessities, his duties, on any occasion call him from his house, or into foreign lands, he is at home still and shall make men sensible by the expression of his countenance that he goes, the missionary of wisdom and virtue, and visits cities and men like a sovereign and not like an interloper or a valet.

I have no churlish objection to the circumnavigation of the globe for the purposes of art, of study, and benevolence, so that the man is first domesticated, or does not go abroad with the hope of finding somewhat greater than he knows. He who travels to be amused, or to get somewhat which he does not carry, travels away from himself, and grows old even in youth among old things. In Thebes, in Palmyra, his will and mind have become old and dilapidated as they. He carries ruins to ruins.

Travelling is a fool's paradise. Our first journeys discover to us the indifference of places. At home I dream that at Naples, at Rome, I can be intoxicated with beauty and lose my sadness. I pack my trunk, embrace my friends, embark on the sea and at last wake up in Naples, and there beside me is the stern fact, the sad self, unrelenting, identical, that I fled from. I seek the Vatican and the palaces. I affect to be intoxicated with sights and suggestions, but I am not intoxicated. My giant goes with me wherever I go.[1]

3. But the rage of travelling is a symptom of a deeper unsoundness affecting the whole intellectual action. The intellect is vagabond, and our system of education fosters restlessness. Our minds travel when our bodies are forced to stay at home. We imitate; and what is imitation but the travelling of the mind? Our houses are built with foreign taste; our shelves are garnished with foreign ornaments; our opinions, our tastes, our faculties, lean, and follow the Past and the Distant. The soul created the arts wherever they have flourished. It was in his own mind that the artist sought his model. It was an application of his own thought to the thing to be done and the conditions to be observed. And why need we copy the Doric or the Gothic model? Beauty, convenience, grandeur of thought and quaint expression are as near to us as to any, and if the American artist will study with hope and love the precise thing to be done by him, considering the climate, the soil,

the length of the day, the wants of the people, the habit and form of the government, he will create a house in which all these will find themselves fitted, and taste and sentiment will be satisfied also.

Insist on yourself; never imitate. Your own gift you can present every moment with the cumulative force of a whole life's cultivation; but of the adopted talent of another you have only an extemporaneous half possession. That which each can do best, none but his Maker can teach him. No man yet knows what it is, nor can, till that person has exhibited it. Where is the master who could have taught Shakspeare? Where is the master who could have instructed Franklin, or Washington, or Bacon, or Newton? Every great man is a unique. The Scipionism of Scipio is precisely that part he could not borrow.[1] Shakspeare will never be made by the study of Shakspeare. Do that which is assigned you, and you cannot hope too much or dare too much. There is at this moment for you an utterance brave and grand as that of the colossal chisel of Phidias, or trowel of the Egyptians, or the pen of Moses or Dante, but different from all these. Not possibly will the soul, all rich, all eloquent, with thousand - cloven tongue, deign to repeat itself; but if you can hear what these patriarchs say, surely you can reply to them in the same pitch of voice; for the ear and the tongue are two organs of one nature. Abide in the simple and noble regions of thy life, obey thy heart, and thou shalt reproduce the Foreworld again.

4. As our Religion, our Education, our Art look abroad, so does our spirit of society. All men plume themselves on the improvement of society, and no man improves.

Society never advances. It recedes as fast on one side as it gains on the other. It undergoes continual changes; it is barbarous, it is civilized, it is christianized, it is rich, it is scientific; but this change is not amelioration. For every thing that is given something is taken. Society acquires new arts and loses old instincts. What a contrast between the well-clad, reading, writing, thinking American, with a watch, a pencil and a bill of exchange in his pocket, and the naked New Zealander, whose property is a club, a spear, a mat and an undivided twentieth of a shed to sleep under! But compare the health of the two men and you shall see that the white man has lost his aboriginal strength. If the traveller tell us truly, strike the savage with a broad-axe and in a day or two the flesh shall unite and heal as if you struck the blow into soft pitch, and the same blow shall send the white to his grave.

The civilized man has built a coach, but has lost the use of his feet. He is supported on crutches, but lacks so much support of muscle. He has a fine Geneva watch, but he fails of the skill to tell the hour by the sun. A Greenwich nautical almanac he has, and so being sure of the information when he wants it, the man in the street does not know a star in the sky. The solstice he does not observe; the equinox he knows as little; and the whole bright calendar of the year is without a dial in his mind. His note-books impair his memory; his libraries overload his wit; the insurance-office increases the number of accidents; and it may be a question whether machinery does not encumber; whether we have not lost by refinement some energy, by a Christianity, entrenched in establishments and forms, some vigor of wild virtue.' For every Stoic was a Stoic; but in Christendom where is the Christian?

There is no more deviation in the moral standard than in the standard of height or bulk. No greater men are now than ever were. A singular equality may be observed between the great men of the first and of the last ages; nor can all the science, art, religion, and philosophy of the nineteenth century avail to educate greater men than Plutarch's heroes, three or four and twenty centuries ago. Not in time is the race progressive. Phocion, Socrates, Anaxagoras, Diogenes, are great men, but they leave no class. He who is really of their class will not be called by their name, but will be his own man, and in his turn the founder of a sect. The arts and inventions of each period are only its costume and do not invigorate men. The harm of the improved machinery may compensate its good. Hudson and Behring accomplished so much in their fishing-boats as to astonish Parry and Franklin, whose equipment exhausted the resources of science and art. Galileo, with an opera-glass, discovered a more splendid series of celestial phenomena than any one since. Columbus found the New World in an undecked boat. It is curious to see the periodical disuse and perishing of means and machinery which were introduced with loud laudation a few years or centuries before. The great genius returns to essential man. We reckoned the improvements of the art of war among the triumphs of science, and yet Napoleon conquered Europe by the bivouac, which consisted of falling back on naked valor and disencumbering it of all aids. The Emperor held it impossible to make a perfect army, says Las Casas, "without abolishing our arms, magazines, commissaries and carriages, until, in imitation of the Roman custom, the soldier should receive his supply of corn, grind it in his hand-mill and bake his bread himself."

Society is a wave. The wave moves onward, but the water of which it is composed does not. The same particle does not rise from the valley to the ridge. Its unity is only phenomenal. The persons who make up a nation to-day, next year die, and their experience dies with them.

And so the reliance on Property, including the reliance on governments which protect it, is the want of self-reliance. Men have looked away from themselves and at things so long that they have come to esteem the religious, learned and civil institutions as guards of property, and they deprecate assaults on these, because they feel them to be assaults on property. They measure their esteem of each other by what each has, and not by what each is. But a cultivated man becomes ashamed of his property, out of new respect for his nature. Especially he hates what he has if he see that it is accidental, — came to him by inheritance, or gift, or crime ; then he feels that it is not having; it does not belong to him, has no root in him and merely lies there because no revolution or no robber takes it away. But that which a man is, does always by necessity acquire ; and what the man acquires, is living property, which does not wait the beck of rulers, or mobs, or revolutions, or fire, or storm, or bankruptcies, but perpetually renews itself wherever the man breathes. "Thy lot or portion of life," said the Caliph Ali, "is seeking after thee ; therefore be at rest from seeking after it."' Our dependence on these foreign goods leads us to our slavish respect for numbers. The political parties meet in numerous conventions; the greater the concourse and with each new uproar of announcement, The delegation from Essex! The Democrats from New Hampshire ! The Whigs of Maine ! the young patriot feels himself stronger than before by a new thousand of eyes and arms. In like manner the reformers summon conventions and vote and resolve in multitude. Not so, O friends ! will the God deign to enter and inhabit you, but by a method precisely the reverse. It is only as a man puts off all foreign support and stands alone that I see him to be strong and to prevail. He is weaker by every recruit to his banner. Is not a man better than a town? Ask nothing of men, and, in the endless mutation, thou only firm column must presently appear the upholder of all that surrounds thee. He who knows that power is inborn, that he is weak because he has looked for good out of him and elsewhere, and, so perceiving, throws himself unhesitatingly on his thought, instantly rights himself, stands in the erect position, commands his limbs, works miracles; just as a man who stands on his feet is stronger than a man who stands on his head.

So use all that is called Fortune. Most men gamble with her, and gain all, and lose all, as her wheel rolls. But do thou leave as unlawful these winnings, and deal with Cause and Effect, the chancellors of God. In the Will work and acquire, and thou hast chained the wheel of Chance, and shall sit hereafter out of fear from her rotations. A political victory, a rise of rents, the recovery of your sick or the return of your absent friend, or some other favorable event raises your spirits, and you think good days are preparing for you. Do not believe it. Nothing can bring you peace but yourself. Nothing can bring you peace but the triumph of principles.

III

COMPENSATION

THE wings of Time are black and white,
Pied with morning and with night.
Mountain tall and ocean deep
Trembling balance duly keep.
In changing moon, in tidal wave,
Glows the feud of Want and Have.
Gauge of more and less through space
Electric star and pencil plays.
The lonely Earth amid the balls
That hurry through the eternal halls,
A makeweight flying to the void,
Supplemental asteroid,
Or compensatory spark,
Shoots across the neutral Dark.

Man's the elm, and Wealth the vine,
Stanch and strong the tendrils twine :
Though the frail ringlets thee deceive,
None from its stock that vine can reave.
Fear not, then, thou child infirm,
There's no god dare wrong a worm.
Laurel crowns cleave to deserts
And power to him who power exerts ;
Hast not thy share ? On wingèd feet,
Lo ! it rushes thee to meet ;
And all that Nature made thy own,
Floating in air or pent in stone,
Will rive the hills and swim the sea
And, like thy shadow, follow thee.

COMPENSATION

EVER since I was a boy I have wished to
write a discourse on Compensation; for it
seemed to me when very young that on this
subject life was ahead of theology and the people knew more than the preachers taught. The
documents too from which the doctrine is to be
drawn, charmed my fancy by their endless variety, and lay always before me, even in sleep; for
they are the tools in our hands, the bread in our
basket, the transactions of the street, the farm
and the dwelling - house ; greetings, relations,
debts and credits, the influence of character, the
nature and endowment of all men. It seemed
to me also that in it might be shown men a ray
of divinity, the present action of the soul of this
world, clean from all vestige of tradition ; and
so the heart of man might be bathed by an inundation of eternal love, conversing with that
which he knows was always and always must be,
because it really is now. It appeared moreover
that if this doctrine could be stated in terms
with any resemblance to those bright intuitions
in which this truth is sometimes revealed to us, it
would be a star in many dark hours and crooked

passages in our journey, that would not suffer
us to lose our way.

I was lately confirmed in these desires by
hearing a sermon at church. The preacher, a
man esteemed for his orthodoxy, unfolded in the
ordinary manner the doctrine of the Last Judgment. He assumed that judgment is not executed in this world; that the wicked are successful; that the good are miserable;[1] and then
urged from reason and from Scripture a compensation to be made to both parties in the next
life. No offence appeared to be taken by the
congregation at this doctrine. As far as I could
observe when the meeting broke up they separated without remark on the sermon.

Yet what was the import of this teaching?
What did the preacher mean by saying that the
good are miserable in the present life? Was it
that houses and lands, offices, wine, horses, dress,
luxury, are had by unprincipled men, whilst the
saints are poor and despised; and that a compensation is to be made to these last hereafter,
by giving them the like gratifications another
day, — bank-stock and doubloons, venison and
champagne? This must be the compensation
intended; for what else? Is it that they are to
have leave to pray and praise? to love and serve

men? Why, that they can do now. The legitimate inference the disciple would draw was, —
'We are to have *such* a good time as the sinners
have now;' — or, to push it to its extreme import, — 'You sin now, we shall sin by and by;
we would sin now, if we could; not being successful we expect our revenge to-morrow.'

The fallacy lay in the immense concession
that the bad are successful; that justice is not
done now. The blindness of the preacher consisted in deferring to the base estimate of the
market of what constitutes a manly success, instead of confronting and convicting the world
from the truth; announcing the presence of the
soul; the omnipotence of the will; and so estab-
lishing the standard of good and ill, of success
and falsehood.

I find a similar base tone in the popular religious works of the day and the same doctrines
assumed by the literary men when occasionally
they treat the related topics. I think that our
popular theology has gained in decorum, and
not in principle, over the superstitions it has dis-
placed. But men are better than their theology.
Their daily life gives it the lie. Every ingenu-
ous and aspiring soul leaves the doctrine behind
him in his own experience, and all men feel

sometimes the falsehood which they cannot demonstrate. For men are wiser than they know.[1]
That which they hear in schools and pulpits
without afterthought, if said in conversation
would probably be questioned in silence. If a
man dogmatize in a mixed company on Providence and the divine laws, he is answered by
a silence which conveys well enough to an observer the dissatisfaction of the hearer, but his
incapacity to make his own statement.

I shall attempt in this and the following chapter[2] to record some facts that indicate the path
of the law of Compensation; happy beyond my
expectation if I shall truly draw the smallest arc
of this circle.

Polarity, or action and reaction, we meet in
every part of nature; in darkness and light; in
heat and cold; in the ebb and flow of waters;
in male and female; in the inspiration and expi-
ration of plants and animals; in the equation of
quantity and quality in the fluids of the animal
body; in the systole and diastole of the heart;
in the undulations of fluids and of sound; in
the centrifugal and centripetal gravity; in electricity, galvanism, and chemical affinity. Superinduce magnetism at one end of a needle, the

opposite magnetism takes place at the other
end. If the south attracts, the north repels. To
empty here, you must condense there. An inevitable dualism bisects nature, so that each
thing is a half, and suggests another thing to
make it whole; as, spirit, matter; man, woman;
odd, even; subjective, objective; in, out; upper,
under; motion, rest; yea, nay.'

Whilst the world is thus dual, so is every one
of its parts. The entire system of things gets
represented in every particle. There is somewhat that resembles the ebb and flow of the sea,
day and night, man and woman, in a single
needle of the pine, in a kernel of corn, in each
individual of every animal tribe. The reaction,
so grand in the elements, is repeated within
these small boundaries. For example, in the
animal kingdom the physiologist has observed
that no creatures are favorites, but a certain
compensation balances every gift and every defect. A surplusage given to one part is paid out
of a reduction from another part of the same
creature. If the head and neck are enlarged,
the trunk and extremities are cut short.

The theory of the mechanic forces is another
example. What we gain in power is lost in
time, and the converse. The periodic or com-

II

pensating errors of the planets is another instance. The influences of climate and soil in
political history is another. The cold climate
invigorates. The barren soil does not breed
fevers, crocodiles, tigers or scorpions.

The same dualism underlies the nature and
condition of man. Every excess causes a defect;
every defect an excess. Every sweet hath its
sour; every evil its good. Every faculty which
is a receiver of pleasure has an equal penalty put
on its abuse. It is to answer for its moderation
with its life. For every grain of wit there is a
grain of folly. For every thing you have missed,
you have gained something else; and for every
thing you gain, you lose something. If riches
increase, they are increased that use them. If
the gatherer gathers too much, Nature takes out
of the man what she puts into his chest; swells
the estate, but kills the owner. Nature hates
monopolies and exceptions. The waves of the
sea do not more speedily seek a level from their
loftiest tossing than the varieties of condition
tend to equalize themselves. There is always
some levelling circumstance that puts down the
overbearing, the strong, the rich, the fortunate,
substantially on the same ground with all others.
Is a man too strong and fierce for society and

by temper and position a bad citizen, — a morose ruffian, with a dash of the pirate in him? — Nature sends him a troop of pretty sons and daughters who are getting along in the dame's classes at the village school, and love and fear for them smooths his grim scowl to courtesy. Thus she contrives to intenerate the granite and felspar, takes the boar out and puts the lamb in and keeps her balance true.[1]

The farmer imagines power and place are fine things. But the President has paid dear for his White House. It has commonly cost him all his peace, and the best of his manly attributes. To preserve for a short time so conspicuous an appearance before the world, he is content to eat dust before the real masters who stand erect behind the throne. Or do men desire the more substantial and permanent grandeur of genius? Neither has this an immunity. He who by force of will or of thought is great and overlooks thousands, has the charges of that eminence. With every influx of light comes new danger. Has he light? he must bear witness to the light, and always outrun that sympathy which gives him such keen satisfaction, by his fidelity to new revelations of the incessant soul. He must hate father and mother, wife and child. Has he all

that the world loves and admires and covets?—
he must cast behind him their admiration and
afflict them by faithfulness to his truth and become a byword and a hissing.

This law writes the laws of cities and nations.
It is in vain to build or plot or combine against
it. Things refuse to be mismanaged long. *Res
nolunt diu male administrari.* Though no checks
to a new evil appear, the checks exist, and will
appear. If the government is cruel, the governor's life is not safe. If you tax too high, the
revenue will yield nothing. If you make the
criminal code sanguinary, juries will not convict.
If the law is too mild, private vengeance comes
in. If the government is a terrific democracy,
the pressure is resisted by an over-charge of energy in the citizen, and life glows with a fiercer
flame. The true life and satisfactions of man
seem to elude the utmost rigors or felicities of
condition and to establish themselves with great
indifferency under all varieties of circumstances.
Under all governments the influence of character remains the same,—in Turkey and in New
England about alike. Under the primeval des-
pots of Egypt, history honestly confesses that
man must have been as free as culture could
make him.

These appearances indicate the fact that the
universe is represented in every one of its particles. Every thing in nature contains all the
powers of nature. Every thing is made of one
hidden stuff; as the naturalist sees one type
under every metamorphosis, and regards a horse
as a running man, a fish as a swimming man, a
bird as a flying man, a tree as a rooted man.
Each new form repeats not only the main character of the type, but part for part all the details,
all the aims, furtherances, hindrances, energies
and whole system of every other. Every occupation, trade, art, transaction, is a compend of
the world and a correlative of every other. Each
one is an entire emblem of human life; of its
good and ill, its trials, its enemies, its course and
its end. And each one must somehow accom-
modate the whole man and recite all his destiny.

The world globes itself in a drop of dew.
The microscope cannot find the animalcule which
is less perfect for being little. Eyes, ears, taste,
smell, motion, resistance, appetite, and organs
of reproduction that take hold on eternity, —
all find room to consist in the small creature.
So do we put our life into every act. The true
doctrine of omnipresence is that God reappears
with all his parts in every moss and cobweb.

The value of the universe contrives to throw itself into every point. If the good is there, so is the evil; if the affinity, so the repulsion; if the force, so the limitation.

Thus is the universe alive. All things are moral. That soul which within us is a sentiment, outside of us is a law. We feel its inspiration; but there in history we can see its fatal strength. "It is in the world, and the world was made by it." Justice is not postponed. A perfect equity adjusts its balance in all parts of life. Ἀεὶ γὰρ εὖ πίπτουσιν οἱ Διὸς κύβοι,' — The dice of God are always loaded. The world looks like a multiplication-table, or a mathematical equation, which, turn it how you will, balances itself. Take what figure you will, its exact value, nor more nor less, still returns to you. Every secret is told, every crime is punished, every virtue rewarded, every wrong redressed, in silence and certainty. What we call retribution is the universal necessity by which the whole appears wherever a part appears. If you see smoke, there must be fire. If you see a hand or a limb, you know that the trunk to which it belongs is there behind.

Every act rewards itself, or in other words integrates itself, in a twofold manner; first in

the thing, or in real nature ; and secondly in the
circumstance, or in apparent nature. Men call'
the circumstance the retribution. The causal
retribution is in the thing and is seen by the
soul. The retribution in the circumstance is seen
by the understanding ; it is inseparable from the
thing, but is often spread over a long time and
so does not become distinct until after many
years. The specific stripes may follow late after
the offence, but they follow because they accompany it. Crime and punishment grow out of one
stem. Punishment is a fruit that unsuspected
ripens within the flower of the pleasure which
concealed it. Cause and effect, means and ends,
seed and fruit, cannot be severed ; for the effect
already blooms in the cause, the end preëxists in
the means, the fruit in the seed.[1]

Whilst thus the world will be whole and refuses to be disparted, we seek to act partially,
to sunder, to appropriate ; for example, — to
gratify the senses we sever the pleasure of the
senses from the needs of the character. The ingenuity of man has always been dedicated to the
solution of one problem, — how to detach the
sensual sweet, the sensual strong, the sensual
bright, etc., from the moral sweet, the moral
deep, the moral fair ; that is, again, to contrive

to cut clean off this upper surface so thin as to
leave it bottomless; to get a *one end*, without an
other end. The soul says, 'Eat;' the body would
feast. The soul says, 'The man and woman
shall be one flesh and one soul;' the body would
join the flesh only. The soul says, 'Have dominion over all things to the ends of virtue;'
the body would have the power over things to
its own ends.

The soul strives amain to live and work
through all things. It would be the only fact.
All things shall be added unto it,— power, pleasure, knowledge, beauty. The particular man
aims to be somebody; to set up for himself; to
truck and higgle for a private good; and, in
particulars, to ride that he may ride; to dress
that he may be dressed; to eat that he may eat;
and to govern, that he may be seen. Men seek
to be great; they would have offices, wealth,
power, and fame. They think that to be great
is to possess one side of nature,— the sweet,
without the other side, the bitter.

This dividing and detaching is steadily coun-
teracted. Up to this day it must be owned no
projector has had the smallest success. The
parted water reunites behind our hand. Pleasure is taken out of pleasant things, profit out

of profitable things, power out of strong things, as soon as we seek to separate them from the whole. We can no more halve things and get the sensual good, by itself, than we can get an inside that shall have no outside, or a light without a shadow. " Drive out Nature with a fork, she comes running back." [1]

Life invests itself with inevitable conditions, which the unwise seek to dodge, which one and another brags that he does not know, that they do not touch him; — but the brag is on his lips, the conditions are in his soul. If he escapes them in one part they attack him in another more vital part. If he has escaped them in form and in the appearance, it is because he has resisted his life and fled from himself, and the retribution is so much death. So signal is the failure of all attempts to make this separation of the good from the tax, that the experiment would not be tried, — since to try it is to be mad, — but for the circumstance that when the disease began in the will, of rebellion and separation, the intellect is at once infected, so that the man ceases to see God whole in each object, but is able to see the sensual allurement of an object and not see the sensual hurt; he sees the mermaid's head but not the dragon's tail, and thinks he can cut off that which he would have from that which he would not have. "How secret art thou who dwellest in the highest heavens in silence, O thou only great God, sprinkling with an unwearied providence certain penal blindnesses upon such as have unbridled desires!"[1]

The human soul is true to these facts in the painting of fable, of history, of law, of proverbs, of conversation. It finds a tongue in literature unawares. Thus the Greeks called Jupiter, Supreme Mind; but having traditionally ascribed to him many base actions, they involuntarily made amends to reason by tying up the hands of so bad a god. He is made as helpless as a king of England. Prometheus knows one secret which Jove must bargain for; Minerva, another. He cannot get his own thunders; Minerva keeps the key of them : —

> " Of all the gods, I only know the keys
> That ope the solid doors within whose vaults
> His thunders sleep." [2]

A plain confession of the in-working of the All and of its moral aim. The Indian mythology ends in the same ethics; and it would seem impossible for any fable to be invented and get any currency which was not moral. Aurora forgot to ask youth for her lover, and though Ti-

thonus is immortal, he is old, Achilles is not
quite invulnerable; the sacred waters did not
wash the heel by which Thetis held him. Sieg-
fried, in the Nibelungen, is not quite immortal,
for a leaf fell on his back whilst he was bathing
in the dragon's blood, and that spot which it
covered is mortal. And so it must be. There is
a crack in every thing God has made. It would
seem there is always this vindictive circumstance
stealing in at unawares even into the wild poesy
in which the human fancy attempted to make
bold holiday and to shake itself free of the old
laws, — this back-stroke, this kick of the gun,
certifying that the law is fatal; that in nature
nothing can be given, all things are sold.

This is that ancient doctrine of Nemesis, who
keeps watch in the universe and lets no offence
go unchastised. The Furies, they said, are at-
tendants on justice, and if the sun in heaven
should transgress his path they would punish
him. The poets related that stone walls and iron
swords and leathern thongs had an occult sympathy with the wrongs of their owners; that the
belt which Ajax gave Hector dragged the Tro-
jan hero over the field at the wheels of the car
of Achilles, and the sword which Hector gave
Ajax was that on whose point Ajax fell. They

recorded that when the Thasians erected a
statue to Theagenes, a victor in the games, one
of his rivals went to it by night and endeavored
to throw it down by repeated blows, until at last
he moved it from its pedestal and was crushed
to death beneath its fall.

This voice of fable has in it somewhat divine.
It came from thought above the will of the
writer. That is the best part of each writer which
has nothing private in it; that which he does
not know; that which flowed out of his constitution and not from his too active invention;
that which in the study of a single artist you
might not easily find, but in the study of many
you would abstract as the spirit of them all.
Phidias it is not, but the work of man in that
early Hellenic world that I would know. The
name and circumstance of Phidias, however convenient for history, embarrass when we come to
the highest criticism. We are to see that which
man was tending to do in a given period, and was
hindered, or, if you will, modified in doing, by
the interfering volitions of Phidias, of Dante,
of Shakspeare, the organ whereby man at the
moment wrought.[1]

Still more striking is the expression of this
fact in the proverbs of all nations, which are al-

ways the literature of reason, or the statements
of an absolute truth without qualification. Proverbs, like the sacred books of each nation, are
the sanctuary of the intuitions. That which the
droning world, chained to appearances, will not
allow the realist to say in his own words, it will
suffer him to say in proverbs without contradiction. And this law of laws, which the pulpit, the
senate and the college deny, is hourly preached
in all markets and workshops by flights of proverbs, whose teaching is as true and as omnipre-
sent as that of birds and flies.

All things are double, one against another. —
Tit for tat; an eye for an eye; a tooth for a
tooth; blood for blood; measure for measure;
love for love. — Give, and it shall be given
you. — He that watereth shall be watered himself. — What will you have? quoth God; pay for
it and take it. — Nothing venture, nothing have.
— Thou shalt be paid exactly for what thou hast
done, no more, no less. — Who doth not work
shall not eat. — Harm watch, harm catch. —
Curses always recoil on the head of him who
imprecates them. — If you put a chain around
the neck of a slave, the other end fastens itself
around your own. — Bad counsel confounds the
adviser. — The Devil is an ass.

It is thus written, because it is thus in life. Our action is overmastered and characterized above our will by the law of nature. We aim at a petty end quite aside from the public good, but our act arranges itself by irresistible magnetism in a line with the poles of the world.

A man cannot speak but he judges himself. With his will or against his will he draws his portrait to the eye of his companions by every word. Every opinion reacts on him who utters it. It is a thread-ball thrown at a mark, but the other end remains in the thrower's bag. Or rather it is a harpoon hurled at the whale, unwinding, as it flies, a coil of cord in the boat, and, if the harpoon is not good, or not well thrown, it will go nigh to cut the steersman in twain or to sink the boat.[1]

You cannot do wrong without suffering wrong. "No man had ever a point of pride that was not injurious to him," said Burke. The exclusive in fashionable life does not see that he excludes himself from enjoyment, in the attempt to appropriate it. The exclusionist in religion does not see that he shuts the door of heaven on himself, in striving to shut out others. Treat men as pawns and ninepins and you shall suffer as well as they. If you leave out their heart,

you shall lose your own. The senses would
make things of all persons; of women, of children, of the poor. The vulgar proverb, " I will
get it from his purse or get it from his skin," is
sound philosophy.

All infractions of love and equity in our social
relations are speedily punished. They are punished by fear. Whilst I stand in simple relations
to my fellow-man, I have no displeasure in meeting him. We meet as water meets water, or as
two currents of air mix, with perfect diffusion
and interpenetration of nature. But as soon as
there is any departure from simplicity and attempt at halfness, or good for me that is not
good for him, my neighbor feels the wrong; he
shrinks from me as far as I have shrunk from
him; his eyes no longer seek mine; there is war
between us; there is hate in him and fear in me.

All the old abuses in society, universal and
particular, all unjust accumulations of property
and power, are avenged in the same manner.
Fear is an instructor of great sagacity and the
herald of all revolutions. One thing he teaches,
that there is rottenness where he appears. He
is a carrion crow, and though you see not well
what he hovers for, there is death somewhere.
Our property is timid, our laws are timid, our

cultivated classes are timid. Fear for ages has boded and mowed and gibbered over government and property. That obscene bird is not there for nothing. He indicates great wrongs which must be revised.

Of the like nature is that expectation of change which instantly follows the suspension of our voluntary activity. The terror of cloudless noon, the emerald of Polycrates,¹ the awe of prosperity, the instinct which leads every generous soul to impose on itself tasks of a noble asceticism and vicarious virtue, are the tremblings of the balance of justice through the. heart and mind of man.

Experienced men of the world know very well that it is best to pay scot and lot as they go along, and that a man often pays dear for a small frugality. The borrower runs in his own debt. Has a man gained any thing who has received a hundred favors and rendered none? Has he gained by borrowing, through indolence or cunning, his neighbor's wares, or horses, or money? There arises on the deed the instant acknowledgment of benefit on the one part and of debt on the other; that is, of superiority and inferiority. The transaction remains in the memory of himself and his neighbor; and every new transaction alters according to its nature their

relation to each other. He may soon come to
see that he had better have broken his own bones
than to have ridden in his neighbor's coach, and
that " the highest price he can pay for a thing is
to ask for it." [1]

A wise man will extend this lesson to all parts
of life, and know that it is the part of prudence
to face every claimant and pay every just demand on your time, your talents, or your heart.
Always pay ; for first or last you must pay your
entire debt. Persons and events may stand for
a time between you and justice, but it is only a
postponement. You must pay at last your own
debt. If you are wise you will dread a prosperity which only loads you with more. Benefit is
the end of nature. But for every benefit which
you receive, a tax is levied. He is great who
confers the most benefits. He is base, — and
that is the one base thing in the universe, — to
receive favors and render none. In the order of
nature we cannot render benefits to those from
whom we receive them, or only seldom. But
the benefit we receive must be rendered again,
line for line, deed for deed, cent for cent, to
somebody. Beware of too much good staying in
your hand. It will fast corrupt and worm worms.
Pay it away quickly in some sort.

Labor is watched over by the same pitiless laws. Cheapest, say the prudent, is the dearest labor. What we buy in a broom, a mat, a wagon, a knife, is some application of good sense to a common want. It is best to pay in your land a skilful gardener, or to buy good sense applied to gardening; in your sailor, good sense applied to navigation; in the house, good sense applied to cooking, sewing, serving; in your agent, good sense applied to accounts and affairs. So do you multiply your presence, or spread yourself throughout your estate. But because of the dual constitution of things, in labor as in life there can be no cheating. The thief steals from himself. The swindler swindles himself. For the real price of labor is knowledge and virtue, whereof wealth and credit are signs. These signs, like paper money, may be counterfeited or stolen, but that which they represent, namely, knowledge and virtue, cannot be counterfeited or stolen. These ends of labor cannot be answered but by real exertions of the mind, and in obedience to pure motives. The cheat, the defaulter, the gambler, cannot extort the knowledge of material and moral nature which his honest care and pains yield to the operative. The law of nature is, Do the thing, and you shall have the power ; but they who do not the thing have not the power.

Human labor, through all its forms, from the sharpening of a stake to the construction of a city or an epic, is one immense illustration of the perfect· compensation of the universe. The absolute balance of Give and Take, the doctrine that every thing has its price, — and if that price is not paid, not that thing but something else is obtained, and that it is impossible to get anything without its price, — is not less sublime in the columns of a leger than in the budgets of states, in the laws of light and darkness, in all the action and reaction of nature. I cannot doubt that the high laws which each man sees implicated in those processes with which he is conversant, the stern ethics which sparkle on his chisel-edge, which are measured out by his plumb and foot-rule, which stand as manifest in the footing of the shop-bill as in the history of a state, — do recommend to him his trade, and though seldom named, exalt his business to his imagination.[1]

The league between virtue and nature engages all things to assume a hostile front to vice. The beautiful laws and substances of the world persecute and whip the traitor. He finds that things are arranged for truth and benefit, but there is no den in the wide world to hide a rogue. Commit a crime, and the earth is made of glass. Commit a crime, and it seems as if a coat of snow fell on the ground, such as reveals in the woods the track of every partridge and fox and squirrel and mole. You cannot recall the spoken word, you cannot wipe out the foot-track, you cannot draw up the ladder, so as to leave no inlet or clew. Some damning circumstance always transpires. The laws and substances of nature, — water, snow, wind, gravitation, — become penalties to the thief.

On the other hand the law holds with equal sureness for all right action. Love, and you shall be loved! All love is mathematically just, as much as the two sides of an algebraic equation. The good man has absolute good, which like fire turns every thing to its own nature, so that you cannot do him any harm ; but as the royal armies sent against Napoleon, when he approached cast down their colors and from enemies became friends, so disasters of all kinds, as sickness, offence, poverty, prove benefactors : —

> " Winds blow and waters roll
> Strength to the brave and power and deity,
> Yet in themselves are nothing." [1]

† Except for that "Self-Reliant" Wellington and that
" — — — — ˒ ˒ ˒ — ̣ ̣ ̣ ̣ ̣ ̣ ̣

The good are befriended even by weakness
and defect. As no man had ever a point of
pride that was not injurious to him, so no man
had ever a defect that was not somewhere made-
useful to him.[+] The stag in the fable admired
his horns and blamed his feet, but when the
hunter came, his feet saved him, and afterwards,
caught in the thicket, his horns destroyed him.
Every man in his lifetime needs to thank his
faults.' As no man thoroughly understands a
truth until he has contended against it, so no
man has a thorough acquaintance with the hindrances or talents of men until he has suffered
from the one and seen the triumph of the other
over his own want of the same. Has he a defect of temper that unfits him to live in society ?
Thereby he is driven to entertain himself alone
and acquire habits of self-help; and thus, like
the wounded oyster, he mends his shell with
pearl.

Our strength grows out of our weakness.
The indignation which arms itself with secret
forces does not awaken until we are pricked and
stung and sorely assailed. A great man is always
willing to be little. Whilst he sits on the cush-
ion of advantages, he goes to sleep. When he
is pushed, tormented, defeated, he has a chance

leprosy,
cancer,
insanity,
idiocy,
Mongolism,

[+] thus Johnson, afflicted with Scrofula, became
a great Lexicographer ?

to learn something; he has been put on his wits, on his manhood; he has gained facts; learns his ignorance; is cured of the insanity of conceit; has got moderation and real skill. The wise man throws himself on the side of his assailants. It is more his interest than it is theirs to find his weak point. The wound cicatrizes and falls off from him like a dead skin, and when they would triumph, lo! he has passed on invulnerable. Blame is safer than praise. I hate to be defended in a newspaper.[†] As long as all that is said is said against me, I feel a certain assurance of success. But as soon as honeyed words of praise are spoken for me I feel as one that lies unprotected before his enemies. In general, every evil to which we do not succumb is a benefactor. As the Sandwich Islander believes that the strength and valor of the enemy he kills passes into himself, so we gain the strength of the temptation we resist.

The same guards which protect us from disaster, defect and enmity, defend us, if we will, from selfishness and fraud. Bolts and bars are not the best of our institutions, nor is shrewdness in trade a mark of wisdom. Men suffer all their life long under the foolish superstition that they can be cheated. But it is as impossi-

[†] So do I.

ble for a man to be cheated by any one but
himself, as for a thing to be and not to be at
the same time. There is a third silent party to
all our bargains. The nature and soul of things
takes on itself the guaranty of the fulfilment of
every contract, so that honest service cannot
come to loss. If you serve an ungrateful master, serve him the more. Put God in your debt.[1]
Every stroke shall be repaid. The longer the
payment is withholden, the better for you ; for
compound interest on compound interest is the
rate and usage of this exchequer.[+]

The history of persecution is a history of endeavors to cheat nature, to make water run up
hill, to twist a rope of sand. It makes no difference whether the actors be many or one, a
tyrant or a mob. A mob is a society of bodies
voluntarily bereaving themselves of reason and
traversing its work. The mob is man voluntarily descending to the nature of the beast. Its
fit hour of activity is night. Its actions are insane, like its whole constitution. It persecutes
a principle ; it would whip a right ; it would
tar and feather justice, by inflicting fire and outrage upon the houses and persons of those who
have these. It resembles the prank of boys,
who run with fire-engines to put out the ruddy

[+] As the preacher said.

aurora streaming to the stars. The inviolate spirit turns their spite against the wrongdoers. The martyr cannot be dishonored. Every lash inflicted is a tongue of fame; every prison a more illustrious abode; every burned book or house enlightens the world; every suppressed or expunged word reverberates through the earth from side to side.[1] Hours of sanity and consideration are always arriving to communities, as to individuals, when the truth is seen and the martyrs are justified.[+]

Thus do all things preach the indifferency of circumstances. The man is all. Every thing has two sides, a good and an evil. Every advantage has its tax. I learn to be content. But the doctrine of compensation is not the doctrine of indifferency. The thoughtless say, on hearing these representations, — What boots it to do well? there is one event to good and evil; if I gain any good I must pay for it; if I lose any good I gain some other; all actions are indifferent.

There is a deeper fact in the soul than compensation, to wit, its own nature. The soul is not a compensation, but a life. The soul is. Under all this running sea of circumstance, whose waters ebb and flow with perfect balance,

[+] "Man never is, but always to be blest..."

YES!

lies the aboriginal abyss of real Being. Essence, or God, is not a relation or a part, but the whole.[1] Being is the vast affirmative, excluding negation, self-balanced, and swallowing up all relations, parts and times within itself. Nature, truth, virtue, are the influx from thence. Vice is the absence or departure of the same. Nothing, Falsehood, may indeed stand as the great Night or shade on which as a background the living universe paints itself forth, but no fact is begotten by it; it cannot work, for it is not. It cannot work any good; it cannot work any harm. It is harm inasmuch as it is worse not to be than to be.

We feel defrauded of the retribution due to evil acts, because the criminal adheres to his vice and contumacy and does not come to a crisis or judgment anywhere in visible nature. There is no stunning confutation of his nonsense before men and angels. Has he therefore outwitted the law? Inasmuch as he carries the malignity and the lie with him he so far deceases from nature. In some manner there will be a demonstration of the wrong to the understanding also; but, should we not see it, this deadly deduction makes square the eternal account.

Neither can it be said, on the other hand, that the gain of rectitude must be bought by any loss. There is no penalty to virtue ; no penalty to wisdom ; they are proper additions of being. In a virtuous action I properly *am ;* in a virtuous act I add to the world; I plant into deserts conquered from Chaos and Nothing and see the darkness receding on the limits of the horizon. There can be no excess to love, none to knowledge, none to beauty, when these attributes are considered in the purest sense. The soul refuses limits, and always affirms an Optimism, never a Pessimism.

His life is a progress, and not a station. His instinct is trust. Our instinct uses " more " and " less" in application to man, of the *presence of the soul,* and not of its absence ; the brave man is greater than the coward ; the true, the bene-volent, the wise, is more a man and not less, than the fool and knave. There is no tax on the good of virtue, for that is the incoming of God himself, or absolute existence, without any comparative. Material good has its tax, and if it came without desert or sweat, has no root in me, and the next wind will blow it away. But all the good of nature is the soul's, and may be had if paid for in nature's lawful coin, that is,

by labor which the heart and the head allow. I
no longer wish to meet a good I do not earn,
for example to find a pot of buried gold, knowing that it brings with it new burdens. I do not
wish more external goods, — neither possessions, nor honors, nor powers, nor persons.
The gain is apparent; the tax is certain. But
there is no tax on the knowledge that the compensation exists and that it is not desirable to
dig up treasure.¹ Herein I rejoice with a serene
eternal peace. I contract the boundaries of possible mischief. I learn the wisdom of St. Ber-
nard, — "Nothing can work me damage except
myself; the harm that I sustain I carry about
with me, and never am a real sufferer but by
my own fault."

In the nature of the soul is the compensation
for the inequalities of condition. The radical
tragedy of nature seems to be the distinction of
More and Less. How can Less not feel the
pain; how not feel indignation or malevolence
towards More? Look at those who have less
faculty, and one feels sad and knows not well
what to make of it. He almost shuns their
eye; he fears they will upbraid God. What
should they do? It seems a great injustice.
But see the facts nearly and these mountainous

inequalities vanish. Love reduces them as the sun melts the iceberg in the sea. The heart and soul of all men being one, this bitterness of *His* and *Mine* ceases. His is mine. I am my brother and my brother is me. If I feel over-shadowed and outdone by great neighbors, I can yet love; I can still receive; and he that loveth maketh his own the grandeur he loves. Thereby I make the discovery that my brother is my guardian, acting for me with the friend-liest designs, and the estate I so admired and envied is my own. It is the nature of the soul to appropriate all things. Jesus and Shakspeare are fragments of the soul, and by love I con-quer and incorporate them in my own conscious domain. His virtue, — is not that mine? His wit, — if it cannot be made mine, it is not wit.

Such also is the natural history of calamity. The changes which break up at short intervals the prosperity of men are advertisements of a nature whose law is growth. Every soul is by this intrinsic necessity quitting its whole system of things, its friends and home and laws and faith, as the shell-fish crawls out of its beautiful but stony case, because it no longer admits of its growth, and slowly forms a new house. In proportion to the vigor of the individual these

revolutions are frequent, until in some happier
mind they are incessant and all worldly relations hang very loosely about him, becoming as
it were a transparent fluid membrane through
which the living form is seen, and not, as in
most men, an indurated heterogeneous fabric of
many dates and of no settled character, in which
the man is imprisoned. Then there can be enlargement, and the man of to-day scarcely recognizes the man of yesterday. And such should
be the outward biography of man in time, a putting off of dead circumstances day by day, as he
renews his raiment day by day. But to us, in
our lapsed estate, resting, not advancing, resist-
ing, not coöperating with the divine expansion,
this growth comes by shocks.

We cannot part with our friends. We cannot
let our angels go. We do not see that they only
go out that archangels may come in.¹ We are
idolaters of the old. We do not believe in the
riches of the soul, in its proper eternity and omnipresence. We do not believe there is any force
in to-day to rival or recreate that beautiful yesterday. We linger in the ruins of the old tent
where once we had bread and shelter and organs,
nor believe that the spirit can feed, cover, and
nerve us again. We cannot again find aught so

dear, so sweet, so graceful. But we sit and weep in vain. The voice of the Almighty saith, 'Up and onward for evermore!' We cannot stay amid the ruins. Neither will we rely on the new; and so we walk ever with reverted eyes, like those monsters who look backwards.

And yet the compensations of calamity are made apparent to the understanding also, after long intervals of time. A fever, a mutilation, a cruel disappointment, a loss of wealth, a loss of friends, seems at the moment unpaid loss, and unpayable. But the sure years reveal the deep remedial force that underlies all facts. The death of a dear friend, wife, brother, lover, which seemed nothing but privation, somewhat later assumes the aspect of a guide or genius; for it commonly operates revolutions in our way of life, terminates an epoch of infancy or of youth which was waiting to be closed, breaks up a wonted occupation, or a household, or style of living, and allows the formation of new ones more friendly to the growth of character. It permits or constrains the formation of new acquaintances and the reception of new influences that prove of the first importance to the next years; and the man or woman who would have remained a sunny garden-flower, with no room for its roots and too much sunshine for its head, by the falling of the walls and the neglect of the gardener is made the banian of the forest, yielding shade and fruit to wide neighborhoods of men.

IV

SPIRITUAL LAWS[1]

THE living Heaven thy prayers respect,
House at once and architect,
Quarrying man's rejected hours,
Builds there with eternal towers;
Sole and self-commanded works,
Fears not undermining days,
Grows by decays,
And, by the famous might that lurks
In reaction and recoil,
Makes flame to freeze and ice to boil;
Forging, through swart arms of Offence,
The silver seat of Innocence.

SPIRITUAL LAWS

WHEN the act of reflection takes place in the mind, when we look at ourselves in the light of thought, we discover that our life is embosomed in beauty. Behind us, as we go, all things assume pleasing forms, as clouds do far off. Not only things familiar and stale, but even the tragic and terrible are comely as they take their place in the pictures of memory. The river-bank, the weed at the water-side, the old house, the foolish person, however neglected in the passing, have a grace in the past. Even the corpse that has lain in the chambers has added a solemn ornament to the house.[1] The soul will not know either deformity or pain. If in the hours of clear reason we should speak the severest truth, we should say that we had never made a sacrifice. In these hours the mind seems so great that nothing can be taken from us that seems much. All loss, all pain, is particular; the universe remains to the heart unhurt.[2] Neither vexations nor calamities abate our trust. No man ever stated his griefs as lightly as he might. Allow for exaggeration in the most patient and sorely ridden hack that ever was driven. For it

is only the finite that has wrought and suffered;
the infinite lies stretched in smiling repose.

The intellectual life may be kept clean and
healthful if man will live the life of nature and
not import into his mind difficulties which are
none of his. No man need be perplexed in his
speculations. Let him do and say what strictly
belongs to him, and though very ignorant of
books, his nature shall not yield him any intellectual obstructions and doubts. Our young people are diseased with the theological problems
of original sin, origin of evil, predestination and
the like. These never presented a practical difficulty to any man, — never darkened across any
man's road who did not go out of his way to
seek them. These are the soul's mumps and
measles and whooping-coughs, and those who
have not caught them cannot describe their
health or prescribe the cure. A simple mind will
not know these enemies.' It is quite another
thing that he should be able to give account of
his faith and expound to another the theory of
his self-union and freedom. This requires rare
gifts. Yet without this self-knowledge there
may be a sylvan strength and integrity in that
which he is. "A few strong instincts and a few
plain rules" suffice us.'

My will never gave the images in my mind the rank they now take. The regular course of studies, the years of academical and professional education have not yielded me better facts than some idle books under the bench at the Latin School. What we do not call education is more precious than that which we call so. We form no guess, at the time of receiving a thought, of its comparative value. And education often wastes its effort in attempts to thwart and balk this natural magnetism, which is sure to select what belongs to it.[1]

In like manner our moral nature is vitiated by any interference of our will. People represent virtue as a struggle, and take to themselves great airs upon their attainments, and the question is everywhere vexed when a noble nature is commended, whether the man is not better who strives with temptation. But there is no merit in the matter. Either God is there or he is not there. We love characters in proportion as they are impulsive and spontaneous. The less a man thinks or knows about his virtues the better we like him. Timoleon's victories are the best victories, which ran and flowed like Homer's verses, Plutarch said. When we see a soul whose acts are all regal, graceful and pleasant as roses, we must thank God that such things can be and are, and not turn sourly on the angel and say 'Crump is a better man with his grunting resistance to all his native devils.'

Not less conspicuous is the preponderance of nature over will in all practical life. There is less intention in history than we ascribe to it. We impute deep-laid far-sighted plans to Cæsar and Napoleon ; but the best of their power was in nature, not in them. Men of an extraordinary success, in their honest moments, have always sung ' Not unto us, not unto us.' According to the faith of their times they have built altars to Fortune, or to Destiny, or to St. Julian. Their success lay in their parallelism to the course of thought, which found in them an unobstructed channel ; and the wonders of which they were the visible conductors seemed to the eye their deed. Did the wires generate the galvanism ? It is even true that there was less in them on which they could reflect than in another ; as the virtue of a pipe is to be smooth and hollow.' That which externally seemed will and immovableness was willingness and self-annihilation. Could Shakspeare give a theory of Shakspeare ? Could ever a man of prodigious mathematical genius convey to others any insight into his methods? If he could communicate that secret it would instantly lose its exaggerated value, blending with the daylight and the vital energy the power to stand and to go.

The lesson is forcibly taught by these observations that our life might be much easier and simpler than we make it; that the world might be a happier place than it is; that there is no need of struggles, convulsions, and despairs, of the wringing of the hands and the gnashing of the teeth; that we miscreate our own evils. We interfere with the optimism of nature; for whenever we get this vantage-ground of the past, or of a wiser mind in the present, we are able to discern that we are begirt with laws which execute themselves.

The face of external nature teaches the same lesson. Nature will not have us fret and fume. She does not like our benevolence or our learning much better than she likes our frauds and wars. When we come out of the caucus, or the bank, or the Abolition-convention, or the Temperance - meeting, or the Transcendental club into the fields and woods, she says to us, 'So hot? my little Sir.' ¹

We are full of mechanical actions. We must needs intermeddle and have things in our own

way, until the sacrifices and virtues of society
are odious. Love should make joy; but our
benevolence is unhappy. Our Sunday-schools
and churches and pauper-societies are yokes
to the neck. We pain ourselves to please nobody. There are natural ways of arriving at the
same ends at which these aim, but do not arrive.
Why should all virtue work in one and the
same way? Why should all give dollars? It is
very inconvenient to us country folk, and we
do not think any good will come of it. We
have not dollars, merchants have; let them
give them. Farmers will give corn; poets. will
sing; women will sew; laborers will lend a
hand; the children will bring flowers. And why
drag this dead weight of a Sunday-school over
the whole Christendom? It is natural and beautiful that childhood should inquire and maturity
should teach; but it is time enough to answer
questions when they are asked. Do not shut
up the young people against their will in a pew
and force the children to ask them questions
for an hour against their will.

If we look wider, things are all alike; laws
and letters and creeds and modes of living seem
a travesty of truth. Our society is encumbered
by ponderous machinery, which resembles the

endless aqueducts which the Romans built over hill and dale and which are superseded by the discovery of the law that water rises to the level of its source. It is a Chinese wall which any nimble Tartar can leap over. It is a standing army, not so good as a peace. It is a graduated, titled, richly appointed empire, quite superfluous when town-meetings are found to answer just as well.

Let us draw a lesson from nature, which always works by short ways. When the fruit is ripe, it falls. When the fruit is despatched, the leaf falls. The circuit of the waters is mere falling. The walking of man and all animals is a falling forward. All our manual labor and works of strength, as prying, splitting, digging, rowing and so forth, are done by dint of continual falling, and the globe, earth, moon, comet, sun, star, fall for ever and ever.

The simplicity of the universe is very different from the simplicity of a machine. He who sees moral nature out and out and thoroughly knows how knowledge is acquired and character formed, is a pedant. The simplicity of nature is not that which may easily be read, but is inexhaustible. The last analysis can no wise be made. We judge of a man's wisdom by his hope, knowing that the perception of the inexhaustibleness of nature is an immortal youth. The wild fertility of nature is felt in comparing our rigid names and reputations with our fluid consciousness. We pass in the world for sects and schools, for erudition and piety, and we are all the time jejune babes. One sees very well how Pyrrhonism grew up.[1] Every man sees that he is that middle point whereof every thing may be affirmed and denied with equal reason. He is old, he is young, he is very wise, he is altogether ignorant. He hears and feels what you say of the seraphim, and of the tin-peddler. There is no permanent wise man except in the figment of the Stoics. We side with the hero, as we read or paint, against the coward and the robber; but we have been ourselves that coward and robber, and shall be again, — not in the low circumstance, but in comparison with the grandeurs possible to the soul.

A little consideration of what takes place around us every day would show us that a higher law than that of our will regulates events; that our painful labors are unnecessary and fruitless; that only in our easy, simple, spontaneous action are we strong, and by contenting ourselves with obedience we become divine.

Belief and love, — a believing love will relieve us of a vast load of care. O my brothers, God exists. There is a soul at the centre of nature and over the will of every man, so that none of us can wrong the universe. It has so infused its strong enchantment into nature that we prosper when we accept its advice, and when we struggle to wound its creatures our hands are glued to our sides, or they beat our own breasts. The whole course of things goes to teach us faith. We need only obey. There is guidance for each of us, and by lowly listening we shall hear the right word. Why need you choose so painfully your place and occupation and associates and modes of action and of entertainment? Certainly there is a possible right for you that precludes the need of balance and wilful election. For you there is a reality, a fit place and congenial duties. Place yourself in the middle of the stream of power and wisdom which animates all whom it floats, and you are without effort impelled to truth, to right and a perfect contentment. Then you put all gainsayers in the wrong. Then you are the world, the measure of right, of truth, of beauty. If we would not be mar-plots with our miserable interferences, the work, the society, letters, arts, science, religion of men would go on far better than now, and the heaven predicted from the beginning of the world, and still predicted from the bottom of the heart, would organize itself, as do now the rose and the air and the sun.

I say, *do not choose*; but that is a figure of speech by which I would distinguish what is commonly called *choice* among men, and which is a partial act, the choice of the hands, of the eyes, of the appetites, and not a whole act of the man.[1] But that which I call right or goodness, is the choice of my constitution ; and that which I call heaven, and inwardly aspire after, is the state or circumstance desirable to my constitution ; and the action which I in all my years tend to do, is the work for my faculties. We must hold a man amenable to reason for the choice of his daily craft or profession. It is not an excuse any longer for his deeds that they are the custom of his trade. What business has he with an evil trade? Has he not a *calling* in his character?

Each man has his own vocation. The talent is the call. There is one direction in which all space is open to him. He has faculties silently inviting him thither to endless exertion. He is like a ship in a river; he runs against obstruc-

tions on every side but one, on that side all obstruction is taken away and he sweeps serenely
over a deepening channel into an infinite sea.
This talent and this call depend on his organization, or the mode in which the general soul in-
carnates itself in him. He inclines to do something which is easy to him and good when it is
done, but which no other man can do. He has
no rival. For the more truly he consults his
own powers, the more difference will his work
exhibit from the work of any other. 'His ambition is exactly proportioned to his powers.' The
height of the pinnacle is determined by the
breadth of the base. Every man has this call
of the power to do somewhat unique, and no
man has any other call. The pretence that he
has another call, a summons by name and personal election and outward " signs that mark
him extraordinary and not in the roll of common men," ¹ is fanaticism, and betrays obtuse-
ness to perceive that there is one mind in all the
individuals, and no respect of persons therein.

By doing his work he makes the need felt
which he can supply, and creates the taste by
which he is enjoyed. By doing his own work
he unfolds himself. It is the vice of our public
speaking that it has not abandonment. Some-

where, not only every orator but every man
should let out all the length of all the reins ;
should find or make a frank and hearty expression of what force and meaning is in him. The
common experience is that the man fits himself
as well as he can to the customary details of that
work or trade he falls into, and tends it as a dog
turns a spit. Then is he a part of the machine
he moves ; the man is lost. Until he can man-
age to communicate himself to others in his full
stature and proportion, he does not yet find his
vocation. He must find in that an outlet for
his character, so that he may justify his work to
their eyes. If the labor is mean, let him by his
thinking and character make it liberal.[1] Whatever he knows and thinks, whatever in his
apprehension is worth doing, that let him communicate, or men will never know and honor
him aright. Foolish, whenever you take the
meanness and formality of that thing you do,
instead of converting it into the obedient spira- ·
cle of your character and aims.

We like only such actions as have already
long had the praise of men, and do not perceive
that any thing man can do may be divinely
done. We think greatness entailed or organ-
ized in some places or duties, in certain offices

or occasions, and do not see that Paganini can extract rapture from a catgut, and Eulenstein from a jews-harp, and a nimble-fingered lad out of shreds of paper with his scissors, and Landseer out of swine, and the hero out of the pitiful habitation and company in which he was hidden. What we call obscure condition or vulgar society is that condition and society whose poetry is not yet written, but which you shall presently make as enviable and renowned as any. In our estimates let us take a lesson from kings. The parts of hospitality, the connection of families, the impressiveness of death, and a thousand other things, royalty makes its own estimate of, and a royal mind will. To make habitually a new estimate, — that is elevation.

What a man does, that he has. What has he to do with hope or fear? In himself is his might. Let him regard no good as solid but that which is in his nature and which must grow out of him as long as he exists. The goods of fortune may come and go like summer leaves; [1] let him scatter them on every wind as the momentary signs of his infinite productiveness.

He may have his own. A man's genius, the quality that differences him from every other, the susceptibility to one class of influences, the

selection of what is fit for him, the rejection of
what is unfit, determines for him the character
of the universe. A man is a method, a progressive arrangement ; a selecting principle, gathering his like to him wherever he goes. He takes
only his own out of the multiplicity that sweeps
and circles round him. He is like one of those
booms which are set out from the shore on
rivers to catch drift-wood, or like the loadstone
amongst splinters of steel. Those facts, words,
persons, which dwell in his memory without his
being able to say why, remain because they have
a relation to him not less real for being as yet
unapprehended. They are symbols of value to
him as they can interpret parts of his consciousness which he would vainly seek words for in
the conventional images of books and other
minds. What attracts my attention shall have
it, as I will go to the man who knocks at my
door, whilst a thousand persons as worthy go
by it, to whom I give no regard. It is enough
that these particulars speak to me. A few anecdotes, a few traits of character, manners, face, a
few incidents, have an emphasis in your memory out of all proportion to their apparent significance if you measure them by the ordinary
standards. They relate to your gift. Let them

have their weight, and do not reject them and cast about for illustration and facts more usual in literature. What your heart thinks great, is great. The soul's emphasis is always right.

Over all things that are agreeable to his nature and genius the man has the highest right. Everywhere he may take what belongs to his spiritual estate, nor can he take anything else though all doors were open, nor can all the force of men hinder him from taking so much. It is vain to attempt to keep a secret from one who has a right to know it. It will tell itself. That mood into which a friend can bring us is his dominion over us. To the thoughts of that state of mind he has a right. All the secrets of that state of mind he can compel. This is a law which statesmen use in practice. All the terrors of the French Republic, which held Austria in awe, were unable to command her diplomacy. But Napoleon sent to Vienna M. de Narbonne, one of the old noblesse, with the morals, manners and name of that interest, saying that it was indispensable to send to the old aristocracy of Europe men of the same connection, which in fact constitutes a sort of free-masonry. M. de Narbonne in less than a fortnight penetrated all the secrets of the imperial cabinet.

II

Nothing seems so easy as to speak and to be understood. Yet a man may come to find *that* the strongest of defences and of ties, — that he has been understood ; and he who has received an opinion may come to find it the most inconvenient of bonds.

If a teacher have any opinion which he wishes to conceal, his pupils will become as fully indoctrinated into that as into any which he publishes. If you pour water into a vessel twisted into coils and angles, it is vain to say, I will pour it only into this or that ; — it will find its level in all. Men feel and act the consequences of your doctrine without being able to show how they follow. Show us an arc of the curve, and a good mathematician will find out the whole figure. We are always reasoning from the seen to the unseen. Hence the perfect intelligence that subsists between wise men of remote ages. A man cannot bury his meanings so deep in his book but time and like-minded men will find them. Plato had a secret doctrine, had he? What secret can he conceal from the eyes of Bacon? of Montaigne? of Kant? Therefore Aristotle said of his works, "They are published and not published."

No man can learn what he has not preparation for learning, however near to his eyes is the object. A chemist may tell his most precious secrets to a carpenter, and he shall be never the wiser, — the secrets he would not utter to a chemist for an estate. God screens us evermore from premature ideas. Our eyes are holden that we cannot see things that stare us in the face, until the hour arrives when the mind is ripened; then we behold them, and the time when we saw them not is like a dream.

Not in nature but in man is all the beauty and worth he sees. The world is very empty, and is indebted to this gilding, exalting soul for all its pride. " Earth fills her lap with splendors " *not* her own.¹ The vale of Tempe, Tivoli and Rome are earth and water, rocks and sky. There are as good earth and water in a thousand places, yet how unaffecting !

People are not the better for the sun and moon, the horizon and the trees; as it is not observed that the keepers of Roman galleries or the valets of painters have any elevation of thought, or that librarians are wiser men than others. There are graces in the demeanor of a polished and noble person which are lost upon the eye of a churl. These are like the stars whose light has not yet reached us.

He may see what he maketh. Our dreams
are the sequel of our waking knowledge.[1] The
visions of the night bear some proportion to
the visions of the day. Hideous dreams are ex-
aggerations of the sins of the day. We see our
evil affections embodied in bad physiognomies.
On the Alps the traveller sometimes beholds his
own shadow magnified to a giant, so that every
gesture of his hand is terrific. " My children,"
said an old man to his boys scared by a figure
in the dark entry, " my children, you will never
see anything worse than yourselves." As in
dreams, so in the scarcely less fluid events of the
world every man sees himself in colossal, without knowing that it is himself. The good, compared to the evil which he sees, is as his own
good to his own evil. Every quality of his mind
is magnified in some one acquaintance, and every
emotion of his heart in some one. He is like
a quincunx of trees, which counts five, — east,
west, north, or south ; or an initial, medial, and
terminal acrostic. And why not? He cleaves
to one person and avoids another, according to
their likeness or unlikeness to himself, truly
seeking himself in his associates and moreover
in his trade and habits and gestures and meats
and drinks, and comes at last to be faithfully

represented by every view you take of his circumstances.

He may read what he writes. What can we see or acquire but what we are? You have observed a skilful man reading Virgil. Well, that author is a thousand books to a thousand persons. Take the book into your two hands and read your eyes out, you will never find what I find. If any ingenious reader would have a monopoly of the wisdom or delight he gets, he is as secure now the book is Englished, as if it were imprisoned in the Pelews' tongue. It is with a good book as it is with good company. Introduce a base person among gentlemen, it is all to no purpose; he is not their fellow. Every society protects itself. The company is perfectly safe, and he is not one of them, though his body is in the room.

What avails it to fight with the eternal laws of mind, which adjust the relation of all persons to each other by the mathematical measure of their havings and beings? Gertrude is enamored of Guy; how high, how aristocratic, how Roman his mien and manners! to live with him were life indeed, and no purchase is too great; and heaven and earth are moved to that end. Well, Gertrude has Guy; but what now avails how high, how aristocratic, how Roman his mien and manners, if his heart and aims are in the senate, in the theatre and in the billiard-room, and she has no aims, no conversation that can enchant her graceful lord ?

He shall have his own society. We can love nothing but nature. The most wonderful talents, the most meritorious exertions really avail very little with us ; but nearness or likeness of nature, — how beautiful is the ease of its victory ! Persons approach us, famous for their beauty, for their accomplishments, worthy of all wonder for their charms and gifts; they dedicate their whole skill to the hour and the company, — with very imperfect result. To be sure it would be ungrateful in us not to praise them loudly. Then, when all is done, a person of related mind, a brother or sister by nature, comes to us so softly and easily, so nearly and intimately, as if it were the blood in our proper veins, that we feel as if some one was gone, instead of another having come ; we are utterly relieved and refreshed ; it is a sort of joyful solitude. We foolishly think in our days of sin that we must court friends by compliance to the customs of society, to its dress, its breeding, and its estimates. But only that soul can be my friend which I encounter on the line of my own march, that soul to which I do not decline and which does not decline to me, but, native of the same celestial latitude, repeats in its own all my experience. The scholar forgets himself and apes the customs and costumes of the man of the world to deserve the smile of beauty, and follows some giddy girl, not yet taught by religious passion to know the noble woman with all that is serene, oracular and beautiful in her soul. Let him be great, and love shall follow him. Nothing is more deeply punished than the neglect of the affinities by which alone society should be formed, and the insane levity of choosing associates by others' eyes.[1]

He may set his own rate. It is a maxim worthy of all acceptation that a man may have that allowance he takes. Take the place and attitude which belong to you, and all men acquiesce. The world must be just. It leaves every man, with profound unconcern, to set his own rate. Hero or driveller, it meddles not in the matter. It will certainly accept your own measure of your doing and being, whether you sneak about and deny your own name, or whether you see your work produced to the concave sphere of the heavens, one with the revolution of the stars.

The same reality pervades all teaching. The man may teach by doing, and not otherwise. If he can communicate himself he can teach, but not by words. He teaches who gives, and he learns who receives. There is no teaching until the pupil is brought into the same state or principle in which you are; a transfusion takes place; he is you and you are he; then is a teaching, and by no unfriendly chance or bad company can he ever quite lose the benefit. But your propositions run out of one ear as they ran in at the other. We see it advertised that Mr. Grand will deliver an oration on the Fourth of July, and Mr. Hand before the Mechanics' Association, and we do not go thither, because we know that these gentlemen will not communicate their own character and experience to the company. If we had reason to expect such a confidence we should go through all inconvenience and opposition. The sick would be carried in litters. But a public oration is an escapade, a non-committal, an apology, a gag, and not a communication, not a speech, not a man.

A like Nemesis presides over all intellectual works. We have yet to learn that the thing uttered in words is not therefore affirmed. It must affirm itself, or no forms of logic or of oath can give it evidence. The sentence must also contain its own apology for being spoken.[1]

The effect of any writing on the public mind is mathematically measurable by its depth of thought. How much water does it draw? If it awaken you to think, if it lift you from your feet with the great voice of eloquence, then the effect is to be wide, slow, permanent, over the minds of men; if the pages instruct you not, they will die like flies in the hour. The way to speak and write what shall not go out of fashion is to speak and write sincerely. The argument which has not power to reach my own practice, I may well doubt will fail to reach yours. But take Sidney's maxim:— "Look in thy heart, and write." He that writes to himself writes to an eternal public. That statement only is fit to be made public which you have come at in attempting to satisfy your own curiosity. The writer who takes his subject from his ear and not from his heart, should know that he has lost as much as he seems to have gained, and when the empty book has gathered all its praise, and half the people say, 'What poetry! what genius!' it still needs fuel to make fire. That only profits which is profitable. Life alone can

impart life; and though we should burst we
can only be valued as we make ourselves valuable. There is no luck in literary reputation.
They who make up the final verdict upon every
book are not the partial and noisy readers of
the hour when it appears, but a court as of angels, a public not to be bribed, not to be en-
treated and not to be overawed, decides upon
every man's title to fame. Only those books
come down which deserve to last. Gilt edges,
vellum and morocco, and presentation - copies
to all the libraries will not preserve a book in
circulation beyond its intrinsic date. It must go
with all Walpole's Noble and Royal Authors
to its fate. Blackmore, Kotzebue or Pollok
may endure for a night, but Moses and Homer
stand for ever. There are not in the world at
any one time more than a dozen persons who
read and understand Plato, — never enough to
pay for an edition of his works; yet to every
generation these come duly down, for the sake
of those few persons, as if God brought them in
his hand. "No book," said Bentley, "was ever
written down by any but itself." The permanence of all books is fixed by no effort, friendly
or hostile, but by their own specific gravity, or
the intrinsic importance of their contents to the

constant mind of man. "Do not trouble yourself too much about the light on your statue,"
said Michel Angelo to the young sculptor; "the
light of the public square will test its value."

In like manner the effect of every action is
measured by the depth of the sentiment from
which it proceeds. The great man knew not
that he was great. It took a century or two for
that fact to appear. What he did, he did because he must; it was the most natural thing in
the world, and grew out of the circumstances of
the moment. But now, every thing he did, even
to the lifting of his finger or the eating of bread,
looks large, all-related, and is called an institution.

These are the demonstrations in a few particulars of the genius of nature; they show the
direction of the stream. But the stream is blood;
every drop is alive. Truth has not single victories; all things are its organs, — not only dust
and stones, but errors and lies. The laws of disease, physicians say, are as beautiful as the laws
of health. Our philosophy is affirmative and
readily accepts the testimony of negative facts,
as every shadow points to the sun. By a divine
necessity every fact in nature is constrained to
offer its testimony.

Human character evermore publishes itself.
The most fugitive deed and word, the mere air
of doing a thing, the intimated purpose, expresses character. If you act you show character; if you sit still, if you sleep, you show it.
You think because you have spoken nothing
when others spoke, and have given no opinion
on the times, on the church, on slavery, on marriage, on socialism, on secret societies, on the
college, on parties and persons, that your verdict is still expected with curiosity as a reserved
wisdom. Far otherwise; your silence answers
very loud. You have no oracle to utter, and
your fellow-men have learned that you cannot
help them; for oracles speak. Doth not Wisdom cry and Understanding put forth her
voice?

Dreadful limits are set in nature to the powers
of dissimulation. Truth tyrannizes over the un-
willing members of the body. Faces never lie,
it is said. No man need be deceived who will
study the changes of expression. When a man
speaks the truth in the spirit of truth, his eye is
as clear as the heavens. When he has base ends
and speaks falsely, the eye is muddy and sometimes asquint.

I have heard an experienced counsellor' say

that he never feared the effect upon a jury of a lawyer who does not believe in his heart that his client ought to have a verdict. If he does not believe it his unbelief will appear to the jury, despite all his protestations, and will become their unbelief. This is that law whereby a work of art, of whatever kind, sets us in the same state of mind wherein the artist was when he made it. That which we do not believe we cannot adequately say, though we may repeat the words never so often. It was this conviction which Swedenborg expressed when he described a group of persons in the spiritual world endeavoring in vain to articulate a proposition which they did not believe; but they could not, though they twisted and folded their lips even to indignation.

A man passes for that he is worth. Very idle is all curiosity concerning other people's estimate of us, and all fear of remaining unknown is not less so. If a man know that he can do any thing, — that he can do it better than any one else, — he has a pledge of the acknowledgment of that fact by all persons. The world is full of judgment-days, and into every assembly that a man enters, in every action he attempts, he is gauged and stamped. In every troop of boys

that whoop and run in each yard and square, a
new-comer is as well and accurately weighed in
the course of a few days and stamped with his
right number, as if he had undergone a formal trial of his strength, speed and temper. A
stranger comes from a distant school, with better
dress, with trinkets in his pockets, with airs and
pretensions ; an older boy says to himself, ' It's
of no use ; we shall find him out to-morrow.'
' What has he done ?' is the divine question
which searches men and transpierces every false
reputation. A fop may sit in any chair of the
world nor be distinguished for his hour from
Homer and Washington ; but there need never
be any doubt concerning the respective ability
of human beings. Pretension may sit still, but
cannot act. Pretension never feigned an act of
real greatness. Pretension never wrote an Iliad,
nor drove back Xerxes, nor christianized the
world, nor abolished slavery.

As much virtue as there is, so much appears ;
as much goodness as there is, so much reverence it commands. All the devils respect virtue. The high, the generous, the self-devoted
sect will always instruct and command mankind.
Never was a sincere word utterly lost. Never
a magnanimity fell to the ground, but there is

some heart to greet and accept it unexpectedly.
A man passes for that he is worth. What he is
engraves itself on his face, on his form, on his
fortunes, in letters of light. Concealment avails
him nothing, boasting nothing. There is confession in the glances of our eyes, in our smiles,
in salutations, and the grasp of hands. His sin
bedaubs him, mars all his good impression.
Men know not why they do not trust him, but
they do not trust him. His vice glasses his eye,
cuts lines of mean expression in his cheek,
pinches the nose, sets the mark of the beast on
the back of the head, and writes O fool! fool!
on the forehead of a king.

If you would not be known to do any thing,
never do it. A man may play the fool in the
drifts of a desert, but every grain of sand shall
seem to see. He may be a solitary eater, but
he cannot keep his foolish counsel. A broken
complexion, a swinish look, ungenerous acts
and the want of due knowledge, — all blab.
Can a cook, a Chiffinch, an Iachimo be mistaken
for Zeno or Paul? Confucius exclaimed, —
"How can a man be concealed? How can a
man be concealed?"

On the other hand, the hero fears not that
if he withhold the avowal of a just and brave

act it will go unwitnessed and unloved. One knows it, — himself, — and is pledged by it to sweetness of peace and to nobleness of aim which will prove in the end a better proclamation of it than the relating of the incident. Virtue is the adherence in action to the nature of things and the nature of things makes it prevalent. It consists in a perpetual substitution of being for seeming, and with sublime propriety God is described as saying, I AM.

The lesson which these observations convey is, Be, and not seem. Let us acquiesce. Let us take our bloated nothingness out of the path of the divine circuits. Let us unlearn our wisdom of the world. Let us lie low in the Lord's power and learn that truth alone makes rich and great.

If you visit your friend, why need you apologize for not having visited him, and waste his time and deface your own act? Visit him now. Let him feel that the highest love has come to see him, in thee its lowest organ. Or why need you torment yourself and friend by secret self-reproaches that you have not assisted him or complimented him with gifts and salutations heretofore? Be a gift and a benediction. Shine with real light and not with the borrowed reflection of gifts. Common men are apologies for men; they bow the head, excuse themselves with prolix reasons, and accumulate appearances because the substance is not.

We are full of these superstitions of sense, the worship of magnitude. We call the poet inactive, because he is not a president, a merchant, or a porter. We adore an institution, and do not see that it is founded on a thought which we have. But real action is in silent moments. The epochs of our life are not in the visible facts of our choice of a calling, our marriage, our acquisition of an office, and the like, but in a silent thought by the wayside as we walk; in a thought which revises our entire manner of life and says, — 'Thus hast thou done, but it were better thus.' And all our after years, like menials, serve and wait on this, and according to their ability execute its will. This revisal or correction is a constant force, which, as a tendency, reaches through our lifetime. The object of the man, the aim of these moments, is to make daylight shine through him, to suffer the law to traverse his whole being without obstruction, so that on what point soever of his doing your eye falls it shall report truly of his character, whether it be his diet, his

II

house, his religious forms, his society, his mirth,
his vote, his opposition. Now he is not homo-
geneous, but heterogeneous, and the ray does
not traverse ; there are no thorough lights, but
the eye of the beholder is puzzled, detecting
many unlike tendencies and a life not yet at
one.

Why should we make it a point with our
false modesty to disparage that man we are and
that form of being assigned to us ? A good
man is contented. I love and honor Epaminondas, but I do not wish to be Epaminondas.
I hold it more just to love the world of this
hour than the world of his hour. Nor can you,
if I am true, excite me to the least uneasiness
by saying, ' He acted and thou sittest still.' I
see action to be good, when the need is, and
sitting still to be also good. Epaminondas, if
he was the man I take him for, would have sat
still with joy and peace, if his lot had been mine.
Heaven is large, and affords space for all modes
of love and fortitude. Why should we be busy-
bodies and superserviceable? Action and inac-
tion are alike to the true. One piece of the tree
is cut for a weathercock and one for the sleeper
of a bridge; the virtue of the wood is apparent
in both.

I desire not to disgrace the soul. The fact
that I am here certainly shows me that the soul
had need of an organ here. Shall I not assume
the post? Shall I skulk and dodge and duck
with my unseasonable apologies and vain modesty and imagine my being here impertinent?
less pertinent than Epaminondas or Homer being there? and that the soul did not know its
own needs? Besides, without any reasoning on
the matter, I have no discontent. The good
soul nourishes me and unlocks new magazines
of power and enjoyment to me every day. I
will not meanly decline the immensity of good,
because I have heard that it has come to others
in another shape.

Besides, why should we be cowed by the
name of Action? 'T is a trick of the senses, —
no more. We know that the ancestor of every
action is a thought. The poor mind does not
seem to itself to be any thing unless it have an
outside badge, — some Gentoo diet, or Quaker
coat, or Calvinistic prayer-meeting, or philan-
thropic society, or a great donation, or a high
office, or, any how, some wild contrasting action
to testify that it is somewhat. The rich mind
lies in the sun and sleeps, and is Nature. To
think is to act.

Let us, if we must have great actions, make our own so. All action is of an infinite elasticity, and the least admits of being inflated with the celestial air until it eclipses the sun and moon. Let us seek *one* peace by fidelity. Let me heed my duties. Why need I go gadding into the scenes and philosophy of Greek and Italian history before I have justified myself to my benefactors? How dare I read Washington's campaigns when I have not answered the letters of my own correspondents? Is not that a just objection to much of our reading? It is a pusillanimous desertion of our work to gaze after our neighbors. It is peeping. Byron says of Jack Bunting, —

He knew not what to say, and so he swore.[1]

I may say it of our preposterous use of books, — He knew not what to do, and so *he read.* I can think of nothing to fill my time with, and I find the Life of Brant. It is a very extravagant compliment to pay to Brant, or to General Schuyler, or to General Washington. My time should be as good as their time, — my facts, my net of relations, as good as theirs, or either of theirs. Rather let me do my work so well that other idlers if they choose may compare my texture with the texture of these and find it identical with the best.

This over-estimate of the possibilities of Paul and Pericles, this under-estimate of our own, comes from a neglect of the fact of an identical nature. Bonaparte knew but one merit, and rewarded in one and the same way the good soldier, the good astronomer, the good poet, the good player. The poet uses the names of Cæsar, of Tamerlane, of Bonduca,[1] of Belisarius; the painter uses the conventional story of the Virgin Mary, of Paul, of Peter. He does not therefore defer to the nature of these accidental men, of these stock heroes. If the poet write a true drama, then he is Cæsar, and not the player of Cæsar; then the selfsame strain of thought, emotion as pure, wit as subtle, motions as swift, mounting, extravagant, and a heart as great, self-sufficing, dauntless, which on the waves of its love and hope can uplift all that is reckoned solid and precious in the world, — palaces, gardens, money, navies, kingdoms, — marking its own incomparable worth by the slight it casts on these gauds of men; — these all are his, and by the power of these he rouses the nations. Let a man believe in God, and not in names and places and persons. Let the great soul incarnated in some woman's form, poor and sad and single, in some Dolly or Joan, go out to service and sweep chambers and scour floors, and its effulgent daybeams cannot be muffled or hid, but to sweep and scour will instantly appear supreme and beautiful actions, the top and radiance of human life, and all people will get mops and brooms; until, lo! suddenly the great soul has enshrined itself in some other form and done some other deed, and that is now the flower and head of all living nature.[1]

We are the photometers, we the irritable gold-leaf and tinfoil that measure the accumulations of the subtle element. We know the authentic effects of the true fire through every one of its million disguises.

V

LOVE

" I WAS as a gem concealed ;
Me my burning ray revealed."

Koran.[1]

LOVE

EVERY promise of the soul has innumerable fulfilments; each of its joys ripens into a new want. Nature, uncontainable, flowing, forelooking, in the first sentiment of kindness anticipates already a benevolence which shall lose all particular regards in its general light. The introduction to this felicity is in a private and tender relation of one to one, which is the enchantment of human life; which, like a certain divine rage and enthusiasm, seizes on man at one period and works a revolution in his mind and body; unites him to his race, pledges him to the domestic and civic relations, carries him with new sympathy into nature, enhances the power of the senses, opens the imagination, adds to his character heroic and sacred attributes, establishes marriage and gives permanence to human society.

The natural association of the sentiment of love with the heyday of the blood seems to require that in order to portray it in vivid tints, which every youth and maid should confess to be true to their throbbing experience, one must not be too old. The delicious fancies of youth reject the least savor of a mature philosophy, as chilling with age and pedantry their purple bloom. And therefore I know I incur the imputation of unnecessary hardness and stoicism from those who compose the Court and Parliament of Love. But from these formidable censors I shall appeal to my seniors. For it is to be considered that this passion of which we speak, though it begin with the young, yet forsakes not the old, or rather suffers no one who is its servant to grow old, but makes the aged participators of it not less than the tender maiden, though in a different and nobler sort. For it is a fire that kindling its first embers in the narrow nook of a private bosom, caught from a wandering spark out of another private heart, glows and enlarges until it warms and beams upon multitudes of men and women, upon the universal heart of all, and so lights up the whole world and all nature with its generous flames. It matters not therefore whether we attempt to describe the passion at twenty, thirty, or at eighty years. He who paints it at the first period will lose some of its later, he who paints it at the last, some of its earlier traits. Only it is to be hoped that by patience and the Muses' aid we may attain to that inward view of the law which

shall describe a truth ever young and beautiful,
so central that it shall commend itself to the eye
at whatever angle beholden.

And the first condition is that we must leave
a too close and lingering adherence to facts, and
study the sentiment as it appeared in hope, and
not in history. For each man sees his own life
defaced and disfigured, as the life of man is not
to his imagination. Each man sees over his own
experience a certain stain of error, whilst that
of other men looks fair and ideal. Let any
man go back to those delicious relations which
make the beauty of his life, which have given
him sincerest instruction and nourishment, he
will shrink and moan. Alas ! I know not why,
but infinite compunctions embitter in mature
life the remembrances of budding joy, and cover
every beloved name.¹ Every thing is beautiful
seen from the point of the intellect, or as truth.
But all is sour if seen as experience. Details
are melancholy ; the plan is seemly and noble.
In the actual world — the painful kingdom of
time and place — dwell care and canker and fear.
With thought, with the ideal, is immortal hilarity, the rose of joy. Round it all the Muses
sing. But grief cleaves to names and persons and
the partial interests of to-day and yesterday.

The strong bent of nature is seen in the proportion which this topic of personal relations
usurps in the conversation of society. What do
we wish to know of any worthy person so much
as how he has sped in the history of this sentiment? What books in the circulating library
circulate? How we glow over these novels of
passion, when the story is told with any spark
of truth and nature! And what fastens attention, in the intercourse of life, like any passage
betraying affection between two parties? Perhaps we never saw them before and never shall
meet them again. But we see them exchange a
glance or betray a deep emotion, and we are no
longer strangers. We understand them and take
the warmest interest in the development of the
romance. All mankind love a lover. The earliest demonstrations of complacency and kindness are nature's most winning pictures.[1] It is
the dawn of civility and grace in the coarse and
rustic. The rude village boy teases the girls
about the school-house door; — but to-day he
comes running into the entry and meets one
fair child disposing her satchel; he holds her
books to help her, and instantly it seems to
him as if she removed herself from him infinitely, and was a sacred precinct. Among the

throng of girls he runs rudely enough, but one
alone distances him; and these two little neighbors, that were so close just now, have learned
to respect each other's personality. Or who can
avert his eyes from the engaging, half-artful,
half-artless ways of school-girls who go into the
country shops to buy a skein of silk or a sheet
of paper, and talk half an hour about nothing
with the broad-faced, good-natured shop-boy.
In the village they are on a perfect equality,
which love delights in, and without any coquetry
the happy, affectionate nature of woman flows
out in this pretty gossip. The girls may have
little beauty, yet plainly do they establish between them and the good boy the most agreeable, confiding relations; what with their fun
and their earnest, about Edgar and Jonas and
Almira, and who was invited to the party, and
who danced at the dancing-school, and when
the singing-school would begin, and other no-
things concerning which the parties cooed. By
and by that boy wants a wife, and very truly
and heartily will he know where to find a sincere and sweet mate, without any risk such as
Milton deplores as incident to scholars and
great men.

I have been told that in some public dis-

·courses of mine my reverence for the intellect has made me unjustly cold to the personal relations. But now I almost shrink at the remembrance of such disparaging words. For persons are love's world, and the coldest philosopher cannot recount the debt of the young soul wandering here in nature to the power of love, without being tempted to unsay, as treasonable to nature, aught derogatory to the social instincts. For though the celestial rapture falling out of heaven seizes only upon those of tender age, and although a beauty overpowering all analysis or comparison and putting us quite beside ourselves we can seldom see after thirty years, yet the remembrance of these visions outlasts all other remembrances, and is a wreath of flowers on the oldest brows. But here is a strange fact; it may seem to many men, in revising their experience, that they have no fairer page in their life's book than the delicious memory of some passages wherein affection contrived to give a witchcraft, surpassing the deep attraction of its own truth, to a parcel of accidental and trivial circumstances. In looking backward they may find that several things which were not the charm have more reality to this groping memory than the charm itself which embalmed them.

But be our experience in particulars what it
may, no man ever forgot the visitations of that
power to his heart and brain, which created
all things anew ; which was the dawn in him
of music, poetry and art ; which made the face
of nature radiant with purple light, the morning and the night varied enchantments ; when a
single tone of one voice could make the heart
bound, and the most trivial circumstance associated with one form is put in the amber of
memory ; when he became all eye when one was
present, and all memory when one was gone ;
when the youth becomes a watcher of windows and studious of a glove, a veil, a ribbon,
or the wheels of a carriage ; when no place is
too solitary and none too silent for him who
has richer company and sweeter conversation in
his new thoughts than any old friends, though
best and purest, can give him ; for the figures,
the motions, the words of the beloved object
are not, like other images, written in water, but,
as Plutarch said, " enamelled in fire," and make
the study of midnight : —

> " Thou art not gone being gone, where'er thou art,
>   Thou leav'st in him thy watchful eyes, in him thy loving
>   heart." [1]

In the noon and the afternoon of life we still

throb at the recollection of days when happiness was not happy enough, but must be drugged with the relish of pain and fear; for he touched the secret of the matter who said of love, —

" All other pleasures are not worth its pains : " [1]

and when the day was not long enough, but the night too must be consumed in keen recollections; when the head boiled all night on the pillow with the generous deed it resolved on; when the moonlight was a pleasing fever and the stars were letters and the flowers ciphers and the air was coined into song; when all business seemed an impertinence, and all the men and women running to and fro in the streets, mere pictures.

The passion rebuilds the world for the youth. It makes all things alive and significant. Nature grows conscious. Every bird on the boughs of the tree sings now to his heart and soul. The notes are almost articulate. The clouds have faces as he looks on them. The trees of the forest, the waving grass and the peeping flowers have grown intelligent; and he almost fears to trust them with the secret which they seem to invite. Yet nature soothes and sympathizes. In the green solitude he finds a dearer home than with men : —

" Fountain-heads and pathless groves,
    Places which pale passion loves,
    Moonlight walks, when all the fowls
    Are safely housed, save bats and owls,
    A midnight bell, a passing groan, —
    These are the sounds we feed upon." [1]

Behold there in the wood the fine madman ! He is a palace of sweet sounds and sights ; he dilates ; he is twice a man ; he walks with arms akimbo ; he soliloquizes ; he accosts the grass and the trees ; he feels the blood of the violet, the clover and the lily in his veins ; and he talks with the brook that wets his foot.[2]

The heats that have opened his perceptions of natural beauty have made him love music and verse. It is a fact often observed, that men have written good verses under the inspiration of passion who cannot write well under any other circumstances.

The like force has the passion over all his nature. It expands the sentiment ; it makes the clown gentle and gives the coward heart. Into the most pitiful and abject it will infuse a heart and courage to defy the world, so only it have the countenance of the beloved object. In giving him to another it still more gives him to himself. He is a new man, with new percep-

II

tions, new and keener purposes, and a religious solemnity of character and aims. He does not longer appertain to his family and society ; *he* is somewhat ; *he* is a person ; *he* is a soul.

And here let us examine a little nearer the nature of that influence which is thus potent over the human youth. Beauty, whose revelation to man we now celebrate, welcome as the sun wherever it pleases to shine, which pleases everybody with it and with themselves, seems sufficient to itself. The lover cannot paint his maiden to his fancy poor and solitary. Like a tree in flower, so much soft, budding, informing loveliness is society for itself ; and she teaches his eye why Beauty was pictured with Loves and Graces attending her steps. Her existence makes the world rich. Though she extrudes all other persons from his attention as cheap and unworthy, she indemnifies him by carrying out her own being into somewhat impersonal, large, mundane, so that the maiden stands to him for a representative of all select things and virtues. For that reason the lover never sees personal resemblances in his mistress to her kindred or to others. His friends find in her a likeness to her mother, or her sisters, or to persons not of her blood. The lover sees no resemblance except to summer evenings and diamond mornings, to rainbows and the song of birds.

The ancients called beauty the flowering of virtue.[1] Who can analyze the nameless charm which glances from one and another face and form? We are touched with emotions of tenderness and complacency, but we cannot find whereat this dainty emotion, this wandering gleam, points. It is destroyed for the imagination by any attempt to refer it to organization. Nor does it point to any relations of friendship or love known and described in society, but, as it seems to me, to a quite other and unattainable sphere, to relations of transcendent delicacy and sweetness, to what roses and violets hint and foreshow. We cannot approach beauty. Its nature is like opaline doves'-neck lustres, hovering and evanescent. Herein it resembles the most excellent things, which all have this rainbow character, defying all attempts at appropriation and use. What else did Jean Paul Richter signify, when he said to music, "Away! away! thou speakest to me of things which in all my endless life I have not found and shall not find." The same fluency may be observed in every work of the plastic arts. The statue is then beautiful when it begins to be incomprehensible, when it is passing out of criticism and can no longer be defined by compass and measuring-wand, but demands an active imagination to go with it and to say what it is in the act of doing. The god or hero of the sculptor is always represented in a transition *from* that which is representable to the senses, *to* that which is not. Then first it ceases to be a stone. The same remark holds of painting. And of poetry the success is not attained when it lulls and satisfies, but when it astonishes and fires us with new endeavors after the unattainable. Concerning it Landor inquires " whether it is not to be referred to some purer state of sensation and existence."

In like manner, personal beauty is then first charming and itself when it dissatisfies us with any end ; when it becomes a story without an end ; when it suggests gleams and visions and not earthly satisfactions ; when it makes the beholder feel his unworthiness ; when he cannot feel his right to it, though he were Cæsar ; he cannot feel more right to it than to the firmament and the splendors of a sunset.

Hence arose the saying, " If I love you, what is that to you ? " We say so because we feel that what we love is not in your will, but above it. It is not you, but your radiance. It is that which you know not in yourself and can never know.

This agrees well with that high philosophy of Beauty which the ancient writers delighted in ; for they said that the soul of man, embodied here on earth, went roaming up and down in quest of that other world of its own out of which it came into this, but was soon stupefied by the light of the natural sun, and unable to see any other objects than those of this world, which are but shadows of real things.[1] Therefore the Deity sends the glory of youth before the soul, that it may avail itself of beautiful bodies as aids to its recollection of the celestial good and fair ; and the man beholding such a person in the female sex runs to her and finds the highest joy in contemplating the form, movement and intelligence of this person, because it suggests to him the presence of that which indeed is within the beauty, and the cause of the beauty.

If however, from too much conversing with material objects, the soul was gross, and misplaced its satisfaction in the body, it reaped nothing but sorrow ; body being unable to fulfil the promise which beauty holds out ; but if, accepting the hint of these visions and suggestions which beauty makes to his mind, the soul passes through the body and falls to admire strokes of character, and the lovers contemplate one another in their discourses and their actions, then they pass to the true palace of beauty, more and more inflame their love of it, and by this love extinguishing the base affection, as the sun puts out fire by shining on the hearth, they become pure and hallowed. By conversation with that which is in itself excellent, magnanimous, lowly, and just, the lover comes to a warmer love of these nobilities, and a quicker apprehension of them. Then he passes from loving them in one to loving them in all, and so is the one beautiful soul only the door through which he enters to the society of all true and pure souls. In the particular society of his mate he attains a clearer sight of any spot, any taint which her beauty has contracted from this world, and is able to point it out, and this with mutual joy that they are now able, without offence, to indicate blemishes and hindrances in each other, and give to each all help and comfort in curing the same. And beholding in many souls the traits of the divine beauty, and separating in each soul that which is divine from the taint which it has contracted in the world, the lover ascends to the highest beauty, to the love and knowledge

of the Divinity, by steps on this ladder of created souls.

Somewhat like this have the truly wise told
us of love in all ages. The doctrine is not old,
nor is it new. If Plato, Plutarch and Apuleius
taught it, so have Petrarch, Angelo and Milton.
It awaits a truer unfolding in opposition and
rebuke to that subterranean prudence which presides at marriages with words that take hold of
the upper world, whilst one eye is prowling in the
cellar; so that its gravest discourse has a savor
of hams and powdering-tubs. Worst, when this
sensualism intrudes into the education of young
women, and withers the hope and affection of
human nature by teaching that marriage signi-
fies nothing but a housewife's thrift, and that
woman's life has no other aim.

But this dream of love, though beautiful, is
only one scene in our play. In the procession
of the soul from within outward, it enlarges its
circles ever, like the pebble thrown into the
pond, or the light proceeding from an orb. The
rays of the soul alight first on things nearest, on
every utensil and toy, on nurses and domestics,
on the house and yard and passengers, on the
circle of household acquaintance, on politics and
geography and history. But things are ever

grouping themselves according to higher or more interior laws. Neighborhood, size, numbers, habits, persons, lose by degrees their power over us. Cause and effect, real affinities, the longing for harmony between the soul and the circumstance, the progressive, idealizing instinct, predominate later, and the step backward from the higher to the lower relations is impossible. Thus even love, which is the deification of persons, must become more impersonal every day. Of this at first it gives no hint. Little think the youth and maiden who are glancing at each other across crowded rooms with eyes so full of mutual intelligence, of the precious fruit long hereafter to proceed from this new, quite external stimulus. The work of vegetation begins first in the irritability of the bark and leaf-buds. From exchanging glances, they advance to acts of courtesy, of gallantry, then to fiery passion, to plighting troth and marriage. Passion beholds its object as a perfect unit. The soul is wholly embodied, and the body is wholly ensouled :—

> " Her pure and eloquent blood
> Spoke in her cheeks, and so distinctly wrought,
> That one might almost say her body thought." [1]

Romeo, if dead, should be cut up into little stars to make the heavens fine. Life, with this pair,

has no other aim, asks no more, than Juliet, —
than Romeo. Night, day, studies, talents, kingdoms, religion, are all contained in this form full
of soul, in this soul which is all form. The lovers delight·in endearments, in avowals of love,
in comparisons of their regards. When alone,
they solace themselves with the remembered image of the other. Does that other see the same
star, the same melting cloud, read the same
book, feel the same emotion, that now delights
me?[1] They try and weigh their affection, and
adding up costly advantages, friends, opportuni-
ties, properties, exult in discovering that will-
ingly, joyfully, they would give all as a ransom
for the beautiful, the beloved head, not one
hair of which shall be harmed. But the lot of
humanity is on these children. Danger, sorrow
and pain arrive to them as to all. Love prays.
It makes covenants with Eternal Power in be-
half of this dear mate. The union which is thus
effected and which adds a new value to every
atom in nature — for it transmutes every thread
throughout the whole web of relation into a
golden ray, and bathes the soul in a new and
sweeter element — is yet a temporary state. Not
always can flowers, pearls, poetry, protestations,
nor even home in another heart, content the

awful soul that dwells in clay. It arouses itself
at last from these endearments, as toys, and puts
on the harness and aspires to vast and universal
aims. The soul which is in the soul of each,
craving a perfect beatitude, detects incongruities,
defects and disproportion in the behavior of the
other. Hence arise surprise, expostulation and
pain. Yet that which drew them to each other
was signs of loveliness, signs of virtue ; and these
virtues are there, however eclipsed. They appear and reappear and continue to attract ; but
the regard changes, quits the sign and attaches
to the substance. This repairs the wounded
affection. Meantime, as life wears on, it proves
a game of permutation and combination of all
possible positions of the parties, to employ all
the resources of each and acquaint each with the
strength and weakness of the other. For it is
the nature and end of this relation, that they
should represent the human race to each other.
All that is in the world, which is or ought to be
known, is cunningly wrought into the texture
of man, of woman : —

> " The person love does to us fit,
> Like manna, has the taste of all in it." [1]

The world rolls ; the circumstances vary every
hour. The angels that inhabit this temple of

the body appear at the windows, and the gnomes
and vices also. By all the virtues they are united.
If there be virtue, all the vices are known as
such ; they confess and·flee. Their once flam-
ing regard is sobered by time in either breast,
and losing in violence what it gains in extent, it
becomes a thorough good understanding. They
resign each other without complaint to the good
offices which man and woman are severally appointed to discharge in time, and exchange the
passion which once could not lose sight of its
object, for a cheerful disengaged furtherance,
whether present or absent, of each other's designs. At last they discover that all which at
first drew them together, — those once sacred
features, that magical play of charms, — was
deciduous, had a prospective end, like the scaf-
folding by which the house was built ; and the
purification of the intellect and the heart from
year to year is the real marriage, foreseen and
prepared from the first, and wholly above their
consciousness. Looking at these aims with which
two persons, a man and a woman, so variously
and correlatively gifted, are shut up in one house
to spend in the nuptial society forty or fifty
years, I do not wonder at the emphasis with
which the heart prophesies this crisis from early

infancy, at the profuse beauty with which the instincts deck the nuptial bower, and nature and intellect and art emulate each other in the gifts and the melody they bring to the epithalamium.

Thus are we put in training for a love which knows not sex, nor person, nor partiality, but which seeks virtue and wisdom everywhere, to the end of increasing virtue and wisdom. We are by nature observers, and thereby learners. That is our permanent state. But we are often made to feel that our affections are but tents of a night. Though slowly and with pain, the objects of the affections change, as the objects of thought do. There are moments when the affections rule and absorb the man and make his happiness dependent on a person or persons. But in health the mind is presently seen again, — its overarching vault, bright with galaxies of immutable lights, and the warm loves and fears, that swept over us as clouds, must lose their finite character and blend with God, to attain their own perfection. But we need not fear that we can lose any thing by the progress of the soul. The soul may be trusted to the end. That which is so beautiful and attractive as these relations, must be succeeded and supplanted only by what is more beautiful, and so on for ever.

VI

FRIENDSHIP

A RUDDY drop of manly blood
The surging sea outweighs;
The world uncertain comes and goes,
The lover rooted stays.
I fancied he was fled,
And, after many a year,
Glowed unexhausted kindliness
Like daily sunrise there.
My careful heart was free again, —
O friend, my bosom said,
Through thee alone the sky is arched,
Through thee the rose is red,
All things through thee take nobler form
And look beyond the earth,
The mill-round of our fate appears
A sun-path in thy worth.
Me too thy nobleness has taught
To master my despair;
The fountains of my hidden life
Are through thy friendship fair.

FRIENDSHIP

WE have a great deal more kindness than is ever spoken. Maugre all the selfishness that chills like east winds the world, the whole human family is bathed with an element of love like a fine ether. How many persons we meet in houses, whom we scarcely speak to, whom yet we honor, and who honor us! How many we see in the street, or sit with in church, whom, though silently, we warmly rejoice to be with! [1] Read the language of these wandering eye-beams. The heart knoweth.

The effect of the indulgence of this human affection is a certain cordial exhilaration. In poetry and in common speech the emotions of benevolence and complacency which are felt towards others are likened to the material effects of fire; so swift, or much more swift, more active, more cheering, are these fine inward irradiations. From the highest degree of passionate love to the lowest degree of good-will, they make the sweetness of life.

Our intellectual and active powers increase with our affection. The scholar sits down to write, and all his years of meditation do not

furnish him with one good thought or happy
expression ; but it is necessary to write a letter
to a friend, — and forthwith troops of gentle
thoughts invest themselves, on every hand, with
chosen words.[1] See, in any house where virtue
and self-respect abide, the palpitation which the
approach of a stranger causes. A commended
stranger is expected and announced, and an uneasiness betwixt pleasure and pain invades all
the hearts of a household. His arrival almost
brings fear to the good hearts that would welcome him. The house is dusted, all things fly
into their places, the old coat is exchanged for
the new, and they must get up a dinner if they
can. Of a commended stranger, only the good
report is told by others, only the good and new
is heard by us. He stands to us for humanity.
He is what we wish. Having imagined and
invested him, we ask how we should stand related in conversation and action with such a
man, and are uneasy with fear. The same idea
exalts conversation with him. We talk better
than we are wont. We have the nimblest fancy,
a richer memory, and our dumb devil has taken
leave for the time. For long hours we can continue a series of sincere, graceful, rich communications, drawn from the oldest, secretest

Mr. Emerson's House in Concord

experience, so that they who sit by, of our own kinsfolk and acquaintance, shall feel a lively surprise at our unusual powers. But as soon as the stranger begins to intrude his partialities, his definitions, his defects into the conversation, it is all over. He has heard the first, the last and best he will ever hear from us. He is no stranger now. Vulgarity, ignorance, misapprehension are old acquaintances. Now, when he comes, he may get the order, the dress and the dinner, — but the throbbing of the heart and the communications of the soul, no more.

What is so pleasant as these jets of affection which make a young world for me again? What so delicious as a just and firm encounter of two, in a thought, in a feeling? How beautiful, on their approach to this beating heart, the steps and forms of the gifted and the true! The moment we indulge our affections, the earth is metamorphosed; there is no winter and no night; all tragedies, all ennuis vanish,—all duties even; nothing fills the proceeding eternity but the forms all radiant of beloved persons. Let the soul be assured that somewhere in the universe it should rejoin its friend, and it would be content and cheerful alone for a thousand years.

II

I awoke this morning with devout thanksgiving for my friends, the old and the new. Shall I not call God the Beautiful, who daily showeth himself so to me in his gifts? I chide society, I embrace solitude, and yet I am not so ungrateful as not to see the wise, the lovely and the noble-minded, as from time to time they pass my gate.¹ Who hears me, who understands me, becomes mine,—a possession for all time. Nor is Nature so poor but she gives me this joy several times, and thus we weave social threads of our own, a new web of relations ; and, as many thoughts in succession substantiate themselves, we shall by and by stand in a new world of our own creation, and no longer strangers and pilgrims in a traditionary globe. My friends have come to me unsought. The great God gave them to me. By oldest right, by the divine affinity of virtue with itself, I find them, or rather not I, but the Deity in me and in them derides and cancels the thick walls of individual character, relation, age, sex, circumstance, at which he usually connives, and now makes many one. High thanks I owe you, excellent lovers, who carry out the world for me to new and noble depths, and enlarge the meaning of all my thoughts. These are new poetry of the first

Bard, — poetry without stop, — hymn, ode and epic, poetry still flowing, Apollo and the Muses chanting still. Will these too separate themselves from me again, or some of them? I know not, but I fear it not; for my relation to them is so pure that we hold by simple affinity, and the Genius of my life being thus social, the same affinity will exert its energy on whomsoever is as noble as these men and women, wherever I may be.

I confess to an extreme tenderness of nature on this point. It is almost dangerous to me to "crush the sweet poison of misused wine"[1] of the affections. A new person is to me a great event and hinders me from sleep. I have often had fine fancies about persons which have given me delicious hours; but the joy ends in the day; it yields no fruit. Thought is not born of it; my action is very little modified. I must feel pride in my friend's accomplishments as if they were mine, and a property in his virtues. I feel as warmly when he is praised, as the lover when he hears applause of his engaged maiden. We over-estimate the conscience of our friend. His goodness seems better than our goodness, his nature finer, his temptations less. Every thing that is his, — his name, his form, his dress, books and instruments,—fancy enhances. Our own thought sounds new and larger from his mouth.[1]

Yet the systole and diastole of the heart are not without their analogy in the ebb and flow of love. Friendship, like the immortality of the soul, is too good to be believed. The lover, beholding his maiden, half knows that she is not verily that which he worships; and in the golden hour of friendship we are surprised with shades of suspicion and unbelief. We doubt that we bestow on our hero the virtues in which he shines, and afterwards worship the form to which we have ascribed this divine inhabitation. In strictness, the soul does not respect men as it respects itself. In strict science all persons underlie the same condition of an infinite remoteness. Shall we fear to cool our love by mining for the metaphysical foundation of this Elysian temple? Shall I not be as real as the things I see? If I am, I shall not fear to know them for what they are. Their essence is not less beautiful than their appearance, though it needs finer organs for its apprehension. The root of the plant is not unsightly to science, though for chaplets and festoons we cut the stem short. And I must hazard the production of the bald fact amidst these pleasing reveries, though it

should prove an Egyptian skull at our banquet.
A man who stands united with his thought con-
ceives magnificently of himself. He is conscious
of a universal success, even though bought by
uniform particular failures.[1] No advantages, no
powers, no gold or force, can be any match for .
him. I cannot choose but rely on my own poverty more than on your wealth. I cannot make
your consciousness tantamount to mine. Only
the star dazzles ; the planet has a faint, moon-
like ray. I hear what you say of the admirable
parts and tried temper of the party you praise,
but I see well that, for all his purple cloaks, I
shall not like him, unless he is at least a poor
Greek like me. I cannot deny it, O friend, that
the vast shadow of the Phenomenal includes
thee also in its pied and painted immensity, —
thee also, compared with whom all else is shadow.
Thou art not Being, as Truth is, as Justice is,
— thou art not my soul, but a picture and effigy
of that. Thou hast come to me lately, and already thou art seizing thy hat and cloak. Is it
not that the soul puts forth friends as the tree
puts forth leaves, and presently, by the germ-
ination of new buds, extrudes the old leaf?[2]
The law of nature is alternation for evermore.
Each electrical state superinduces the opposite.

The soul environs itself with friends that it may enter into a grander self-acquaintance or solitude ; and it goes alone for a season that it may exalt its conversation or society. This method betrays itself along the whole history of our personal relations. The instinct of affection revives the hope of union with our mates, and the returning sense of insulation recalls us from the chase. Thus every man passes his life in the search after friendship, and if he should record his true sentiment, he might write a letter like this to each new candidate for his love : —

DEAR FRIEND,

If I was sure of thee, sure of thy capacity, sure to match my mood with thine, I should never think again of trifles in relation to thy comings and goings. I am not very wise ; my moods are quite attainable, and I respect thy genius ; it is to me as yet unfathomed ; yet dare I not presume in thee a perfect intelligence of me, and so thou art to me a delicious torment. Thine ever, or never.

Yet these uneasy pleasures and fine pains are for curiosity and not for life. They are not to be indulged. This is to weave cobweb, and not cloth. Our friendships hurry to short and poor

conclusions, because we have made them a texture of wine and dreams, instead of the tough
fibre of the human heart. The laws of friendship are austere and eternal, of one web with
the laws of nature and of morals. But we have
aimed at a swift and petty benefit, to suck a
sudden sweetness. We snatch at the slowest
fruit in the whole garden of God, which many
summers and many winters must ripen. We seek
our friend not sacredly, but with an adulterate
passion which would appropriate him to ourselves. In vain. We are armed all over with
subtle antagonisms, which, as soon as we meet,
begin to play, and translate all poetry into stale
prose.[1] Almost all people descend to meet. All
association must be a compromise, and, what is
worst, the very flower and aroma of the flower
of each of the beautiful natures disappears as
they approach each other. What a perpetual
disappointment is actual society, even of the
virtuous and gifted! After interviews have been
compassed with long foresight we must be tormented presently by baffled blows, by sudden,
unseasonable apathies, by epilepsies of wit and
of animal spirits, in the heyday of friendship
and thought. Our faculties do not play us true,
and both parties are relieved by solitude.

I ought to be equal to every relation. It makes no difference how many friends I have and what content I can find in conversing with each, if there be one to whom I am not equal. If I have shrunk unequal from one contest, the joy I find in all the rest becomes mean and cowardly. I should hate myself, if then I made my other friends my asylum : —

> " The valiant warrior famousèd for fight,
> After a hundred victories, once foiled,
> Is from the book of honor razèd quite
> And all the rest forgot for which he toiled." [1]

Our impatience is thus sharply rebuked. Bashfulness and apathy are a tough husk in which a delicate organization is protected from premature ripening. It would be lost if it knew itself before any of the best souls were yet ripe enough to know and own it. Respect the *naturlangsamkeit* which hardens the ruby in a million years, and works in duration in which Alps and Andes come and go as rainbows. The good spirit of our life has no heaven which is the price of rashness. Love, which is the essence of God, is not for levity, but for the total worth of man. Let us not have this childish luxury in our regards, but the austerest worth ; let us approach our friend with an audacious trust in the truth of his heart, in the breadth, impossible to be overturned, of his foundations.

The attractions of this subject are not to be resisted, and I leave, for the time, all account of subordinate social benefit, to speak of that select and sacred relation which is a kind of absolute, and which even leaves the language of love suspicious and common, so much is this purer, and nothing is so much divine.

I do not wish to treat friendships daintily, but with roughest courage. When they are real, they are not glass threads or frostwork, but the solidest thing we know. For now, after so many ages of experience, what do we know of nature or of ourselves? Not one step has man taken toward the solution of the problem of his destiny. In one condemnation of folly stand the whole universe of men. But the sweet sincerity of joy and peace which I draw from this alliance with my brother's soul is the nut itself whereof all nature and all thought is but the husk and shell. Happy is the house that shelters a friend! It might well be built, like a festal bower or arch, to entertain him a single day. Happier, if he know the solemnity of that relation and honor its law! He who offers himself a candidate for that covenant comes up, like an

Olympian, to the great games where the first-born of the world are the competitors. He proposes himself for contests where Time, Want, Danger, are in the lists, and he alone is victor who has truth enough in his constitution to preserve the delicacy of his beauty from the wear and tear of all these. The gifts of fortune may be present or absent, but all the speed in that contest depends on intrinsic nobleness and the contempt of trifles. There are two elements that go to the composition of friendship, each so sovereign that I can detect no superiority in either, no reason why either should be first named. One is truth. [A friend is a person with whom I may be sincere. Before him I may think aloud. I am arrived at last in the presence of a man so real and equal that I may drop even those undermost garments of dissimulation, courtesy, and second thought, which men never put off, and may deal with him with the simplicity and wholeness with which one chemical atom meets another. Sincerity is the luxury allowed, like diadems and authority, only to the highest rank; *that* being permitted to speak truth, as having none above it to court or conform unto.[1] Every man alone is sincere.[2]. At the entrance of a second person, hypocrisy begins. We parry and

fend the approach of our fellow-man by compliments, by gossip, by amusements, by affairs.
We cover up our thought from him under
a hundred folds. I knew a man who under a
certain religious frenzy cast. off this drapery,
and omitting all compliment and commonplace,
spoke to the conscience of every person he en-
countered, and that with great insight and beauty.
At first he was resisted, and all men agreed he
was mad. But persisting — as indeed he could
not help doing — for some time in this course,
he attained to the advantage of bringing every·
man of his acquaintance into true relations with
him. No man would think of speaking falsely
with him, or of putting him off with any chat
of markets or reading-rooms. But every man
was constrained by so much sincerity to the
like plaindealing, and what love of nature, what
poetry, what symbol of truth he had, he did
certainly show him.¹ But to most of us society
shows not its face and eye, but its side and its
back. To stand in true relations with men in a
false age is worth a fit of insanity, is it not? We
can seldom go erect. Almost every man we meet
requires some civility — requires to be humored;
he has some fame, some talent, some whim of
religion or philanthropy in his head that is not

to be questioned, and which spoils all conversation with him. But a friend is a sane man who exercises not my ingenuity, but me. My friend gives me entertainment without requiring any stipulation on my part. A friend therefore is a sort of paradox in nature. I who alone am, I who see nothing in nature whose existence I can affirm with equal evidence to my own, behold now the semblance of my being, in all its height, variety and curiosity, reiterated in a foreign form; so that a friend may well be reckoned the master-piece of nature.

The other element of friendship is tenderness. We are holden to men by every sort of tie, by blood, by pride, by fear, by hope, by lucre, by lust, by hate, by admiration, by every circumstance and badge and trifle, — but we can scarce believe that so much character can subsist in another as to draw us by love. Can another be so blessed and we so pure that we can offer him tenderness? When a man becomes dear to me I have touched the goal of fortune. I find very little written directly to the heart of this matter in books. And yet I have one text which I cannot choose but remember. My author ' says, — " I offer myself faintly and bluntly to those whose I effectually am, and

tender myself least to him to whom I am the
most devoted." I wish that friendship should
have feet, as well as eyes and eloquence. It
must plant itself on the ground, before it vaults
over the moon. I wish it to be a little of a citizen, before it is quite a cherub. We chide the
citizen because he makes love a commodity. It
is an exchange of gifts, of useful loans; it is
good neighborhood; it watches with the sick;
it holds the pall at the funeral; and quite loses
sight of the delicacies and nobility of the relation. But though we cannot find the god under
this disguise of a sutler, yet on the other hand
we cannot forgive·the poet if he spins his thread
too fine and does not substantiate his romance
by the municipal virtues of justice, punctual-
ity, fidelity and pity. I hate the prostitution of
the name of friendship to signify modish and
worldly alliances. I much prefer the company
of ploughboys and tin-peddlers to the silken and
perfumed amity which celebrates its days of
encounter by a frivolous display, by rides in a
curricle and dinners at the best taverns. The
end of friendship is a commerce the most strict
and homely that can be joined; more strict than
any of which we have experience. It is for aid
and comfort through all the relations and passages

of life and death. It is fit for serene days and
graceful gifts and country rambles, but also for
rough roads and hard fare, shipwreck, poverty
and persecution. It keeps company with the
sallies of the wit and the trances of religion. We
are to dignify to each other the daily needs and
offices of man's life, and embellish it by courage,
wisdom and unity. It should never fall into
something usual and settled, but should be alert
and inventive and add rhyme and reason to what
was drudgery.

Friendship may be said to require natures so
rare and costly, each so well tempered and so
happily adapted, and withal so circumstanced
(for even in that particular, a poet says, love
demands that the parties be altogether paired),
that its satisfaction can very seldom be assured.
It cannot subsist in its perfection, say some of
those who are learned in this warm lore of the
heart, betwixt more than two. I am not quite
so strict in my terms, perhaps because I have
never known so high a fellowship as others. I
please my imagination more with a circle of godlike men and women variously related to each
other and between whom subsists a lofty intelligence. But I find this law of *one to one* peremp-
tory for conversation, which is the practice and

consummation of friendship.[1] Do not mix waters too much. The best mix as ill as good and bad. You shall have very useful and cheering discourse at several times with two several men, but let all three of you come together and you shall not have one new and hearty word. Two may talk and one may hear, but three cannot take part in a conversation of the most sincere and searching sort. In good company there is never such discourse between two, across the table, as takes place when you leave them alone. In good company the individuals merge their egotism into a social soul exactly co-extensive with the several consciousnesses there present. No partialities of friend to friend, no fondnesses of brother to sister, of wife to husband, are there pertinent, but quite otherwise. Only he may then speak who can sail on the common thought of the party, and not poorly limited to his own. Now this convention, which good sense demands, destroys the high freedom of great conversation, which requires an absolute running of two souls into one.

No two men but being left alone with each other enter into simpler relations. Yet it is affinity that determines *which* two shall converse. Unrelated men give little joy to each other, will never suspect the latent powers of each. We talk sometimes of a great talent for conversation, as if it were a permanent property in some individuals. Conversation is an evanescent relation, — no more. A man is reputed to have thought and eloquence; he cannot, for all that, say a word to his cousin or his uncle. They accuse his silence with as much reason as they would blame the insignificance of a dial in the shade. In the sun it will mark the hour. Among those who enjoy his thought he will regain his tongue.

Friendship requires that rare mean betwixt likeness and unlikeness that piques each with the presence of power and of consent in the other party. Let me be alone to the end of the world, rather than that my friend should overstep, by a word or a look, his real sympathy. I am equally balked by antagonism and by compliance. Let him not cease an instant to be himself. The only joy I have in his being mine, is that the *not mine* is *mine*. I hate, where I looked for a manly furtherance or at least a manly resistance, to find a mush of concession. Better be a nettle in the side of your friend than his echo. The condition which high friendship demands is ability to do without it. That high office requires great and sublime parts.¹ There must be very two, before

there can be very one. Let it be an alliance of
two large, formidable natures, mutually beheld,
mutually feared, before yet they recognize the
deep identity which, beneath these disparities,
unites them.

He only is fit for this society who is magnanimous ; who is sure that greatness and goodness
are always economy ; who is not swift to intermeddle with his fortunes. Let him not intermeddle with this. Leave to the diamond its ages
to grow, nor expect to accelerate the births of
the eternal. Friendship demands a religious
treatment. We talk of choosing our friends, but
friends are self-elected. Reverence is a great
part of it. Treat your friend as a spectacle. Of
course he has merits that are not yours, and that
you cannot honor if you must needs hold him
close to your person. Stand aside ; give those
merits room ; let them mount and expand. Are
you the friend of your friend's buttons, or of his
thought? To a great heart he will still be a
stranger in a thousand particulars, that he may
come near in the holiest ground. Leave it to
girls and boys to regard a friend as property,
and to suck a short and all-confounding pleasure, instead of the noblest benefit.[1]

Let us buy our entrance to this guild by a

II

long probation. Why should we desecrate noble and beautiful souls by intruding on them? Why insist on rash personal relations with your friend? Why go to his house, or know his mother and brother and sisters? Why be visited by him at your own? Are these things material to our covenant? Leave this touching and clawing. Let him be to me a spirit. A message, a thought, a sincerity, a glance from him, I want, but not news, nor pottage. I can get politics and chat and neighborly conveniences from cheaper companions. Should not the society of my friend be to me poetic, pure, universal and great as nature itself? Ought I to feel that our tie is profane in comparison with yonder bar of cloud that sleeps on the horizon, or that clump of waving grass that divides the brook? Let us not vilify, but raise it to that standard. That great defying eye, that scornful beauty of his mien and action, do not pique yourself on reducing, but rather fortify and enhance. Worship his superiorities; wish him not less by a thought, but hoard and tell them all. Guard him as thy counterpart. Let him be to thee for ever a sort of beautiful enemy, untamable, devoutly revered, and not a trivial conveniency to be soon outgrown and cast aside. The hues of the opal, the light of the diamond, are not to be seen if the eye is too near. To my friend I write a letter and from him I receive a letter. That seems to you a little. It suffices me. It is a spiritual gift, worthy of him to give and of me to receive. It profanes nobody. In these warm lines the heart will trust itself, as it will not to the tongue, and pour out the prophecy of a godlier existence than all the annals of heroism have yet made good.

Respect so far the holy laws of this fellowship as not to prejudice its perfect flower by your impatience for its opening. We must be our own before we can be another's. There is at least this satisfaction in crime, according to the Latin proverb; — you can speak to your accomplice on even terms. *Crimen quos inquinat, æquat.* To those whom we admire and love, at first we cannot. Yet the least defect of self-possession vitiates, in my judgment, the entire relation. There can never be deep peace between two spirits, never mutual respect, until in their dialogue each stands for the whole world.

What is so great as friendship, let us carry with what grandeur of spirit we can. Let us be silent, — so we may hear the whisper of the gods. Let us not interfere. Who set you to cast about what you should say to the select souls, or how to say any thing to such? No matter how in-genious, no matter how graceful and bland. There are innumerable degrees of folly and wis-dom, and for you to say aught is to be frivolous. Wait, and thy heart shall speak. Wait until the necessary and everlasting overpowers you, until day and night avail themselves of your lips.[1] The only reward of virtue is virtue; the only way to have a friend is to be one. You shall not come nearer a man by getting into his house. If unlike, his soul only flees the faster from you, and you shall never catch a true glance of his eye. We see the noble afar off and they repel us; why should we intrude? .Late,—very late,—we perceive that no arrangements, no intro-ductions, no consuetudes or habits of society would be of any avail to establish us in such relations with them as we desire,—but solely the uprise of nature in us to the same degree it is in them; then shall we meet as water with water; and if we should not meet them then, we shall not want them, for we are already they. In the last analysis, love is only the reflection of a man's own worthiness from other men. Men have sometimes exchanged names with their friends, as if they would signify that in their friend each loved his own soul.

The higher the style we demand of friendship, of course the less easy to establish it with flesh and blood. We walk alone in the world. Friends such as we desire are dreams and fables. But a sublime hope cheers ever the faithful heart, that elsewhere, in other regions of the universal power, souls are now acting, enduring and daring, which can love us and which we can love.[1] We may congratulate ourselves that the period of nonage, of follies, of blunders and of shame, is passed in solitude, and when we are finished men we shall grasp heroic hands in heroic hands. Only be admonished by what you already see, not to strike leagues of friendship with cheap persons, where no friendship can be. Our impatience betrays us into rash and foolish alliances which no god attends. By persisting in your path, though you forfeit the little you gain the great. You demonstrate yourself, so as to put yourself out of the reach of false relations, and you draw to you the first-born of the world, — those rare pilgrims whereof only one or two wander in nature at once, and before whom the vulgar great show as spectres and shadows merely.

It is foolish to be afraid of making our ties too spiritual, as if so we could lose any genuine

love. Whatever correction of our popular views
we make from insight, nature will be sure to
bear us out in, and though it seem to rob us
of some joy, will repay us with a greater. Let us
feel if we will the absolute insulation of man.
We are sure that we have all in us. We go to
Europe, or we pursue persons, or we read books,
in the instinctive faith that these will call it out
and reveal us to ourselves. Beggars all. The
persons are such as we; the Europe, an old
faded garment of dead persons; the books, their
ghosts. Let us drop this idolatry. Let us give
over this mendicancy. Let us even bid our
dearest friends farewell, and defy them, saying
'Who are you? Unhand me: I will be dependent no more.' Ah! seest thou not, O brother, that thus we part only to meet again on a
higher platform, and only be more each other's
because we are more our own? A friend is
Janus-faced; he looks to the past and the future.
He is the child of all my foregoing hours, the
prophet of those to come, and the harbinger of
a greater friend.'

I do then with my friends as I do with my
books. I would have them where I can find
them, but I seldom use them. We must have
society on our own terms, and admit or exclude

it on the slightest cause. I cannot afford to
speak much with my friend. If he is great he
makes me so great that I cannot descend to
converse. In the great days, presentiments
hover before me in the firmament. I ought
then to dedicate myself to them. I go in that
I may seize them, I go out that I may seize
them. I fear only that I may lose them receding into the sky in which now they are only a
patch of brighter light. Then, though I prize
my friends, I cannot afford to talk with them
and study their visions, lest I lose my own. It
would indeed give me a certain household joy
to quit this lofty seeking, this spiritual astronomy or search of stars, and come down to warm
sympathies with you ; but then I know well I
shall mourn always the vanishing of my mighty
gods. It is true, next week I shall have languid
moods, when I can well afford to occupy myself with foreign objects; then I shall regret the
lost literature of your mind, and wish you were
by my side again. But if you come, perhaps
you will fill my mind only with new visions;
not with yourself but with your lustres,[1] and I
shall not be able any more than now to converse
with you. So I will owe to my friends this
evanescent intercourse. I will receive from them

not what they have but what they are. They
shall give me that which properly they cannot
give, but which emanates from them. But they
shall not hold me by any relations less subtile
and pure.¹ We will meet as though we met not,
and part as though we parted not.

It has seemed to me lately more possible than
I knew, to carry a friendship greatly, on one
side, without due correspondence on the other.
Why should I cumber myself with regrets that
the receiver is not capacious? It never troubles
the sun that some of his rays fall wide and vain
into ungrateful space, and only a small part on
the reflecting planet. Let your greatness educate the crude and cold companion. If he is
unequal, he will presently pass away; but thou
art enlarged by thy own shining, and no longer
a mate for frogs and worms, dost soar and burn
with the gods of the empyrean. It is thought
a disgrace to love unrequited. But the great
will see that true love cannot be unrequited.
True love transcends the unworthy object and
dwells and broods on the eternal, and when the
poor interposed mask crumbles, it is not sad,
but feels rid of so much earth and feels its independency the surer. Yet these things may

hardly be said without a sort of treachery to the relation. The essence of friendship is entireness, a total magnanimity and trust. It must not surmise or provide for infirmity. It treats its object as a god, that it may deify both.[1]

VII

PRUDENCE

THEME no poet gladly sung,
Fair to old and foul to young ;
Scorn not thou the love of parts,
And the articles of arts.
Grandeur of the perfect sphere
Thanks the atoms that cohere.

--

PRUDENCE

WHAT right have I to write on Prudence, whereof I have little, and that of the negative sort? My prudence consists in avoiding and going without, not in the inventing of means and methods, not in adroit steering, not in gentle repairing. I have no skill to make money spend well, no genius in my economy, and whoever sees my garden discovers that I must have some other garden.[1] Yet I love facts, and hate lubricity and people without perception. Then I have the same title to write on prudence that I have to write on poetry or holiness. We write from aspiration and antagonism, as well as from experience. We paint those qualities which we do not possess. The poet admires the man of energy and tactics; the merchant breeds his son for the church or the bar; and where a man is not vain and egotistic you shall find what he has not by his praise. Moreover it would be hardly honest in me not to balance these fine lyric words of Love and Friendship with words of coarser sound, and whilst my debt to my senses is real and constant, not to own it in passing.[2]

Prudence is the virtue of the senses. It is the science of appearances. It is the outmost action of the inward life. It is God taking thought for oxen. It moves matter after the laws of matter. It is content to seek health of body by complying with physical conditions, and health of mind by the laws of the intellect.

The world of the senses is a world of shows; it does not exist for itself, but has a symbolic character; and a true prudence or law of shows recognizes the co-presence of other laws and knows that its own office is subaltern; knows that it is surface and not centre where it works. Prudence is false when detached. It is legitimate when it is the Natural History of the soul incarnate, when it unfolds the beauty of laws within the narrow scope of the senses.[1]

There are all degrees of proficiency in knowledge of the world. It is sufficient to our present purpose to indicate three. One class live to the utility of the symbol, esteeming health and wealth a final good. Another class live above this mark to the beauty of the symbol, as the poet and artist and the naturalist and man of science. A third class live above the beauty of the symbol to the beauty of the thing signified; these are wise men. The first class have common sense; the second, taste; and the third, spiritual perception. Once in a long time, a man traverses the whole scale, and sees and enjoys the symbol solidly, then also has a clear eye for its beauty, and lastly, whilst he pitches his tent on this sacred volcanic isle of nature, does not offer to build houses and barns thereon, — reverencing the splendor of the God which he sees bursting through each chink and cranny.[1]

The world is filled with the proverbs and acts and winkings of a base prudence, which is a devotion to matter, as if we possessed no other faculties than the palate, the nose, the touch, the eye and ear; a prudence which adores the Rule of Three, which never subscribes, which never gives, which seldom lends, and asks but one question of any project, — Will it bake bread?[2] This is a disease like a thickening of the skin until the vital organs are destroyed. But culture, revealing the high origin of the apparent world and aiming at the perfection of the man as the end, degrades every thing else, as health and bodily life, into means. It sees prudence not to be a several faculty, but a name for wisdom and virtue conversing with the body and its wants. Cultivated men always feel and speak so, as if a great fortune, the achievement of a civil or social measure, great personal influence, a graceful and commanding address, had their value as proofs of the energy of the spirit. If a man lose his balance and immerse himself in any trades or pleasures for their own sake, he may be a good wheel or pin, but he is not a cultivated man.

The spurious prudence, making the senses final, is the god of sots and cowards, and is the subject of all comedy. It is nature's joke, and therefore literature's. The true prudence limits this sensualism by admitting the knowledge of an internal and real world. This recognition once made, the order of the world and the distribution of affairs and times, being studied with the co-perception of their subordinate place, will reward any degree of attention. For our existence, thus apparently attached in nature to the sun and the returning moon and the periods which they mark, — so susceptible to climate and to country, so alive to social good and evil, so fond of splendor and so tender to hunger and cold and debt, — reads all its primary lessons out of these books.

Prudence does not go behind nature and ask whence it is. It takes the laws of the world whereby man's being is conditioned, as they are, and keeps these laws that it may enjoy their proper good. It respects space and time, climate, want, sleep, the law of polarity, growth and death. There revolve, to give bound and period to his being on all sides, the sun and moon, the great formalists in the sky: here lies stubborn matter, and will not swerve from its chemical routine. Here is a planted globe, pierced and belted with natural laws and fenced and distributed externally with civil partitions and properties which impose new restraints on the young inhabitant.

We eat of the bread which grows in the field. We live by the air which blows around us and we are poisoned by the air that is too cold or too hot, too dry or too wet. Time, which shows so vacant, indivisible and divine in its coming, is slit and peddled into trifles and tatters. A door is to be painted, a lock to be repaired. I want wood or oil, or meal or salt; the house smokes, or I have a headache; then the tax, and an affair to be transacted with a man without heart or brains, and the stinging recollection of an injurious or very awkward word,— these eat up the hours. Do what we can, summer will have its flies; if we walk in the woods we must feed mosquitos; if we go a-fishing we must

II

expect a wet coat. Then climate is a great im-
pediment to idle persons; we often resolve to
give up the care of the weather, but still we regard the clouds and the rain.[1]

We are instructed by these petty experiences
which usurp the hours and years. The hard soil
and four months of snow make the inhabitant
of the northern temperate zone wiser and abler
than his fellow who enjoys the fixed smile of
the tropics. The islander may ramble all day at
will. At night he may sleep on a mat under the
moon, and wherever a wild date-tree grows, nature has, without a prayer even, spread a table for
his morning meal. The northerner is perforce
a householder. He must brew, bake, salt and
preserve his food, and pile wood and coal. But
as it happens that not one stroke can labor
lay to without some new acquaintance with nature, and as nature is inexhaustibly significant,
the inhabitants of these climates have always
excelled the southerner in force.[2] Such is the
value of these matters that a man who knows
other things can never know too much of
these. Let him have accurate perceptions. Let
him, if he have hands, handle; if eyes, measure and discriminate; let him accept and hive
every fact of chemistry, natural history and eco-

nomics ; the more he has, the less is he willing to spare any one. Time is always bringing
the occasions that disclose their value. Some
wisdom comes out of every natural and innocent action. The domestic man, who loves no
music so well as his kitchen clock and the airs
which the logs sing to him as they burn on the
hearth, has solaces which others never dream
of. The application of means to ends insures
victory and the songs of victory not less in a
farm or a shop than in the tactics of party or
of war. The good husband finds method as
efficient in the packing of fire-wood in a shed
or in the harvesting of fruits in the cellar, as in
Peninsular campaigns or the files of the Department of State. In the rainy day he builds a
work-bench, or gets his tool-box set in the corner of the barn-chamber, and stored with 'nails,
gimlet, pincers, screwdriver and chisel. Herein
he tastes an old joy of youth and childhood, the
cat-like love of garrets, presses and corn-cham-
bers, and of the conveniences of long house-
keeping. His garden or his poultry-yard tells
him many pleasant anecdotes. One might find
argument for optimism in the abundant flow
of this saccharine element of pleasure in every
suburb and extremity of the good world. Let

a man keep the law, — any law, — and his way
will be strown with satisfactions. There is more
difference in the quality of our pleasures than in
the amount.

On the other hand, nature punishes any neglect of prudence. If you think the senses final,
obey their law. If you believe in the soul, do
not clutch at sensual sweetness before it is ripe
on the slow tree of cause and effect. It is vine-
gar to the eyes to deal with men of loose and imperfect perception. Dr. Johnson is reported to
have said, — "If the child says he looked out
of this window, when he looked out of that, —
whip him." Our American character is marked
by a more than average delight in accurate perception, which is shown by the currency of the
byword, "No mistake." But the discomfort
of unpunctuality, of confusion of thought about
facts, inattention to the wants of to-morrow, is
of no nation. The beautiful laws of time and
space, once dislocated by our inaptitude, are
holes and dens. If the hive be disturbed by
rash and stupid hands, instead of honey it will
yield us bees. Our words and actions to be fair
must be timely. A gay and pleasant sound is
the whetting of the scythe in the mornings of
June, yet what is more lonesome and sad than

the sound of a whetstone or mower's rifle when
it is too late in the season to make hay? Scat-
ter-brained and "afternoon" men spoil much
more than their own affair in spoiling the temper of those who deal with them. I have seen
a criticism on some paintings, of which I am reminded when I see the shiftless and unhappy
men who are not true to their senses. The last
Grand Duke of Weimar, a man of superior
understanding, said, — "I have sometimes re-
marked in the presence of great works of art,
and just now especially in Dresden, how much
a certain property contributes to the effect which
gives life to the figures, and to the life an irresistible truth. This property is the hitting, in
all the figures we draw, the right centre of gravity. I mean the placing the figures firm upon
their feet, making the hands grasp, and fastening
the eyes on the spot where they should look.
Even lifeless figures, as vessels and stools — let
them be drawn ever so correctly — lose all effect
so soon as they lack the resting upon their centre
of gravity, and have a certain swimming and oscil-
lating appearance. The Raphael in the Dresden
gallery (the only great affecting picture which
I have seen) is the quietest and most passionless
piece you can imagine; a couple of saints who

worship the Virgin and Child. Nevertheless it awakens a deeper impression than the contortions of ten crucified martyrs. For beside all the resistless beauty of form, it possesses in the highest degree the property of the perpendicularity of all the figures." This perpendicularity we demand of all the figures in this picture of life. Let them stand on their feet, and not float and swing. Let us know where to find them. Let them discriminate between what they remember and what they dreamed, call a spade a spade, give us facts, and honor their own senses with trust.'

But what man shall dare task another with imprudence? Who is prudent? The men we call greatest are least in this kingdom. There is a certain fatal dislocation in our relation to nature, distorting our modes of living and making every law our enemy, which seems at last to have aroused all the wit and virtue in the world to ponder the question of Reform. We must call the highest prudence to counsel, and ask why health and beauty and genius should now be the exception rather than the rule of human nature? We do not know the properties of plants and animals and the laws of nature, through our sympathy with the same; but this

remains the dream of poets.[1] Poetry and prudence should be coincident. Poets should be
lawgivers ; that is, the boldest lyric inspiration
should not chide and insult, but should announce
and lead the civil code and the day's work. But
now the two things seem irreconcilably parted.
We have violated law upon law until we stand
amidst ruins, and when by chance we espy a
coincidence between reason and the phenomena,
we are surprised. Beauty should be the dowry
of every man and woman, as invariably as sensation; but it is rare. Health or sound organization should be universal. Genius should be the
child of genius and every child should be inspired ;
but now it is not to be predicted of any child,
and nowhere is it pure. We call partial half-
lights, by courtesy, genius ; talent which converts itself to money ; talent which glitters to-
day that it may dine and sleep well to-morrow ;
and society is officered by *men of parts*, as they
are properly called, and not by divine men.
These use their gift to refine luxury, not to
abolish it. Genius is always ascetic, and piety,
and love. Appetite shows to the finer souls as
a disease, and they find beauty in rites and
bounds that resist it.

We have found out fine names to cover our

sensuality withal, but no gifts can raise intemperance. The man of talent affects to call his transgressions of the laws of the senses trivial and to count them nothing considered with his devotion to his art. His art never taught him lewdness, nor the love of wine, nor the wish to reap where he had not sowed. His art is less for every deduction from his holiness, and less for every defect of common sense. On him who scorned the world, as he said, the scorned world wreaks its revenge. He that despiseth small things will perish by little and little.[1] Goethe's Tasso is very likely to be a pretty fair historic portrait, and that is true tragedy. It does not seem to me so genuine grief when some tyrannous Richard the Third oppresses and slays a score of innocent persons, as when Antonio and Tasso, both apparently right, wrong each other. One living after the maxims of this world and consistent and true to them, the other fired with all divine sentiments, yet grasping also at the pleasures of sense, without submitting to their law. That is a grief we all feel, a knot we cannot untie. Tasso's is no unfrequent case in modern biography. A man of genius, of an ardent temperament, reckless of physical laws, self-indulgent, becomes

presently unfortunate, querulous, a " discomfort-
able cousin," a thorn to himself and to others.

The scholar shames us by his bifold life.
Whilst something higher than prudence is active, he is admirable ; when common sense is
wanted, he is an encumbrance. Yesterday, Cæsar was not so great ; to-day, the felon at the
gallows' foot is not more miserable. Yesterday, radiant with the light of an ideal world
in which he lives, the first of men ; and now
oppressed by wants and by sickness, for which
he must thank himself.¹ He resembles the pitiful drivellers whom travellers describe as fre-
quenting the bazaars of Constantinople, who
skulk about all day, yellow, emaciated, ragged,
sneaking ; and at evening, when the bazaars
are open, slink to the opium-shop, swallow their
morsel and become tranquil and glorified seers.
And who has not seen the tragedy of imprudent
genius struggling for years with paltry pecuniary difficulties, at last sinking, chilled, exhausted
and fruitless, like a giant slaughtered by pins ?

Is it not better that a man should accept the
first pains and mortifications of this sort, which
nature is not slack in sending him, as hints that
he must expect no other good than the just
fruit of his own labor and self-denial ? Health,

bread, climate, social position, have their importance, and he will give them their due. Let him esteem Nature a perpetual counsellor, and her perfections the exact measure of our deviations. Let him make the night night, and the day day. Let him control the habit of expense. Let him see that as much wisdom may be expended on a private economy as on an empire, and as much wisdom may be drawn from it. The laws of the world are written out for him on every piece of money in his hand. There is nothing he will not be the better for knowing, were it only the wisdom of Poor Richard, or the State-Street prudence of buying by the acre to sell by the foot; or the thrift of the agriculturist, to stick a tree between whiles, because it will grow whilst he sleeps; or the prudence which consists in husbanding little strokes of the tool, little portions of time, particles of stock and small gains. The eye of prudence may never shut. Iron, if kept at the ironmonger's, will rust; beer, if not brewed in the right state of the atmosphere, will sour; timber of ships will rot at sea, or if laid up high and dry, will strain, warp and dry-rot; money, if kept by us, yields no rent and is liable to loss; if invested, is liable to depreciation of the particu-

lar kind of stock.   Strike, says the smith, the
iron is white; keep the rake, says the haymaker,
as nigh the scythe as you can, and the cart as
nigh the rake. Our Yankee trade is reputed to
be very much on the extreme of this prudence.
It takes bank-notes, good, bad, clean, ragged,
and saves itself by the speed with which it passes
them off. Iron cannot rust, nor beer sour, nor
timber rot, nor calicoes go out of fashion, nor
money stocks depreciate, in the few swift moments in which the Yankee suffers any one of
them to remain in his possession. In skating
over thin ice our safety is in our speed.[1]

Let him learn a prudence of a higher strain.
Let him learn that every thing in nature, even
motes and feathers, go by law and not by luck,
and that what he sows he reaps. By diligence
and self-command let him put the bread he eats
at his own disposal, that he may not stand in
bitter and false relations to other men ; for the
best good of wealth is freedom. Let him practise the minor virtues. How much of human
life is lost in waiting! let him not make his
fellow-creatures wait. How many words and
promises are promises of conversation! Let his
be words of fate. When he sees a folded and
sealed scrap of paper float round the globe in

a pine ship and come safe to the eye for which
it was written, amidst a swarming population,
let him likewise feel the admonition to integrate
his being across all these distracting forces, and
keep a slender human word among the storms,
distances and accidents that drive us hither and
thither, and, by persistency, make the paltry
force of one man reappear to redeem its pledge
after months and years in the most distant climates.

We must not try to write the laws of any one
virtue, looking at that only. Human nature
loves no contradictions, but is symmetrical.
The prudence which secures an outward well-
being is not to be studied by one set of men,
whilst heroism and holiness are studied by another, but they are reconcilable. Prudence concerns the present time, persons, property and
existing forms. But as every fact hath its roots
in the soul, and if the soul were changed would
cease to be, or would become some other thing,
— the proper administration of outward things
will always rest on a just apprehension of their
cause and origin ; that is, the good man will be
the wise man, and the single-hearted the politic
man. Every violation of truth is not only a sort
of suicide in the liar, but is a stab at the health

of human society. On the most profitable lie
the course of events presently lays a destructive
tax ; whilst frankness invites frankness, puts the
parties on a convenient footing and makes their
business a friendship. Trust men and they will
be true to you ; treat them greatly and they will
show themselves great, though they make an exception in your favor to all their rules of trade.

So, in regard to disagreeable and formidable
things, prudence does not consist in evasion or
in flight, but in courage. He who wishes to
walk in the most peaceful parts of life with any
serenity must screw himself up to resolution.
Let him front the object of his worst apprehension, and his stoutness will commonly make his
fear groundless. The Latin proverb says, " In
battles the eye is first overcome." [1] Entire self-
possession may make a battle very little more
dangerous to life than a match at foils or at foot-
ball. Examples are cited by soldiers of men
who have seen the cannon pointed and the fire
given to it, and who have stepped aside from the
path of the ball. The terrors of the storm are
chiefly confined to the parlor and the cabin.
The drover, the sailor, buffets it all day, and his
health renews itself at as vigorous a pulse under
the sleet as under the sun of June.

In the occurrence of unpleasant things among neighbors, fear comes readily to heart and magnifies the consequence of the other party; but it is a bad counsellor. Every man is actually weak and apparently strong. To himself he seems weak; to others, formidable. You are afraid of Grim; but Grim also is afraid of you. You are solicitous of the good-will of the meanest person, uneasy at his ill-will. But the sturdiest offender of your peace and of the neighborhood, if you rip up *his* claims, is as thin and timid as any, and the peace of society is often kept, because, as children say, one is afraid and the other dares not. Far off, men swell, bully and threaten; bring them hand to hand, and they are a feeble folk.

It is a proverb that 'courtesy costs nothing;' but calculation might come to value love for its profit. Love is fabled to be blind, but kindness is necessary to perception; love is not a hood, but an eye-water. If you meet a sectary or a hostile partisan, never recognize the dividing lines, but meet on what common ground remains, — if only that the sun shines and the rain rains for both; the area will widen very fast, and ere you know it, the boundary mountains on which the eye had fastened have melted into air. If they

set out to contend, Saint Paul will lie and Saint
John will hate. What low, poor, paltry, hypocritical people an argument on religion will
make of the pure and chosen souls ! They will
shuffle and crow, crook and hide, feign to confess here, only that they may brag and conquer
there, and not a thought has enriched either
party, and not an emotion of bravery, modesty,
or hope.[1] So neither should you put yourself
in a false position with your contemporaries
by indulging a vein of hostility and bitterness.
Though your views are in straight antagonism
to theirs, assume an identity of sentiment, assume that you are saying precisely that which
all think, and in the flow of wit and love roll out
your paradoxes in solid column, with not the
infirmity of a doubt. So at least shall you get
an adequate deliverance. The natural motions
of the soul are so much better than the voluntary ones that you will never do yourself justice in dispute. The thought is not then taken
hold of by the right handle, does not show itself proportioned and in its true bearings, but
bears extorted, hoarse, and half witness. But assume a consent and it shall presently be granted,
since really and underneath their external diver-
sities, all men are of one heart and mind.[2]

Wisdom will never let us stand with any man or men on an unfriendly footing. We refuse sympathy and intimacy with people, as if we waited for some better sympathy and intimacy to come. But whence and when? To-morrow will be like to-day. Life wastes itself whilst we are preparing to live. Our friends and fellow-workers die off from us. Scarcely can we say we see new men, new women, approaching us. We are too old to regard fashion, too old to expect patronage of any greater or more powerful. Let us suck the sweetness of those affections and consuetudes that grow near us. These old shoes are easy to the feet. Undoubtedly we can easily pick faults in our company, can easily whisper names prouder, and that tickle the fancy more. Every man's imagination hath its friends; and life would be dearer with such companions. But if you cannot have them on good mutual terms, you cannot have them. If not the Deity but our ambition hews and shapes the new relations, their virtue escapes, as strawberries lose their flavor in garden-beds.

Thus truth, frankness, courage, love, humility and all the virtues range themselves on the side of prudence, or the art of securing a present well-being. I do not know if all matter will be found to be made of one element, as oxygen or hydrogen, at last, but the world of manners and actions is wrought of one stuff, and begin where we will, we are pretty sure in a short space to be mumbling our ten commandments.

VIII

HEROISM

" Paradise is under the shadow of swords."
Mahomet.

Ruby wine is drunk by knaves,
 Sugar spends to fatten slaves,
Rose and vine-leaf deck buffoons ;
Thunderclouds are Jove's festoons,
Drooping oft in wreaths of dread
Lightning-knotted round his head:
The hero is not fed on sweets,
Daily his own heart he eats ;
Chambers of the great are jails,
And head-winds right for royal sails.

HEROISM

IN the elder English dramatists, and mainly in the plays of Beaumont and Fletcher, there is a constant recognition of gentility, as if a noble behavior were as easily marked in the society of their age as color is in our American population. When any Rodrigo, Pedro or Valerio enters, though he be a stranger, the duke or governor exclaims, ' This is a gentleman,'— and proffers civilities without end ; but all the rest are slag and refuse. In harmony with this delight in personal advantages there is in their plays a certain heroic cast of character and dialogue, — as in Bonduca, Sophocles,[1] the Mad Lover, the Double Marriage, — wherein the speaker is so earnest and cordial and on such deep grounds of character, that the dialogue, on the slightest additional incident in the plot, rises naturally into poetry. Among many texts take the following. The Roman Martius has conquered Athens, — all but the invincible spirits of Sophocles, the duke of Athens, and Dorigen, his wife. The beauty of the latter inflames Martius, and he seeks to save her husband; but Sophocles will not ask his life, although assured

that a word will save him, and the execution of
both proceeds : —

    Valerius.   Bid thy wife farewell.
    Soph. No, I will take no leave. My Dorigen,
Yonder, above, 'bout Ariadne's crown,
My spirit shall hover for thee. Prithee, haste.
    Dor. Stay, Sophocles, — with this tie up my sight;
Let not soft nature so transfòrmèd be,
And lose her gentler sexed humanity,
To make me see my lord bleed. So, 't is well;
Never one object underneath the sun
Will I behold before my Sophocles :
Farewell ; now teach the Romans how to die.
    Mar. Dost know what 't is to die ?
    Soph.   Thou dost not, Martius,
And, therefore, not what 't is to live ; to die
Is to begin to live. It is to end
An old, stale, weary work and to commence
A newer and a better. 'T is to leave
Deceitful knaves for the society
Of gods and goodness. Thou thyself must part
At last from all thy garlands, pleasures, triumphs,
And prove thy fortitude what then 't will do.
    Val. But art not grieved nor vexed to leave thy life thus ?
    Soph. Why should I grieve or vex for being sent
To them I ever loved best ? Now I 'll kneel,
But with my back toward thee : 't is the last duty
This trunk can do the gods.
    Mar.   Strike, strike, Valerius,
Or Martius' heart will leap out at his mouth.
This is a man, a woman. Kiss thy lord,

And live with all the freedom you were wont.
O love ! thou doubly hast afflicted me
With virtue and with beauty. Treacherous heart,
My hand shall cast thee quick into my urn,
Ere thou transgress this knot of piety.
    Val. What ails my brother ?
    Soph.   Martius, O Martius,
Thou now hast found a way to conquer me.
    Dor. O star of Rome ! what gratitude can speak
Fit words to follow such a deed as this ?
    Mar. This admirable duke, Valerius,
With his disdain of fortune and of death,
Captived himself, has captivated me,
And though my arm hath ta'en his body here,
His soul hath subjugated Martius' soul.
By Romulus, he is all soul, I think ;
He hath no flesh, and spirit cannot be gyved,
Then we have vanquished nothing ; he is free,
And Martius walks now in captivity."

I do not readily remember any poem, play, sermon, novel or oration that our press vents in the last few years, which goes to the same tune. We have a great many flutes and flageolets, but not often the sound of any fife. Yet Wordsworth's " Laodamia," and the ode of " Dion," and some sonnets, have a certain noble music ; and Scott will sometimes draw a stroke like the portrait of Lord Evandale given by Balfour of Burley.[1] Thomas Carlyle, with his natural taste for what is manly and daring in character, has suffered no heroic trait in his favorites to drop from his biographical and historical pictures. Earlier, Robert Burns has given us a song or two. In the Harleian Miscellanies there is an account of the battle of Lutzen which deserves to be read. And Simon Ockley's History of the Saracens recounts the prodigies of individual valor, with admiration all the more evident on the part of the narrator that he seems to think that his place in Christian Oxford requires of him some proper protestations of abhorrence. But if we explore the literature of Heroism we shall quickly come to Plutarch, who is its Doctor and historian. To him we owe the Brasidas, the Dion, the Epaminondas, the Scipio of old, and I must think we are more deeply indebted to him than to all the ancient writers. Each of his " Lives " is a refutation to the despondency and cowardice of our religious and political theorists. A wild courage, a Stoicism not of the schools but of the blood, shines in every anecdote, and has given that book its immense fame.[1]

We need books of this tart cathartic virtue more than books of political science or of private economy. Life is a festival only to the

wise. Seen from the nook and chimney - side
of prudence, it wears a ragged and dangerous
front. The violations of the laws of nature by
our predecessors and our contemporaries are
punished in us also. The disease and deformity
around us certify the infraction of natural, intellectual and moral laws, and often violation on
violation to breed such compound misery. A
lock-jaw that bends a man's head back to his
heels ; hydrophobia that makes him bark at his
wife and babes ; insanity that makes him eat
grass ; war, plague, cholera, famine, indicate a
certain ferocity in nature, which, as it had its
inlet by human crime, must have its outlet by
human suffering. Unhappily no man exists
who has not in his own person become to some
amount a stockholder in the sin, and so made
himself liable to a share in the expiation.

Our culture therefore must not omit the arm-
ing of the man. Let him hear in season that he
is born into the state of war, and that the com-
monwealth and his own well-being require that
he should not go dancing in the weeds of peace,
but warned, self-collected and neither defying
nor dreading the thunder, let him take both
reputation and life in his hand, and with perfect
urbanity dare the gibbet and the mob by the

absolute truth of his speech and the rectitude
of his behavior.[1]

Towards all this external evil the man within
the breast assumes a warlike attitude, and affirms
his ability to cope single-handed with the infinite army of enemies. To this military attitude
of the soul we give the name of Heroism. Its
rudest form is the contempt for safety and ease,
which makes the attractiveness of war. It is a
self-trust which slights the restraints of prudence,
in the plenitude of its energy and power to re-
pair the harms it may suffer. The hero is a
mind of such balance that no disturbances can
shake his will, but pleasantly and as it were
merrily he advances to his own music, alike in
frightful alarms and in the tipsy mirth of universal dissoluteness. There is somewhat not
philosophical in heroism; there is somewhat
not holy in it; it seems not to know that other
souls are of one texture with it; it has pride;
it is the extreme of individual nature. Nevertheless we must profoundly revere it. There
is somewhat in great actions which does not
allow us to go behind them. Heroism feels and
never reasons, and therefore is always right;
and although a different breeding, different religion and greater intellectual activity would

have modified or even reversed the particular
action, yet for the hero that thing he does is
the highest deed, and is not open to the censure
of philosophers or divines. It is the avowal of
the unschooled man that he finds a quality in
him that is negligent of expense, of health, of
life, of danger, of hatred, of reproach, and knows
that his will is higher and more excellent than
all actual and all possible antagonists.

Heroism works in contradiction to the voice
of mankind and in contradiction, for a time, to
the voice of the great and good. Heroism is
an obedience to a secret impulse of an individual's character. Now to no other man can its
wisdom appear as it does to him, for every man
must be supposed to see a little farther on his
own proper path than any one else. Therefore
just and wise men take umbrage at his act, until
after some little time be past ; then they see it
to be in unison with their acts. All prudent
men see that the action is clean contrary to a
sensual prosperity ; for every heroic act measures
itself by its contempt of some external good.
But it finds its own success at last, and then the
prudent also extol.[1]

Self-trust is the essence of heroism. It is the
state of the soul at war, and its ultimate objects

are the last defiance of falsehood and wrong, and
the power to bear all that can be inflicted by evil
agents. It speaks the truth and it is just, generous, hospitable, temperate, scornful of petty
calculations and scornful of being scorned. It
persists ; it is of an undaunted boldness and of
a fortitude not to be wearied out. Its jest is
the littleness of common life. That false prudence which dotes on health and wealth is the
butt and merriment of heroism. Heroism, like
Plotinus, is almost ashamed of its body. What
shall it say then to the sugar-plums and cats'-
cradles, to the toilet, compliments, quarrels, cards
and custard, which rack the wit of all society ?
What joys has kind nature provided for us dear
creatures ! There seems to be no interval between greatness and meanness. When the spirit
is not master of the world, then it is its dupe.
Yet the little man takes the great hoax so inno-
cently, works in it so headlong and believing,
is born red, and dies gray, arranging his toilet,
attending on his own health, laying traps for
sweet food and strong wine, setting his heart on
a horse or a rifle, made happy with a little gossip or a little praise, that the great soul cannot
choose but laugh at such earnest nonsense. "Indeed, these humble considerations make me out

of love with greatness. What a disgrace is it to me to take note how many pairs of silk stockings thou hast, namely, these and those that were the peach-colored ones; or to bear the inventory of thy shirts, as one for superfluity, and one other for use! " [1]

Citizens, thinking after the laws of arithmetic, consider the inconvenience of receiving strangers at their fireside, reckon narrowly the loss of time and the unusual display; the soul of a better quality thrusts back the unreasonable economy into the vaults of life, and says, I will obey the God, and the sacrifice and the fire he will provide. Ibn Haukal, the Arabian geographer, describes a heroic extreme in the hospitality of Sogd, in Bukharia. " When I was in Sogd I saw a great building, like a palace, the gates of which were open and fixed back to the wall with large nails. I asked the reason, and was told that the house had not been shut, night or day, for a hundred years. Strangers may present themselves at any hour and in whatever number; the master has amply provided for the reception of the men and their animals, and is never happier than when they tarry for some time. Nothing of the kind have I seen in any other country." [2] The magnanimous know very well

that they who give time, or money, or shelter,
to the stranger, — so it be done for love and
not for ostentation, — do, as it were, put God
under obligation to them, so perfect are the
compensations of the universe. In some way
the time they seem to lose is redeemed and the
pains they seem to take remunerate themselves.
These men fan the flame of human love and
raise the standard of civil virtue among mankind.
But hospitality must be for service and not for
show, or it pulls down the host. The brave soul
rates itself too high to value itself by the splendor of its table and draperies. It gives what it
hath, and all it hath, but its own majesty can
lend a better grace to bannocks and fair water
than belong to city feasts.'

The temperance of the hero proceeds from
the same wish to do no dishonor to the worthiness he has. But he loves it for its elegancy, not
for its austerity. It seems not worth his while
to be solemn and denounce with bitterness flesh-
eating or wine-drinking, the use of tobacco, or
opium, or tea, or silk, or gold. A great man
scarcely knows how he dines, how he dresses; but
without railing or precision his living is natural
and poetic. John Eliot, the Indian Apostle,
drank water, and said of wine, — "It is a noble,

generous liquor and we should be humbly thank-
ful for it, but, as I remember, water was made
before it." Better still is the temperance of King
David, who poured out on the ground unto the
Lord the water which three of his warriors had
brought him to drink at the peril of their lives.

It is told of Brutus, that when he fell on his
sword after the battle of Philippi, he quoted a
line of Euripides, — " O Virtue ! I have followed thee through life, and I find thee at last
but a shade." I doubt not the hero is slandered
by this report. The heroic soul does not sell
its justice and its nobleness. It does not ask to
dine nicely and to sleep warm. The essence of
greatness is the perception that virtue is enough.
Poverty is its ornament. It does not need plenty,
and can very well abide its loss.

But that which takes my fancy most in the
heroic class, is the good-humor and hilarity they
exhibit. It is a height to which common duty
can very well attain, to suffer and to dare with
solemnity. But these rare souls set opinion, success, and life at so cheap a rate that they will
not soothe their enemies by petitions, or the
show of sorrow, but wear their own habitual
greatness. Scipio, charged with peculation, refuses to do himself so great a disgrace as to wait

for justification, though he had the scroll of his
accounts in his hands, but tears it to pieces before the tribunes.[1] Socrates's condemnation of
himself to be maintained in all honor in the
Prytaneum, during his life, and Sir Thomas
More's playfulness at the scaffold, are of the
same strain. In Beaumont and Fletcher's "Sea
Voyage," Juletta tells the stout captain and his
company, —

> *Jul.* Why, slaves, 't is in our power to hang ye.
> *Master.*   Very likely,
> 'T is in our powers, then, to be hanged, and scorn ye.

These replies are sound and whole. Sport is the
bloom and glow of a perfect health. The great
will not condescend to take any thing seriously;
all must be as gay as the song of a canary,
though it were the building of cities or the
eradication of old and foolish churches and nations which have cumbered the earth long thousands of years. Simple hearts put all the history
and customs of this world behind them, and play
their own game in innocent defiance of the Blue-
Laws of the world; and such would appear,
could we see the human race assembled in vision,
like little children frolicking together, though to
the eyes of mankind at large they wear a stately
and solemn garb of works and influences.

The interest these fine stories have for us, the power of a romance over the boy who grasps the forbidden book under his bench at school, our delight in the hero, is the main fact to our purpose.¹ All these great and transcendent properties are ours. If we dilate in beholding the Greek energy, the Roman pride, it is that we are already domesticating the same sentiment. Let us find room for this great guest in our small houses. The first step of worthiness will be to disabuse us of our superstitious associations with places and times, with number and size. Why should these words, Athenian, Roman, Asia and England, so tingle in the ear? Where the heart is, there the muses, there the gods sojourn, and not in any geography of fame. Massachusetts, Connecticut River and Boston Bay you think paltry places, and the ear loves names of foreign and classic topography. But here we are; and, if we will tarry a little, we may come to learn that here is best. See to it only that thyself is here, and art and nature, hope and fate, friends, angels and the Supreme Being shall not be absent from the chamber where thou sittest. Epaminondas, brave and affectionate, does not seem to us to need Olympus to die upon, nor the Syrian sunshine. He 'lies very well where he is. The Jerseys were handsome ground enough for Washington to tread, and London streets for the feet of Milton. A great man makes his climate genial in the imagination of men, and its air the beloved element of all delicate spirits. That country is the fairest which is inhabited by the noblest minds. The pictures which fill the imagination in reading the actions of Pericles, Xenophon, Columbus, Bayard, Sidney, Hampden, teach us how needlessly mean our life is; that we, by the depth of our living, should deck it with more than regal or national splendor, and act on principles that should interest man and nature in the length of our days.'

We have seen or heard of many extraordinary young men who never ripened, or whose performance in actual life was not extraordinary. When we see their air and mien, when we hear them speak of society, of books, of religion, we admire their superiority; they seem to throw contempt on our entire polity and social state; theirs is the tone of a youthful giant who is sent to work revolutions. But they enter an active profession and the forming Colossus shrinks to the common size of man. The magic they used was the ideal tendencies, which always make the

Actual ridiculous; but the tough world had its
revenge the moment they put their horses of
the sun to plough in its furrow. They found
no example and no companion, and their heart
fainted. What then? The lesson they gave in
their first aspirations is yet true; and a better
valor and a purer truth shall one day organize
their belief. Or why should a woman liken herself to any historical woman, and think, because
Sappho, or Sévigné, or De Staël, or the clois-
tered souls who have had genius and cultivation
do not satisfy the imagination and the serene
Themis, none can, — certainly not she? Why
not? She has a new and unattempted problem
to solve, perchance that of the happiest nature
that ever bloomed. Let the maiden, with erect
soul, walk serenely on her way, accept the hint
of each new experience, search in turn all the
objects that solicit her eye, that she may learn
the power and the charm of her new-born being,
which is the kindling of a new dawn in the
recesses of space. The fair girl who repels interference by a decided and proud choice of
influences, so careless of pleasing, so wilful and
lofty, inspires every beholder with somewhat of
her own nobleness. The silent heart encourages
her; O friend, never strike sail to a fear! Come

into port greatly, or sail with God the seas.
Not in vain you live, for every passing eye is
cheered and refined by the vision.

The characteristic of heroism is its persistency. All men have wandering impulses, fits
and starts of generosity. But when you have
chosen your part, abide by it, and do not weakly
try to reconcile yourself with the world. The
heroic cannot be the common, nor the common
the heroic. Yet we have the weakness to expect
the sympathy of people in those actions whose
excellence is that they outrun sympathy and
appeal to a tardy justice. If you would serve
your brother, because it is fit for you to serve
him, do not take back your words when you
find that prudent people do not commend you.
Adhere to your own act, and congratulate yourself if you have done something strange and
extravagant and broken the monotony of a
decorous age. It was a high counsel that I
once heard given to a young person, — "Always do what you are afraid to do."[1] A simple
manly character need never make an apology,
but should regard its past action with the calm-
ness of Phocion, when he admitted that the
event of the battle was happy, yet did not regret his dissuasion from the battle.

There is no weakness or exposure for which we cannot find consolation in the thought — this is a part of my constitution, part of my relation and office to my fellow-creature. Has nature covenanted with me that I should never appear to disadvantage, never make a ridiculous figure? Let us be generous of our dignity as well as of our money. Greatness once and for ever has done with opinion. We tell our charities, not because we wish to be praised for them, not because we think they have great merit, but for our justification. It is a capital blunder; as you discover when another man recites his charities.

To speak the truth, even with some austerity, to live with some rigor of temperance, or some extremes of generosity, seems to be an asceticism which common good-nature would appoint to those who are at ease and in plenty, in sign that they feel a brotherhood with the great multitude of suffering men. And not only need we breathe and exercise the soul by assuming the penalties of abstinence, of debt, of solitude, of unpopularity, — but it behooves the wise man to look with a bold eye into those rarer dangers which sometimes invade men, and to familiarize himself with disgusting forms of disease, with sounds of execration, and the vision of violent death.

Times of heroism are generally times of terror, but the day never shines in which this element may not work. The circumstances of man, we say, are historically somewhat better in this country and at this hour than perhaps ever before. More freedom exists for culture. It will not now run against an axe at the first step out of the beaten track of opinion. But whoso is heroic will always find crises to try his edge. Human virtue demands her champions and martyrs, and the trial of persecution always proceeds. It is but the other day that the brave Lovejoy gave his breast to the bullets of a mob, for the rights of free speech and opinion, and died when it was better not to live.[1]

I see not any road of perfect peace which a man can walk, but after the counsel of his own bosom. Let him quit too much association, let him go home much, and stablish himself in those courses he approves.[2] The unremitting retention of simple and high sentiments in obscure duties is hardening the character to that temper which will work with honor, if need be in the tumult, or on the scaffold. Whatever outrages have happened to men may befall a

man again; and very easily in a republic, if
there appear any signs of a decay of religion.
Coarse slander, fire, tar and feathers and the
gibbet, the youth may freely bring home to his
mind and with what sweetness of temper he can,
and inquire how fast he can fix his sense of
duty, braving such penalties, whenever it may
please the next newspaper and a sufficient number of his neighbors to pronounce his opinions
incendiary.

It may calm the apprehension of calamity in
the most susceptible heart to see how quick a
bound Nature has set to the utmost infliction
of malice. We rapidly approach a brink over
which no enemy can follow us : —

> " Let them rave :
> Thou art quiet in thy grave." [1]

In the gloom of our ignorance of what shall be,
in the hour when we are deaf to the higher
voices, who does not envy those who have seen
safely to an end their manful endeavor ? Who
that sees the meanness of our politics but inly
congratulates Washington that he is long already
wrapped in his shroud, and for ever safe ; that
he was laid sweet in his grave, the hope of humanity not yet subjugated in him ? Who does
not sometimes envy the good and brave who are

no more to suffer from the tumults of the natural world, and await with curious complacency
the speedy term of his own conversation with
finite nature? And yet the love that will be
annihilated sooner than treacherous has already
made death impossible, and affirms itself no
mortal but a native of the deeps of absolute and
inextinguishable being.

IX

THE OVER-SOUL

"But souls that of his own good life partake,
He loves as his own self; dear as his eye
They are to Him: He'll never them forsake:
When they shall die, then God himself shall die:
They live, they live in blest eternity."

Henry More.

Space is ample, east and west,
But two cannot go abreast,
Cannot travel in it two:
Yonder masterful cuckoo
Crowds every egg out of the nest,
Quick or dead, except its own;
A spell is laid on sod and stone,
Night and Day 've been tampered with,
Every quality and pith
Surcharged and sultry with a power
That works its will on age and hour.

THE OVER–SOUL

THERE is a difference between one and
another hour of life in their authority
and subsequent effect. Our faith comes in moments ; our vice is habitual. Yet there is a depth
in those brief moments which constrains us to
ascribe more reality to them than to all other
experiences. For this reason the argument which
is always forthcoming to silence those who con-
ceive extraordinary hopes of man, namely the
appeal to experience, is for ever invalid and vain.
We give up the past to the objector, and yet we
hope. He must explain this hope. We grant
that human life is mean, but how did we find out
that it was mean ? ' What is the ground of this
uneasiness of ours ; of this old discontent? What
is the universal sense of want and ignorance, but
the fine innuendo by which the soul makes its
enormous claim? Why do men feel that the
natural history of man has never been written,
but he is always leaving behind what you have
said of him, and it becomes old, and books of
metaphysics worthless ? The philosophy of six
thousand years has not searched the chambers
and magazines of the soul. In its experiments

there has always remained, in the last analysis, a
residuum it could not resolve. Man is a stream
whose source is hidden.[1] Our being is descending into us from we know not whence. The
most exact calculator has no prescience that
somewhat incalculable may not balk the very
next moment. I am constrained every moment
to acknowledge a higher origin for events than
the will I call mine.

As with events, so is it with thoughts. When
I watch that flowing river, which, out of regions I
see not, pours for a season its streams into me,
I see that I am a pensioner; not a cause but a
surprised spectator of this ethereal water; that
I desire and look up and put myself in the attitude of reception, but from some alien energy
the visions come.[2]

The Supreme Critic on the errors of the past
and the present, and the only prophet of that
which must be, is that great nature in which we
rest as the earth lies in the soft arms of the atmosphere; that Unity, that Over-Soul, within which
every man's particular being is contained and
made one with all other; that common heart of
which all sincere conversation is the worship, to
which all right action is submission; that over-
powering reality which confutes our tricks and

talents, and constrains every one to pass for what
he is, and to speak from his character and not
from his tongue, and which evermore tends to
pass into our thought and hand and become wisdom and virtue and power and beauty. We live
in succession, in division, in parts, in particles.
Meantime within man is the soul of the whole;
the wise silence; the universal beauty, to which
every part and particle is equally related; the
eternal ONE. 'And this deep power in which we
exist and whose beatitude is all accessible to us,
is not only self-sufficing and perfect in every
hour, but the act of seeing and the thing seen,
the seer and the spectacle, the subject and the
object, are one.' We see the world piece by piece,
as the sun, the moon, the animal, the tree; but
the whole, of which these are the shining parts,
is the soul.' Only by the vision of that Wisdom
can the horoscope of the ages be read, and by
falling back on our better thoughts, by yielding
to the spirit of prophecy which is innate in every
man, we can know what it saith. Every man's
words who speaks from that life must sound
vain to those who do not dwell in the same
thought on their own part. I dare not speak
for it. My words do not carry its august sense;
they fall short and cold. Only itself can inspire

whom it will, and behold ! their speech shall be
lyrical, and sweet, and universal as the rising of
the wind. Yet I desire, even by profane words,
if I may not use sacred, to indicate the heaven
of this deity and to report what hints I have collected of the transcendent simplicity and energy
of the Highest Law.[1]

If we consider what happens in conversation,
in reveries, in remorse, in times of passion, in
surprises, in the instructions of dreams, wherein
often we see ourselves in masquerade,—the droll
disguises only magnifying and enhancing a real
element and forcing it on our distant notice, —
we shall catch many hints that will broaden and
lighten into knowledge of the secret of nature.[2]
All goes to show that the soul in man is not an
organ, but animates and exercises all the organs ;
is not a function, like the power of memory,
of calculation, of comparison, but uses these as
hands and feet ; is not a faculty, but a light ; is
not the intellect or the will, but the master of the
intellect and the will ; is the background of our
being, in which they lie, — an immensity not
possessed and that cannot be possessed.[3] From
within or from behind, a light shines through us
upon things and makes us aware that we are
nothing, but the light is all. A man is the façade

of a temple wherein all wisdom and all good
abide. What we commonly call man, the eating, drinking, planting, counting man, does not,
as we know him, represent himself, but misre-
presents himself. Him we do not respect, but
the soul, whose organ he is, would he let it appear through his action, would make our knees
bend. When it breathes through his intellect,
it is genius ; when it breathes through his will,
it is virtue ; when it flows through his affection,
it is love. And the blindness of the intellect
begins when it would be something of itself.[1]
The weakness of the will begins when the individual would be something of himself. All reform aims in some one particular to let the soul
have its way through us ; in other words, to engage us to obey.

Of this pure nature every man is at some
time sensible. Language cannot paint it with
his colors. It is too subtile. It is undefinable,
unmeasurable ; but we know that it pervades
and contains us. We know that all spiritual being is in man. A wise old proverb says, "God
comes to see us without bell ; "[2] that is, as there
is no screen or ceiling between our heads and
the infinite heavens, so is there no bar or wall
in the soul, where man, the effect, ceases, and

God, the cause, begins. The walls are taken away. We lie open on one side to the deeps of spiritual nature, to the attributes of God. Justice we see and know, Love, Freedom, Power. These natures no man ever got above, but they tower over us, and most in the moment when our interests tempt us to wound them.

The sovereignty of this nature whereof we speak is made known by its independency of those limitations which circumscribe us on every hand. The soul circumscribes all things. As I have said, it contradicts all experience. In like manner it abolishes time and space. The influence of the senses has in most men overpowered the mind to that degree that the walls of time and space have come to look real and insurmountable; and to speak with levity of these limits is, in the world, the sign of insanity. Yet time and space are but inverse measures of the force of the soul. The spirit sports with time,—

> " Can crowd eternity into an hour,
> Or stretch an hour to eternity.''

We are often made to feel that there is another youth and age than that which is measured from the year of our natural birth. Some thoughts always find us young, and keep us so.' Such a thought is the love of the universal and eternal beauty. Every man parts from that contemplation with the feeling that it rather belongs to ages than to mortal life. The least activity of the intellectual powers redeems us in a degree from the conditions of time. In sickness, in languor, give us a strain of poetry or a profound sentence, and we are refreshed; or produce a volume of Plato or Shakspeare, or remind us of their names, and instantly we come into a feeling of longevity. See how the deep divine thought reduces centuries and millenniums, and makes itself present through all ages. Is the teaching of Christ less effective now than it was when first his mouth was opened? The emphasis of facts and persons in my thought has nothing to do with time. And so always the soul's scale is one, the scale of the senses and the understanding is another. Before the revelations of the soul, Time, Space and Nature shrink away. In common speech we refer all things to time, as we habitually refer the immensely sundered stars to one concave sphere. And so we say that the Judgment is distant or near, that the Millennium approaches, that a day of certain political, moral, social reforms is at hand, and the like, when we mean that in the nature of things one of the facts we contemplate is

external and fugitive, and the other is permanent
and connate with the soul. The things we now
esteem fixed shall, one by one, detach themselves like ripe fruit from our experience, and
fall. The wind shall blow them none knows
whither. The landscape, the figures, Boston,
London, are facts as fugitive as any institution
past, or any whiff of mist or smoke, and so is
society, and so is the world. The soul looketh
steadily forwards, creating a world before her,
leaving worlds behind her. She has no dates,
nor rites, nor persons, nor specialties nor men.
The soul knows only the soul; the web of
events is the flowing robe in which she is
clothed.[1]

After its own law and not by arithmetic is the
rate of its progress to be computed. The soul's
advances are not made by gradation, such as can
be represented by motion in a straight line, but
rather by ascension of state, such as can be represented by metamorphosis, — from the egg to
the worm, from the worm to the fly. The growths
of genius are of a certain *total* character, that
does not advance the elect individual first over
John, then Adam, then Richard, and give to
each the pain of discovered inferiority,— but by
every throe of growth the man expands there

where he works, passing, at each pulsation, classes, populations, of men. With each divine impulse the mind rends the thin rinds of the visible and finite, and comes out into eternity, and inspires and expires its air. It converses with truths that have always been spoken in the world, and becomes conscious of a closer sympathy with Zeno and Arrian than with persons in the house.

This is the law of moral and of mental gain. The simple rise as by specific levity not into a particular virtue, but into the region of all the virtues. They are in the spirit which contains them all.[1] The soul requires purity, but purity is not it; requires justice, but justice is not that; requires beneficence, but is somewhat better; so that there is a kind of descent and accommodation felt when we leave speaking of moral nature to urge a virtue which it enjoins. To the well-born child all the virtues are natural, and not painfully acquired. Speak to his heart, and the man becomes suddenly virtuous.[2]

Within the same sentiment is the germ of intellectual growth, which obeys the same law. Those who are capable of humility, of justice, of love, of aspiration, stand already on a platform that commands the sciences and arts, speech and poetry, action and grace. For whoso dwells in this moral beatitude already anticipates those special powers which men prize so highly. The lover has no talent, no skill, which passes for quite nothing with his enamored maiden, however little she may possess of related faculty; and the heart which abandons itself to the Supreme Mind finds itself related to all its works, and will travel a royal road to particular knowledges and powers. In ascending to this primary and aboriginal sentiment we have come from our remote station on the circumference instantaneously to the centre of the world, where, as in the closet of God, we see causes, and anticipate the universe, which is but a slow effect.[1]

One mode of the divine teaching is the incarnation of the spirit in a form, — in forms, like my own. I live in society; with persons who answer to thoughts in my own mind, or express a certain obedience to the great instincts to which I live. I see its presence to them. I am certified of a common nature; and these other souls, these separated selves, draw me as nothing else can. They stir in me the new emotions we call passion; of love, hatred, fear, admiration, pity; thence come conversation, competition, persuasion, cities and war. Persons are supplementary to the primary teaching of the soul. In youth we are mad for persons. Childhood and youth see all the world in them. But the larger experience of man discovers the identical nature appearing through them all. Persons themselves acquaint us with the impersonal. In all conversation between two persons tacit reference is made, as to a third party, to a common nature. That third party or common nature is not social; it is impersonal; is God. And so in groups where debate is earnest, and especially on high questions, the company become aware that the thought rises to an equal level in all bosoms, that all have a spiritual property in what was said, as well as the sayer. They all become wiser than they were. It arches over them like a temple, this unity of thought in which every heart beats with nobler sense of power and duty, and thinks and acts with unusual solemnity. All are conscious of attaining to a higher self-possession. It shines for all. There is a certain wisdom of humanity which is common to the greatest men with the lowest, and which our ordinary education often labors to silence and obstruct. The mind is one, and the best minds, who love truth for its own sake, think much less of property in truth. They accept it thankfully everywhere, and do not label or stamp it with any man's name, for it is theirs long beforehand, and from eternity.[1] The learned and the studious of thought have no monopoly of wisdom. Their violence of direction in some degree disqualifies them to think truly. We owe many valuable observations to people who are not very acute or profound, and who say the thing without effort which we want and have long been hunting in vain. The action of the soul is oftener in that which is felt and left unsaid than in that which is said in any conversation. It broods over every society, and they unconsciously seek for it in each other. We know better than we do.[2] We do not yet possess ourselves, and we know at the same time that we are much more. I feel the same truth how often in my trivial conversation with my neighbors, that somewhat higher in each of us overlooks this by-play, and Jove nods to Jove from behind each of us.[3]

Men descend to meet. In their habitual and mean service to the world, for which they forsake their native nobleness, they resemble those Arabian sheiks who dwell in mean houses and affect an external poverty, to escape the rapa-

city of the Pacha, and reserve all their display
of wealth for their interior and guarded retire-
ments.

As it is present in all persons, so it is in
every period of life. It is adult already in the
infant man. In my dealing with my child, my
Latin and Greek, my accomplishments and my
money stead me nothing; but as much soul as
I have avails. If I am wilful, he sets his will
against mine, one for one, and leaves me, if I
please, the degradation of beating him by my
superiority of strength. But if I renounce my
will and act for the soul, setting that up as um-
pire between us two, out of his young eyes looks
the same soul; he reveres and loves with me.'

The soul is the perceiver and revealer of
truth. We know truth when we see it, let scep-
tic and scoffer say what they choose. Foolish
people ask you, when you have spoken what
they do not wish to hear, 'How do you know
it is truth, and not an error of your own?' We
know truth when we see it, from opinion, as we
know when we are awake that we are awake. It
was a grand sentence of Emanuel Swedenborg,
which would alone indicate the greatness of that
man's perception, — " It is no proof of a man's
understanding to be able to affirm whatever he

pleases ; but to be able to discern that what is
true is true, and that what is false is false, —
this is the mark and character of intelligence."
In the book I read, the good thought returns
to me, as every truth will, the image of the
whole soul. To the bad thought which I find
in it, the same soul becomes a discerning, separating sword, and lops it away. We are wiser
than we know. If we will not interfere with our
thought, but will act entirely, or see how the
thing stands in God, we know the particular
thing, and every thing, and every man. For
the Maker of all things and all persons stands
behind us and casts his dread omniscience through
us over things.

But beyond this recognition of its own in
particular passages of the individual's experience, it also reveals truth. And here we should
seek to reinforce ourselves by its very presence,
and to speak with a worthier, loftier strain of
that advent. For the soul's communication of
truth is the highest event in' nature, since it
then does not give somewhat from itself, but it
gives itself, or passes into and becomes that man
whom it enlightens; or in proportion to that
truth he receives, it takes him to itself.

We distinguish the announcements of the

soul, its manifestations of its own nature, by the
term *Revelation*. These are always attended by
the emotion of the sublime. For this communication is an influx of the Divine mind into
our mind.[1] It is an ebb of the individual rivulet
before the flowing surges of the sea of life.
Every distinct apprehension of this central com-
mandment agitates men with awe and delight.
A thrill passes through all men at the reception
of new truth, or at the performance of a great
action, which comes out of the heart of nature.
In these communications the power to see is
not separated from the will to do, but the insight proceeds from obedience, and the obedience proceeds from a joyful perception.[2] Every
moment when the individual feels himself in-
vaded by it is memorable. By the necessity of
our constitution a certain enthusiasm attends the
individual's consciousness of that divine presence. The character and duration of this enthusiasm vary with the state of the individual, from
an ecstasy and trance and prophetic inspiration,
— which is its rarer appearance, — to the faintest glow of virtuous emotion, in which form it
warms, like our household fires, all the families
and associations of men, and makes society
possible. A certain tendency to insanity has

always attended the opening of the religious sense in men, as if they had been " blasted with excess of light." [1] The trances of Socrates, the "union " of Plotinus, the vision of Porphyry, the conversion of · Paul, the aurora of Behmen, the convulsions of George Fox and his Quakers, the illumination of Swedenborg, are of this kind. What was in the case of these remarkable persons a ravishment, has, in innumerable instances in common life, been exhibited in less striking manner. Everywhere the history of religion betrays a tendency to enthusiasm. The rapture of the Moravian and Quietist; the opening of the eternal sense of the Word, in the language of the New Jerusalem Church; the *revival* of the Calvinistic churches; the *experiences* of the Methodists, are varying forms of that shudder of awe and delight with which the individual soul always mingles with the universal soul.

The nature of these revelations is the same; they are perceptions of the absolute law. They are solutions of the soul's own questions. They do not answer the questions which the understanding asks. The soul answers never by words, but by the thing itself that is inquired after. [2]

Revelation is the disclosure of the soul. The

popular notion of a revelation is that it is a
telling of fortunes. In past oracles of the soul
the understanding seeks to find answers to sensual questions, and undertakes to tell from God
how long men shall exist, what their hands shall
do and who shall be their company, adding
names and dates and places. But we must pick
no locks. We must check this low curiosity.[1]
An answer in words is delusive ; it is really
no answer to the questions you ask. Do not
require a description of the countries towards
which you sail. The description does not describe them to you, and to-morrow you arrive
there and know them by inhabiting them. Men
ask concerning the immortality of the soul, the
employments of heaven, the state of the sinner,
and so forth. They even dream that Jesus has
left replies to precisely these interrogatories.
Never a moment did that sublime spirit speak
in their *patois*. To truth, justice, love, the attributes of the soul, the idea of immutableness
is essentially associated. Jesus, living in these
moral sentiments, heedless of sensual fortunes,
heeding only the manifestations of these, never
made the separation of the idea of duration from
the essence of these attributes, nor uttered a
syllable concerning the duration of the soul. It

was left to his disciples to sever duration from
the moral elements, and to teach the immortality
of the soul as a doctrine, and maintain it by
evidences. The moment the doctrine of the
immortality is separately taught, man is already
fallen. In the flowing of love, in the adoration
of humility, there is no question of continuance.
No inspired man ever asks this question or con-
descends to these evidences. For the soul is
true to itself, and the man in whom it is shed
abroad cannot wander from the present, which
is infinite, to a future which would be finite.[1]

These questions which we lust to ask about
the future are a confession of sin. God has no
answer for them. No answer in words can reply
to a question of things. It is not in an arbitrary
"decree of God," but in the nature of man, that
a veil shuts down on the facts of to-morrow;
for the soul will not have us read any other
cipher than that of cause and effect. By this veil
which curtains events it instructs the children
of men to live in to-day. The only mode of
obtaining an answer to these questions of the
senses is to forego all low curiosity, and, accepting the tide of being which floats us into the
secret of nature, work and live, work and live,
and all unawares the advancing soul has built

and forged for itself a new condition, and the question and the answer are one.[1]

By the same fire, vital, consecrating, celestial, which burns until it shall dissolve all things into the waves and surges of an ocean of light, we see and know each other, and what spirit each is of. Who can tell the grounds of his knowledge of the character of the several individuals in his circle of friends? No man. Yet their acts and words do not disappoint him. In that man, though he knew no ill of him, he put no trust. In that other, though they had seldom met, authentic signs had yet passed, to signify that he might be trusted as one who had an interest in his own character. We know each other very well, — which of us has been just to himself and whether that which we teach or behold is only an aspiration or is our honest effort also.

We are all discerners of spirits. That diagnosis lies aloft in our life or unconscious power. The intercourse of society, its trade, its religion, its friendships, its quarrels, is one wide judicial investigation of character. In full court, or in small committee, or confronted face to face, accuser and accused, men offer themselves to be judged. Against their will they exhibit those decisive trifles by which character is read. But who judges? and what? Not our understanding. We do not read them by learning or craft. No; the wisdom of the wise man consists herein, that he does not judge them; he lets them judge themselves and merely reads and records their own verdict.

By virtue of this inevitable nature, private will is overpowered, and, maugre our efforts or our imperfections, your genius will speak from you, and mine from me. That which we are, we shall teach, not voluntarily but involuntarily. Thoughts come into our minds by avenues which we never left open, and thoughts go out of our minds through avenues which we never voluntarily opened.[1] Character teaches over our head. The infallible index of true progress is found in the tone the man takes.[2] Neither his age, nor his breeding, nor company, nor books, nor actions, nor talents, nor all together can hinder him from being deferential to a higher spirit than his own. If he have not found his home in God, his manners, his forms of speech, the turn of his sentences, the build, shall I say, of all his opinions will involuntarily confess it, let him brave it out how he will. If he have found his centre, the Deity will shine through

him, through all the disguises of ignorance, of
ungenial temperament, of unfavorable circumstance. The tone of seeking is one, and the
tone of having is another.

The great distinction between teachers sacred
or literary, — between poets like Herbert, and
poets like Pope, — between philosophers like
Spinoza, Kant and Coleridge, and philosophers
like Locke, Paley, Mackintosh and Stewart, —
between men of the world who are reckoned
accomplished talkers, and here and there a fer-
vent mystic, prophesying half insane under the
infinitude of his thought, — is that one class
speak *from within*, or from experience, as parties
and possessors of the fact; and the other class
from without, as spectators merely, or perhaps
as acquainted with the fact on the evidence of
third persons. It is of no use to preach to me
from without. I can do that too easily myself.
Jesus speaks always from within, and in a degree that transcends all others. In that is the
miracle. I believe beforehand that it ought so
to be. All men stand continually in the expectation of the appearance of such a teacher. But
if a man do not speak from within the veil,
where the word is one with that it tells of, let
him lowly confess it.

The same Omniscience flows into the intellect and makes what we call genius. Much of the wisdom of the world is not wisdom, and the most illuminated class of men are no doubt superior to literary fame, and are not writers. Among the multitude of scholars and authors we feel no hallowing presence; we are sensible of a knack and skill rather than of inspiration; they have a light and know not whence it comes and call it their own ; their talent is some exaggerated faculty, some overgrown member, so that their strength is a disease. In these instances the intellectual gifts do not make the impression of virtue, but almost of vice ; and we feel that a man's talents stand in the way of his advancement in truth. But genius is religious.[1] It is a larger imbibing of the common heart. It is not anomalous, but more like and not less like other men. There is in all great poets a wisdom of humanity which is superior to any talents they exercise. The author, the wit, the partisan, the fine gentleman, does not take place of the man. Humanity shines in Homer, in Chaucer, in Spenser, in Shakspeare, in Milton. They are content with truth. They use the positive degree. They seem frigid and phlegmatic to those who have been spiced with the frantic passion and violent coloring of inferior but popular writers. For they are poets by the free course which they allow to the informing soul, which through their eyes beholds again and blesses the things which it hath made. The soul is superior to its knowledge, wiser than any of its works.[1] The great poet makes us feel our own wealth, and then we think less of his compositions. His best communication to our mind is to teach us to despise all he has done. Shakspeare carries us to such a lofty strain of intelligent activity as to suggest a wealth which beggars his own ; and we then feel that the splendid works which he has created, and which in other hours we extol as a sort of self-existent poetry, take no stronger hold of real nature than the shadow of a passing traveller on the rock.[2] The inspiration which uttered itself in Hamlet and Lear could utter things as good from day to day for ever. Why then should I make account of Hamlet and Lear, as if we had not the soul from which they fell as syllables from the tongue?

This energy does not descend into individual life on any other condition than entire possession. It comes to the lowly and simple; it comes to whomsoever will put off what is foreign and proud ; it comes as insight ; it comes as serenity

and grandeur. When we see those whom it inhabits, we are apprised of new degrees of greatness. From that inspiration the man comes back
with a changed tone. He does not talk with
men with an eye to their opinion. He tries them.
It requires of us to be plain and true. The vain
traveller attempts to embellish his life by quoting my lord and the prince and the countess,
who thus said or did to *him*. The ambitious vulgar show you their spoons and brooches and
rings, and preserve their cards and compliments.
The more cultivated, in their account of their
own experience, cull out the pleasing, poetic circumstance, — the visit to Rome, the man of
genius they saw, the brilliant friend they know;
still further on perhaps the gorgeous landscape,
the mountain lights, the mountain thoughts they
enjoyed yesterday, — and so seek to throw a
romantic color over their life. But the soul that
ascends to worship the great God is plain and
true; has no rose-color, no fine friends, no chivalry, no adventures; does not want admiration;
dwells in the hour that now is, in the earnest
experience of the common day, — by reason of
the present moment and the mere trifle having
become porous to thought and bibulous of the
sea of light.

Converse with a mind that is grandly simple,
and literature looks like word-catching. The
simplest utterances are worthiest to be written,
yet are they so cheap and so things of course,
that in the infinite riches of the soul it is like
gathering a few pebbles off the ground, or bot-
tling a little air in a phial, when the whole earth
and the whole atmosphere are ours. Nothing
can pass there, or make you one of the circle,
but the casting aside your trappings and dealing
man to man in naked truth, plain confession
and omniscient affirmation.

Souls such as these treat you as gods would,
walk as gods in the earth, accepting without any
admiration your wit, your bounty, your virtue
even, — say rather your act of duty, for your
virtue they own as their proper blood, royal as
themselves, and over-royal, and the father of
the gods. But what rebuke their plain fraternal
bearing casts on the mutual flattery with which
authors solace each other and wound themselves! These flatter not. I do not wonder that
these men go to see Cromwell and Christina
and Charles the Second and James the First
and the Grand Turk. For they are, in their
own elevation, the fellows of kings, and must
feel the servile tone of conversation in the world.

They must always be a godsend to princes, for
they confront them, a king to a king, without
ducking or concession, and give a high nature
the refreshment and satisfaction of resistance, of
plain humanity, of even companionship and of
new ideas. They leave them wiser and superior
men. Souls like these make us feel that sincerity
is more excellent than flattery. Deal so plainly
with man and woman as to constrain the utmost sincerity and destroy all hope of trifling
with you. It is the highest compliment you can
pay. Their "highest praising," said Milton, "is
not flattery, and their plainest advice is a kind
of praising."

Ineffable is the union of man and God in
every act of the soul. The simplest person who
in his integrity worships God, becomes God;
yet for ever and ever the influx of this better
and universal self is new and unsearchable.[1]
It inspires awe and astonishment. How dear,
how soothing to man, arises the idea of God,
peopling the lonely place, effacing the scars of
our mistakes and disappointments! When we
have broken our god of tradition and ceased
from our god of rhetoric, then may God fire
the heart with his presence.[2] It is the doubling
of the heart itself, nay, the infinite enlargement

of the heart with a power of growth to a new infinity on every side. It inspires in man an infallible trust. He has not the conviction, but the sight, that the best is the true, and may in that thought easily dismiss all particular uncertainties and fears, and adjourn to the sure revelation of time the solution of his private riddles. He is sure that his welfare is dear to the heart of being. In the presence of law to his mind he is overflowed with a reliance so universal that it sweeps away all cherished hopes and the most stable projects of mortal condition in its flood. He believes that he cannot escape from his good. The things that are really for thee gravitate to thee.[1] You are running to seek your friend. Let your feet run, but your mind need not. If you do not find him, will you not acquiesce that it is best you should not find him? for there is a power, which, as it is in you, is in him also, and could therefore very well bring you together, if it were for the best. You are preparing with eagerness to go and render a service to which your talent and your taste invite you, the love of men and the hope of fame. Has it not occurred to you that you have no right to go, unless you are equally willing to be prevented from going?[2] O, believe, as thou livest,

that every sound that is spoken over the round
world, which thou oughtest to hear, will vibrate
on thine ear! Every proverb, every book, every
byword that belongs to thee for aid or comfort,
shall surely come home through open or wind-
ing passages. Every friend whom not thy fantastic will but the great and tender heart in thee
craveth, shall lock thee in his embrace. And
this because the heart in thee is the heart of all;
not a valve, not a wall, not an intersection is
there anywhere in nature, but one blood rolls
uninterruptedly an endless circulation through
all men, as the water of the globe is all one sea,
and, truly seen, its tide is one.

Let man then learn the revelation of all nature and all thought to his heart; this, namely;
that the Highest dwells with him; that the
sources of nature are in his own mind, if the
sentiment of duty is there. But if he would
know what the great God speaketh, he must
'go into his closet and shut the door,' as Jesus
said. God will not make himself manifest to
cowards. He must greatly listen to himself,
withdrawing himself from all the accents of
other men's devotion. Even their prayers are
hurtful to him, until he have made his own.
Our religion vulgarly stands on numbers of

believers. Whenever the appeal is made, — no
matter how indirectly, — to numbers, proclamation is then and there made that religion is not.
He that finds God a sweet enveloping thought
to him never counts his company. When I sit
in that presence, who shall dare to come in?
When I rest in perfect humility, when I burn
with pure love, what can Calvin or Swedenborg
say?

It makes no difference whether the appeal is
to numbers or to one. The faith that stands
on authority is not faith. The reliance on
authority measures the decline of religion, the
withdrawal of the soul. The position men have
given to Jesus, now for many centuries of history, is a position of authority. It characterizes
themselves. It cannot alter the eternal facts.
Great is the soul, and plain. It is no flatterer,
it is no follower; it never appeals from itself.
It believes in itself. Before the immense possibilities of man all mere experience, all past biography, however spotless and sainted, shrinks
away. Before that heaven which our presentiments foreshow us, we cannot easily praise any
form of life we have seen or read of. We not
only affirm that we have few great men, but,
absolutely speaking, that we have none; that

we have no history, no record of any character
or mode of living that entirely contents us.
The saints and demigods whom history worships we are constrained to accept with a grain
of allowance. Though in our lonely hours we
draw a new strength out of their memory, yet,
pressed on our attention, as they are by the
thoughtless and customary, they fatigue and invade. The soul gives itself, alone, original and
pure, to the Lonely, Original and Pure, who,
on that condition, gladly inhabits, leads and
speaks through it. Then is it glad, young and
nimble. It is not wise, but it sees through all
things. It is not called religious, but it is innocent. It calls the light its own, and feels that
the grass grows and the stone falls by a law inferior to, and dependent on, its nature. Behold,
it saith, I am born into the great, the universal
mind. I, the imperfect, adore my own Perfect.
I am somehow receptive of the great soul, and
thereby I do overlook the sun and the stars and
feel them to be the fair accidents and effects
which change and pass. More and more the
surges of everlasting nature enter into me, and
I become public and human in my regards and
actions. So come I to live in thoughts and act
with energies which are immortal. Thus rever-

ing the soul, and learning, as the ancient said,
that " its beauty is immense," man will come to
see that the world is the perennial miracle which
the soul worketh, and be less astonished at particular wonders ; he will learn that there is no
profane history; that all history is sacred ; that ;
the universe is represented in an atom, in a ;
moment of time.¹ He will weave no longer a
spotted life of shreds and patches, but he will
live with a divine unity. He will cease from
what is base and frivolous in his life and be content with all places and with any service he can
render. He will calmly front the morrow in
the negligency of that trust which carries God
with it and so hath already the whole future in
the bottom of the heart.

X

CIRCLES

NATURE centres into balls,
And her proud ephemerals,
Fast to surface and outside,
Scan the profile of the sphere;
Knew they what that signified,
A new genesis were here.

CIRCLES

THE eye is the first circle; the horizon which it forms is the second; and throughout nature this primary figure is repeated without end. It is the highest emblem in the cipher of the world. St. Augustine described the nature of God as a circle whose centre was everywhere and its circumference nowhere.[1] We are all our lifetime reading the copious sense of this first of forms. One moral we have already deduced in considering the circular or compensatory character of every human action. Another analogy we shall now trace, that every action admits of being outdone. Our life is an apprenticeship to the truth that around every circle another can be drawn; that there is no end in nature, but every end is a beginning; that there is always another dawn risen on mid-noon, and under every deep a lower deep opens.[2]

This fact, as far as it symbolizes the moral fact of the Unattainable, the flying Perfect, around which the hands of man can never meet, at once the inspirer and the condemner of every success, may conveniently serve us to connect many illustrations of human power in every department.

There are no fixtures in nature. The universe
is fluid and volatile. Permanence is but a word
of degrees. Our globe seen by God is a transparent law, not a mass of facts. The law dissolves the fact and holds it fluid.' Our culture
is the predominance of an idea which draws
after it this train of cities and institutions. Let
us rise into another idea; they will disappear.
The Greek sculpture is all melted away, as if it
had been statues of ice; here and there a solitary figure or fragment remaining, as we see
flecks and scraps of snow left in cold dells and
mountain clefts in June and July. For the genius
that created it creates now somewhat else. The
Greek letters last a little longer, but are already
passing under the same sentence and tumbling
into the inevitable pit which the creation of new
thought opens for all that is old. The new con-
tinents are built out of the ruins of an old planet;
the new races fed out of the decomposition
of the foregoing. New arts destroy the old. See
the investment of capital in aqueducts, made
useless by hydraulics; fortifications, by gun-
powder; roads and canals, by railways; sails,
by steam; steam by electricity.

You admire this tower of granite, weathering
the hurts of so many ages. Yet a little waving

hand.built this huge wall, and that which builds
is better than that which is built. The hand that
built can topple it down much faster. Better
than the hand and nimbler was the invisible
thought which wrought through it; and thus
ever, behind the coarse effect, is a fine cause,
which, being narrowly seen, is itself the effect
of a finer cause. Everything looks permanent
until its secret is known. A rich estate appears
to women a firm and lasting fact; to a merchant,
one easily created out of any materials, and easily
lost. An orchard, good tillage, good grounds,
seem a fixture, like a gold mine, or a river, to a
citizen; but to a large farmer, not much more
fixed than the state of the crop. Nature looks
provokingly stable and secular, but it has a cause
like all the rest; and when once I comprehend
that, will these fields stretch so immovably wide,
these leaves hang so individually considerable?
Permanence is a word of degrees. Every thing
is medial. Moons are no more bounds to spiritual power than bat-balls.[1]

The key to every man is his thought. Sturdy
and defying though he look, he has a helm which
he obeys, which is the idea after which all his
facts are classified. He can only be reformed by
showing him a new idea which commands his

own. The life of man is a self-evolving circle, which, from a ring imperceptibly small, rushes on all sides outwards to new and larger circles, and that without end.[1] The extent to which this generation of circles, wheel without wheel, will go, depends on the force or truth of the individual soul. For it is the inert effort of each thought, having formed itself into a circular wave of circumstance, — as for instance an empire, rules of an art, a local usage, a religious rite, — to heap itself on that ridge and to solidify and hem in the life. But if the soul is quick and strong it bursts over that boundary on all sides and expands another orbit on the great deep, which also runs up into a high wave, with attempt again to stop and to bind. But the heart refuses to be imprisoned; in its first and narrowest pulses it already tends outward with a vast force and to immense and innumerable expansions.[2]

Every ultimate fact is only the first of a new series. Every general law only a particular fact of some more general law presently to disclose itself. There is no outside, no inclosing wall, no circumference to us. The man finishes his story, — how good! how final! how it puts a new face on all things! He fills the sky. Lo! on the other side rises also a man and draws a circle around the circle we had just pronounced the outline of the sphere. Then already is our first speaker not man, but only a first speaker. His only redress is forthwith to draw a circle outside of his antagonist. And so men do by themselves. The result of to-day, which haunts the mind and cannot be escaped, will presently be abridged into a word, and the principle that seemed to explain nature will itself be included as one example of a bolder generalization. In the thought of to-morrow there is a power to upheave all thy creed, all the creeds, all the literatures of the nations, and marshal thee to a heaven which no epic dream has yet depicted. Every man is not so much a workman in the world as he is a suggestion of that he should be. Men walk as prophecies of the next age.

Step by step we scale this mysterious ladder; the steps are actions, the new prospect is power. Every several result is threatened and judged by that which follows. Every one seems to be contradicted by the new; it is only limited by the new. The new statement is always hated by the old, and, to those dwelling in the old, comes like an abyss of scepticism. But the eye soon gets wonted to it, for the eye and it are effects of one cause; then its innocency and benefit appear, and presently, all its energy spent, it pales and dwindles before the revelation of the new hour.

Fear not the new generalization. Does the fact look crass and material, threatening to degrade thy theory of spirit? Resist it not; it goes to refine and raise thy theory of matter just as much.

There are no fixtures to men, if we appeal to consciousness. Every man supposes himself not to be fully understood; and if there is any truth in him, if he rests at last on the divine soul, I see not how it can be otherwise. The last chamber, the last closet, he must feel was never opened; there is always a residuum unknown, unanalyzable. That is, every man believes that he has a greater possibility.

Our moods do not believe in each other. To-day I am full of thoughts and can write what I please. I see no reason why I should not have the same thought, the same power of expression, to-morrow. What I write, whilst I write it, seems the most natural thing in the world; but yesterday I saw a dreary vacuity in this direction in which now I see so much; and a month hence, I doubt not, I shall wonder who he was that wrote so many continuous pages. Alas for this infirm faith, this will not strenuous, this vast ebb of a vast flow! I am God in nature; I am a weed by the wall.

The continual effort to raise himself above himself, to work a pitch above his last height, betrays itself in a man's relations.[1] We thirst for approbation, yet cannot forgive the approver. The sweet of nature is love; yet if I have a friend I am tormented by my imperfections. The love of me accuses the other party. If he were high enough to slight me, then could I love him, and rise by my affection to new heights. A man's growth is seen in the successive choirs of his friends. For every friend whom he loses for truth, he gains a better. I thought as I walked in the woods and mused on my friends, why should I play with them this game of idolatry? I know and see too well, when not voluntarily blind, the speedy limits of persons called high and worthy. Rich, noble and great they are by the liberality of our speech, but truth is sad. O blessed Spirit, whom I forsake for these, they are not thou! Every personal consideration that we allow costs us heavenly state. We sell the thrones of angels for a short and turbulent pleasure.[2]

How often must we learn this lesson? Men

cease to interest us when we find their limitations. The only sin is limitation. As soon as you once come up with a man's limitations, it is all over with him. Has he talents? has he enterprise? has he knowledge? It boots not. Infinitely alluring and attractive was he to you yesterday, a great hope, a sea to swim in; now, you have found his shores, found it a pond, and you care not if you never see it again.

Each new step we take in thought reconciles twenty seemingly discordant facts, as expressions of one law. Aristotle and Plato are reckoned the respective heads of two schools. A wise man will see that Aristotle platonizes. By going one step farther back in thought, discordant opinions are reconciled by being seen to be two extremes of one principle, and we can never go so far back as to preclude a still higher vision.[1]

Beware when the great God lets loose a thinker on this planet. Then all things are at risk. It is as when a conflagration has broken out in a great city, and no man knows what is safe, or where it will end. There is not a piece of science but its flank may be turned to-morrow; there is not any literary reputation, not the so-called eternal names of fame, that may not be revised and condemned. The very hopes

of man, the thoughts of his heart, the religion
of nations, the manners and morals of mankind
are all at the mercy of a new generalization.
Generalization is always a new influx of the
divinity into the mind. Hence the thrill that
attends it.

Valor consists in the power of self-recovery,
so that a man cannot have his flank turned, cannot be out-generalled, but put him where you
will, he stands. This can only be by his pre-
ferring truth to his past apprehension of truth,
and his alert acceptance of it from whatever
quarter; the intrepid conviction that his laws,
his relations to society, his Christianity, his
world, may at any time be superseded and de-
cease.

There are degrees in idealism. We learn first
to play with it academically, as the magnet was
once a toy. Then we see in the heyday of youth
and poetry that it may be true, that it is true in
gleams and fragments. Then its countenance
waxes stern and grand, and we see that it must
be true. It now shows itself ethical and practical. We learn that God is; that he is in me;
and that all things are shadows of him. The
idealism of Berkeley is only a crude statement
of the idealism of Jesus, and that again is a

crude statement of the fact that all nature is the rapid efflux of goodness executing and organizing itself. Much more obviously is history and the state of the world at any one time directly dependent on the intellectual classification then existing in the minds of men. The things which are dear to men at this hour are so on account of the ideas which have emerged on their mental horizon, and which cause the present order of things, as a tree bears its apples. A new degree of culture would instantly revolutionize the entire system of human pursuits.

Conversation is a game of circles. In conversation we pluck up the *termini* which bound the common of silence on every side. The parties are not to be judged by the spirit they partake and even express under this Pentecost. To-morrow they will have receded from this high-water mark. To-morrow you shall find them stooping under the old pack-saddles. Yet let us enjoy the cloven flame whilst it glows on our walls. When each new speaker strikes a new light, emancipates us from the oppression of the last speaker to oppress us with the greatness and exclusiveness of his own thought, then yields us to another redeemer, we seem to recover our rights, to become men. O, what

truths profound and executable only in ages
and orbs, are supposed in the announcement
of every truth ! In common hours, society
sits cold and statuesque. We all stand waiting,
empty, — knowing, possibly, that we can be
full, surrounded by mighty symbols which are
not symbols to us, but prose and trivial toys.
Then cometh the god and converts the statues
into fiery men, and by a flash of his eye burns
up the veil which shrouded all things, and the
meaning of the very furniture, of cup and sau-
cer, of chair and clock and tester, is manifest. The
facts which loomed so large in the fogs of yesterday, — property, climate, breeding, personal
beauty and the like, have strangely changed
their proportions. All that we reckoned settled
shakes and rattles ; and literatures, cities, climates, religions, leave their foundations and dance
before our eyes.[1] And yet here again see the swift
circumscription ! Good as is discourse, silence
is better, and shames it. The length of the discourse indicates the distance of thought betwixt
the speaker and the hearer. If they were at a
perfect understanding in any part, no words
would be necessary thereon. If at one in all
parts, no words would be suffered.

Literature is a point outside of our hodiernal

circle through which a new one may be described. The use of literature is to afford us a
platform whence we may command a view of
our present life, a purchase by which we may
move it. We fill ourselves with ancient learning, install ourselves the best we can in Greek,
in Punic, in Roman houses, only that we may
wiselier see French, English and American
houses and modes of living. In like manner
we see literature best from the midst of wild
nature, or from the din of affairs, or from a high
religion. The field cannot be well seen from
within the field. The astronomer must have
his diameter of the earth's orbit as a base to
find the parallax of any star.[1]

Therefore we value the poet. All the argument and all the wisdom is not in the encyclopædia, or the treatise on metaphysics, or
the Body of Divinity, but in the sonnet or the
play. In my daily work I incline to repeat my
old steps, and do not believe in remedial force,
in the power of change and reform. But some
Petrarch or Ariosto, filled with the new wine
of his imagination, writes me an ode or a brisk
romance, full of daring thought and action. He
smites and arouses me with his shrill tones,
breaks up my whole chain of habits, and I open

my eye on my own possibilities. He claps
wings to the sides of all the solid old lumber of
the world, and I am capable once more of choosing a straight path in theory and practice.

We have the same need to command a view
of the religion of the world. We can never see
Christianity from the catechism : — from the pas-
tures, from a boat in the pond, from amidst the
songs of wood-birds we possibly may. Cleansed
by the elemental light and wind, steeped in the
sea of beautiful forms which the field offers us,
we may chance to cast a right glance back upon
biography. Christianity is rightly dear to the
best of mankind ; yet was there never a young
philosopher whose breeding had fallen into the
Christian church by whom that brave text of
Paul's was not specially prized : " Then shall
also the Son be subject unto Him who put all
things under him, that God may be all in all."
Let the claims and virtues of persons be never
so great and welcome, the instinct of man presses
eagerly onward to the impersonal and illimitable, and gladly arms itself against the dogmatism of bigots with this generous word out of
the book itself.'

The natural world may be conceived of as a
system of concentric circles, and we now and

then detect in nature slight dislocations which apprise us that this surface on which we now stand is not fixed, but sliding. These manifold tenacious qualities, this chemistry and vegetation, these metals and animals, which seem to stand there for their own sake, are means and methods only, — are words of God, and as fugitive as other words.[1] Has the naturalist or chemist learned his craft, who has explored the gravity of atoms and the elective affinities, who has not yet discerned the deeper law whereof this is only a partial or approximate statement, namely that like draws to like, and that the goods which belong to you gravitate to you and need not be pursued with pains and cost?[2] Yet is that statement approximate also, and not final. Omnipresence is a higher fact. Not through subtle subterranean channels need friend and fact be drawn to their counterpart, but, rightly considered, these things proceed from the eternal generation of the soul. Cause and effect are two sides of one fact.

The same law of eternal procession ranges all that we call the virtues, and extinguishes each in the light of a better. The great man will not be prudent in the popular sense; all his prudence will be so much deduction from his grandeur.

But it behooves each to see, when he sacrifices
prudence, to what god he devotes it; if to ease
and pleasure, he had better be prudent still; if
to a great trust, he can well spare his mule and
panniers who has a winged chariot instead.
Geoffrey draws on his boots to go through the
woods, that his feet may be safer from the bite
of snakes; Aaron never thinks of such a peril.
In many years neither is harmed by such an
accident. Yet it seems to me that with every
precaution you take against such an evil you
put yourself into the power of the evil. I suppose that the highest prudence is the lowest
prudence. Is this too sudden a rushing from
the centre to the verge of our orbit? Think
how many times we shall fall back into pitiful
calculations before we take up our rest in the
great sentiment, or make the verge of to-day
the new centre. Besides, your bravest sentiment
is familiar to the humblest men. The poor and
the low have their way of expressing the last
facts of philosophy as well as you. " Blessed be
nothing " and " The worse things are, the better they are " are proverbs which express the
transcendentalism of common life.

One man's justice is another's injustice; one
man's beauty another's ugliness; one man's wis-

dom another's folly; as one beholds the same
objects from a higher point. One man thinks
justice consists in paying debts, and has no
measure in his abhorrence of another who is
very remiss in this duty and makes the creditor
wait tediously. But that second man has his
own way of looking at things; asks himself
Which debt must I pay first, the debt to the
rich, or the debt to the poor? the debt of
money, or the debt of thought to mankind, of
genius to nature? For you, O broker, there is
no other principle but arithmetic. For me, commerce is of trivial import; love, faith, truth of
character, the aspiration of man, these are sacred; nor can I detach one duty, like you, from
all other duties, and concentrate my forces me-
chanically on the payment of moneys. Let me
live onward; you shall find that, though slower,
the progress of my character will liquidate all
these debts without injustice to higher claims.
If a man should dedicate himself to the payment of notes, would not this be injustice?
Does he owe no debt but money? And are all
claims on him to be postponed to a landlord's
or a banker's?

There is no virtue which is final; all are
initial. The virtues of society are vices of the

saint. The terror of reform is the discovery that
we must cast away our virtues, or what we have
always esteemed such, into the same pit that
has consumed our grosser vices : —

> " Forgive his crimes, forgive his virtues too,
>   Those smaller faults, half converts to the right." [1]

It is the highest power of divine moments
that they abolish our contritions also. I accuse myself of sloth and unprofitableness day
by day ; but when these waves of God flow into
me I no longer reckon lost time. I no longer
poorly compute my possible achievement by
what remains to me of the month or the year ;
for these moments confer a sort of omnipresence and omnipotence which asks nothing of
duration, but sees that the energy of the mind
is commensurate with the work to be done, without time.

And thus, O circular philosopher, I hear
some reader exclaim, you have arrived at a fine
Pyrrhonism,[2] at an equivalence and indifferency
of all actions, and would fain teach us that *if
we are true*, forsooth, our crimes may be lively
stones out of which we shall construct the temple of the true God !

I am not careful to justify myself. I own I
am gladdened by seeing the predominance of

the saccharine principle throughout vegetable
nature, and not less by beholding in morals that
unrestrained inundation of the principle of good
into every chink and hole that selfishness has
left open, yea into selfishness and sin itself; so
that no evil is pure, nor hell itself without its
extreme satisfactions.[1] But lest I should mislead
any when I have my own head and obey my
whims, let me remind the reader that I am only
an experimenter. Do not set the least value on
what I do, or the least discredit on what I do
not, as if I pretended to settle any thing as true
or false. I unsettle all things. No facts are to
me sacred; none are profane; I simply experiment, an endless seeker with no Past at my
back.[2]

Yet this incessant movement and progression
which all things partake could never become
sensible to us but by contrast to some principle
of fixture or stability in the soul. Whilst the
eternal generation of circles proceeds, the eternal
generator abides. That central life is somewhat
superior to creation, superior to knowledge and
thought, and contains all its circles. Forever it
labors to create a life and thought as large and
excellent as itself, but in vain, for that which is
made instructs how to make a better.

Thus there is no sleep, no pause, no preservation, but all things renew, germinate and spring. Why should we import rags and relics into the new hour? Nature abhors the old, and old age seems the only disease; all others run into this one. We call it by many names, — fever, intemperance, insanity, stupidity and crime; they are all forms of old age; they are rest, conservatism, appropriation, inertia; not newness, not the way onward. We grizzle every day. I see no need of it. Whilst we converse with what is above us, we do not grow old, but grow young. Infancy, youth, receptive, aspiring, with religious eye looking upward, counts itself nothing and abandons itself to the instruction flowing from all sides. But the man and woman of seventy assume to know all, they have outlived their hope, they renounce aspiration, accept the actual for the necessary and talk down to the young. Let them then become organs of the Holy Ghost; let them be lovers; let them behold truth; and their eyes are uplifted, their wrinkles smoothed, they are perfumed again with hope and power.[1] This old age ought not to creep on a human mind. In nature every moment is new; the past is always swallowed and forgotten; the coming only is sacred. Nothing is secure but life, transition, the energizing spirit. No love can be bound by oath or covenant to secure it against a higher love. No truth so sublime but it may be trivial to-morrow in the light of new thoughts. People wish to be settled; only as far as they are unsettled is there any hope for them.

Life is a series of surprises. We do not guess to-day the mood, the pleasure, the power of to-morrow, when we are building up our being. Of lower states, of acts of routine and sense, we can tell somewhat; but the masterpieces of God, the total growths and universal movements of the soul, he hideth; they are incalculable. I can know that truth is divine and helpful; but how it shall help me I can have no guess, for *so to be* is the sole inlet of *so to know*. The new position of the advancing man has all the powers of the old, yet has them all new. It carries in its bosom all the energies of the past, yet is itself an exhalation of the morning. I cast away in this new moment all my once hoarded knowledge, as vacant and vain. Now for the first time seem I to know any thing rightly. The simplest words, — we do not know what they mean except when we love and aspire.

The difference between talents and character

is adroitness to keep the old and trodden round, and power and courage to make a new road to new and better goals. Character makes an over-powering present; a cheerful, determined hour, which fortifies all the company by making them see that much is possible and excellent that was not thought of. Character dulls the impression of particular events. When we see the conqueror we do not think much of any one battle or suc-cess. We see that we had exaggerated the dif-ficulty. It was easy to him. The great man is not convulsible or tormentable; events pass over him without much impression. People say some-times, 'See what I have overcome; see how cheerful I am; see how completely I have tri-umphed over these black events.' Not if they still remind me of the black event. True con-quest is the causing the calamity to fade and dis-appear as an early cloud of insignificant result in a history so large and advancing.

The one thing which we seek with insatiable desire is to forget ourselves, to be surprised out of our propriety, to lose our sempiternal memory and to do something without knowing how or why; in short to draw a new circle. Nothing great was ever achieved without enthusiasm. The way of life is wonderful; it is by abandonment. The great moments of history are the facilities of performance through the strength of ideas, as the works of genius and religion. " A man," said Oliver Cromwell, " never rises so high as when he knows not whither he is going." Dreams and drunkenness, the use of opium and alcohol are the semblance and counterfeit of this oracular genius, and hence their dangerous attraction for men. For the like reason they ask the aid of wild passions, as in gaming and war, to ape in some manner these flames and generosities of the heart.

XI

INTELLECT

Go, speed the stars of Thought
On to their shining goals; —
The sower scatters broad his seed;
The wheat thou strew'st be souls.

INTELLECT

EVERY substance is negatively electric to
that which stands above it in the chemical
tables, positively to that which stands below it.
Water dissolves wood and iron and salt; air dissolves water; electric fire dissolves air, but the
intellect dissolves fire, gravity, laws, method, and
the subtlest unnamed relations of nature in its
resistless menstruum.[1] Intellect lies behind genius, which is intellect constructive. Intellect is
the simple power anterior to all action or construction. Gladly would I unfold in calm degrees a natural history of the intellect, but what
man has yet been able to mark the steps and
boundaries of that transparent essence? The
first questions are always to be asked, and the
wisest doctor is gravelled by the inquisitiveness
of a child. How can we speak of the action of
the mind under any divisions, as of its knowledge, of its ethics, of its works, and so forth,
since it melts will into perception, knowledge
into act? Each becomes the other. Itself alone
is. Its vision is not like the vision of the eye,
but is union with the things known.

Intellect and intellection signify to the com-

mon ear consideration of abstract truth. The
considerations of time and place, of you and me,
of profit and hurt, tyrannize over most men's
minds. Intellect separates the fact considered,
from *you*, from all local and personal reference,
and discerns it as if it existed for its own sake.
Heraclitus looked upon the affections as dense
and colored mists. In the fog of good and evil
affections it is hard for man to walk forward in
a straight line. Intellect is void of affection and
sees an object as it stands in the light of science,
cool and disengaged. The intellect goes out of
the individual, floats over its own personality,
and regards it as a fact, and not as *I* and *mine*.
He who is immersed in what concerns person
or place cannot see the problem of existence.
This the intellect always ponders. Nature shows
all things formed and bound. The intellect
pierces the form, overleaps the wall, detects
intrinsic likeness between remote things and
reduces all things into a few principles.

The making a fact the subject of thought
raises it. All that mass of mental and moral
phenomena which we do not make objects of
voluntary thought, come within the power of
fortune; they constitute the circumstance of daily
life ; they are subject to change, to fear and

Mr. Emerson's Study

hope. Every man beholds his human condition
with a degree of melancholy. As a ship aground
is battered by the waves, so man, imprisoned in
mortal life, lies open to the mercy of coming
events. But a truth, separated by the intellect,
is no longer a subject of destiny. We behold it
as a god upraised above care and fear. And so
any fact in our life, or any record of our fancies or
reflections, disentangled from the web of our unconsciousness, becomes an object impersonal and
immortal. It is the past restored, but embalmed.
A better art than that of Egypt has taken fear
and corruption out of it. It is eviscerated of care.
It is offered for science. What is addressed to
us for contemplation does not threaten us but
makes us intellectual beings.[1]

The growth of the intellect is spontaneous in
every expansion. The mind that grows could
not predict the times, the means, the mode of
that spontaneity. God enters by a private door
into every individual.[2] Long prior to the age
of reflection is the thinking of the mind. Out of
darkness it came insensibly into the marvellous
light of to-day. In the period of infancy it ac-
cepted and disposed of all impressions from the
surrounding creation after its own way. Whatever any mind doth or saith is after a law, and

this native law remains over it after it has come to reflection or conscious thought. In the most worn, pedantic, introverted self-tormentor's life, the greatest part is incalculable by him, unforeseen, unimaginable, and must be, until he can take himself up by his own ears. What am I? What has my will done to make me that I am? Nothing. I have been floated into this thought, this hour, this connection of events, by secret currents of might and mind, and my ingenuity and wilfulness have not thwarted, have not aided to an appreciable degree.[1]

Our spontaneous action is always the best. You cannot with your best deliberation and heed come so close to any question as your spontaneous glance shall bring you, whilst you rise from your bed, or walk abroad in the morning after meditating the matter before sleep on the previous night. Our thinking is a pious reception. Our truth of thought is therefore vitiated as much by too violent direction given by our will, as by too great negligence. We do not determine what we will think. We only open our senses, clear away as we can all obstruction from the fact, and suffer the intellect to see. We have little control over our thoughts. We are the prisoners of ideas. They catch us up for mo-

ments into their heaven and so fully engage us
that we take no thought for the morrow, gaze
like children, without an effort to make them our
own. By and by we fall out of that rapture, be-
think us where we have been, what we have seen,
and repeat as truly as we can what we have beheld. As far as we can recall these ecstasies we
carry away in the ineffaceable memory the result,
and all men and all the ages confirm it. It is
called truth. But the moment we cease to report
and attempt to correct and contrive, it is not
truth.

If we consider what persons have stimulated
and profited us, we shall perceive the superiority of the spontaneous or intuitive principle over
the arithmetical or logical. The first contains
the second, but virtual and latent. We want in
every man a long logic; we cannot pardon the
absence of it, but it must not be spoken. Logic
is the procession or proportionate unfolding of
the intuition; but its virtue is as silent method;
the moment it would appear as propositions and
have a separate value, it is worthless.[1]

In every man's mind, some images, words
and facts remain, without effort on his part to
imprint them, which others forget, and afterwards these illustrate to him important laws.

All our progress is an unfolding, like the vegetable bud. You have first an instinct, then an opinion, then a knowledge, as the plant has root, bud and fruit. Trust the instinct to the end, though you can render no reason. It is vain to hurry it. By trusting it to the end, it shall ripen into truth and you shall know why you believe.

Each mind has its own method. A true man never acquires after college rules. What you have aggregated in a natural manner surprises and delights when it is produced. For we cannot oversee each other's secret. And hence the differences between men in natural endowment are insignificant in comparison with their common wealth. Do you think the porter and the cook have no anecdotes, no experiences, no wonders for you? Everybody knows as much as the savant. The walls of rude minds are scrawled all over with facts, with thoughts. They shall one day bring a lantern and read the inscriptions. Every man, in the degree in which he has wit and culture, finds his curiosity inflamed concerning the modes of living and thinking of other men, and especially of those classes whose minds have not been subdued by the drill of school education.

This instinctive action never ceases in a
healthy mind, but becomes richer and more
frequent in its informations through all states
of culture. At last comes the era of reflection,
when we not only observe, but take pains to
observe ; when we of set purpose sit down to
consider an abstract truth ; when we keep the
mind's eye open whilst we converse, whilst we
read, whilst we act, intent to learn the secret
law of some class of facts.

What is the hardest task in the world ? To
think. I would put myself in the attitude to
look in the eye an abstract truth, and I cannot. I blench and withdraw on this side and
on that. I seem to know what he meant who
said, No man can see God face to face and live.
For example, a man explores the basis of civil
government. Let him intend his mind without
respite, without rest, in one direction. His best
heed long time avails him nothing. Yet thoughts
are flitting before him. We all but apprehend,
we dimly forebode the truth. We say I will
walk abroad, and the truth will take form and
clearness to me. We go forth, but cannot find
it. It seems as if we needed only the stillness
and composed attitude of the library to seize
the thought. But we come in, and are as far

from it as at first. Then, in a moment, and
unannounced, the truth appears. A certain
wandering light appears, and is the distinction,
the principle, we wanted. But the oracle comes
because we had previously laid siege to the
shrine. It seems as if the law of the intellect
resembled that law of nature by which we now
inspire, now expire the breath; by which the
heart now draws in, then hurls out the blood,
— the law of undulation. So now you must
labor with your brains, and now you must forbear your activity and see what the great Soul
showeth.

The immortality of man is as legitimately
preached from the intellections as from the
moral volitions. Every intellection is mainly
prospective. Its present value is its least.' In-
spect what delights you in Plutarch, in Shakspeare, in Cervantes. Each truth that a writer
acquires is a lantern which he turns full on what
facts and thoughts lay already in his mind, and
behold, all the mats and rubbish which had
littered his garret become precious. Every trivial fact in his private biography becomes an
illustration of this new principle, revisits the
day, and delights all men by its piquancy and
new charm. Men say, Where did he get this?

and think there was something divine in his
life. But no; they have myriads of facts just
as good, would they only get a lamp to ransack
their attics withal.[1]

We are all wise. The difference between persons is not in wisdom but in art. I knew, in an
academical club, a person who always deferred
to me; who, seeing my whim for writing, fancied that my experiences had somewhat superior; whilst I saw that his experiences were as
good as mine. Give them to me and I would
make the same use of them. He held the old;
he holds the new; I had the habit of tacking
together the old and the new which he did not
use to exercise. This may hold in the great
examples. Perhaps, if we should meet Shakspeare we should not be conscious of any steep
inferiority; no, but of a great equality, — only
that he possessed a strange skill of using, of
classifying his facts, which we lacked. For notwithstanding our utter incapacity to produce
anything like Hamlet and Othello, see the perfect reception this wit and immense knowledge
of life and liquid eloquence find in us all.

If you gather apples in the sunshine, or make
hay, or hoe corn, and then retire within doors
and shut your eyes and press them with your

hand, you shall still see apples hanging in the bright light with boughs and leaves thereto, or the tasselled grass, or the corn-flags, and this for five or six hours afterwards. There lie the impressions on the retentive organ, though you knew it not. So lies the whole series of natural images with which your life has made you acquainted, in your memory, though you know it not; and a thrill of passion flashes light on their dark chamber, and the active power seizes instantly the fit image, as the word of its momentary thought.

It is long ere we discover how rich we are. Our history, we are sure, is quite tame : we have nothing to write, nothing to infer. But our wiser years still run back to the despised recollections of childhood, and always we are fishing up some wonderful article out of that pond; until by and by we begin to suspect that the biography of the one foolish person we know is, in reality, nothing less than the miniature paraphrase of the hundred volumes of the Universal History.

In the intellect constructive, which we popularly designate by the word Genius, we observe the same balance of two elements as in intellect receptive. The constructive intellect produces

thoughts, sentences, poems, plans, designs, systems.[1] It is the generation of the mind, the
marriage of thought with nature. To genius
must always go two gifts, the thought and the
publication. The first is revelation, always a
miracle, which no frequency of occurrence or
incessant study can ever familiarize, but which
must always leave the inquirer stupid with wonder. It is the advent of truth into the world, a
form of thought now for the first time bursting
into the universe, a child of the old eternal soul,
a piece of genuine and immeasurable greatness.
It seems, for the time, to inherit all that has yet
existed and to dictate to the unborn. It affects
every thought of man and goes to fashion every
institution. But to make it available it needs a
vehicle or art by which it is conveyed to men.
To be communicable it must become picture
or sensible object. We must learn the language
of facts. The most wonderful inspirations die
with their subject if he has no hand to paint
them to the senses. The ray of light passes invisible through space and only when it falls on
an object is it seen. When the spiritual energy
is directed on something outward, then it is a
thought. The relation between it and you first
makes you, the value of you, apparent to me.

The rich inventive genius of the painter must be smothered and lost for want of the power of drawing, and in our happy hours we should be inexhaustible poets if once we could break through the silence into adequate rhyme. As all men have some access to primary truth, so all have some art or power of communication in their head, but only in the artist does it descend into the hand. There is an inequality, whose laws we do not yet know, between two men and between two moments of the same man, in respect to this faculty. In common hours we have the same facts as in the uncommon or inspired, but they do not sit for their portrait; they are not detached, but lie in a web. The thought of genius is spontaneous; but the power of picture or expression, in the most enriched and flowing nature, implies a mixture of will, a certain control over the spontaneous states, without which no production is possible.¹ It is a conversion of all nature into the rhetoric of thought, under the eye of judgment, with a strenuous exercise of choice. And yet the imaginative vocabulary seems to be spontaneous also. It does not flow from experience only or mainly, but from a richer source. Not by any conscious imitation of particular forms are the

grand strokes of the painter executed, but by
repairing to the fountain-head of all forms in
his mind. Who is the first drawing-master?
Without instruction we know very well the ideal
of the human form. A child knows if an arm
or a leg be distorted in a picture; if the attitude
be natural or grand or mean; though he has
never received any instruction in drawing or
heard any conversation on the subject, nor can
himself draw with correctness a single feature.
A good form strikes all eyes pleasantly, long
before they have any science on the subject, and
a beautiful face sets twenty hearts in palpitation,
prior to all consideration of the mechanical proportions of the features and head. We may owe
to dreams some light on the fountain of this
skill; for as soon as we let our will go and let
the unconscious states ensue, see what cunning
draughtsmen we are! We entertain ourselves
with wonderful forms of men, of women, of animals, of gardens, of woods and of monsters, and
the mystic pencil wherewith we then draw has
no awkwardness or inexperience, no meagreness
or poverty; it can design well and group well;
its composition is full of art, its colors are well
laid on and the whole canvas which it paints is
lifelike and apt to touch us with terror, with

II

tenderness, with desire and with grief. Neither are the artist's copies from experience ever mere copies, but always touched and softened by tints from this ideal domain.

The conditions essential to a constructive mind do not appear to be so often combined but that a good sentence or verse remains fresh and memorable for a long time. Yet when we write with ease and come out into the free air of thought, we seem to be assured that nothing is easier than to continue this communication at pleasure. Up, down, around, the kingdom of thought has no inclosures, but the Muse makes us free of her city. Well, the world has a million writers. One would think then that good thought would be as familiar as air and water, and the gifts of each new hour would exclude the last. Yet we can count all our good books; nay, I remember any, beautiful verse for twenty years. It is true that the discerning intellect of the world is always much in advance of the creative, so that there are many competent judges of the best book, and few writers of the best books. But some of the conditions of intellectual construction are of rare occurrence. The intellect is a whole and demands integrity in every work. This is resisted equally by a man's devotion to a single thought and by his ambition to combine too many.

Truth is our element of life, yet if a man fasten his attention on a single aspect of truth and apply himself to that alone for a long time, the truth becomes distorted and not itself but falsehood; herein resembling the air, which is our natural element and the breath of our nostrils, but if a stream of the same be directed on the body for a time, it causes cold, fever, and even death. How wearisome the grammarian, the phrenologist, the political or religious fanatic, or indeed any possessed mortal whose balance is lost by the exaggeration of a single topic. It is incipient insanity. Every thought is a prison also. I cannot see what you see, because I am caught up by a strong wind and blown so far in one direction that I am out of the hoop of your horizon.[1]

Is it any better if the student, to avoid this offence and to liberalize himself, aims to make a mechanical whole of history, or science, or philosophy, by a numerical addition of all the facts that fall within his vision? The world refuses to be analyzed by addition and subtraction. When we are young we spend much time and pains in filling our note-books with all defini-

tions of Religion, Love, Poetry, Politics, Art,
in the hope that in the course of a few years
we shall have condensed into our encyclopædia
the net value of all the theories at which the
world has yet arrived. But year after year our
tables get no completeness, and at last we discover that our curve is a parabola, whose arcs
will never meet.

Neither by detachment, neither by aggrega-
tion is the integrity of the intellect transmitted
to its works, but by a vigilance which brings the
intellect in its greatness and best state to operate
every moment. ʿIt must have the same wholeness which nature has! Although no diligence
can rebuild the universe in a model by the best
accumulation or disposition of details, yet does
the world reappear in miniature in every event,
so that all the laws of nature may be read in the
smallest fact.ʾ The intellect must have the like
perfection in its apprehension and in its works.
For this reason, an index or mercury of intellectual proficiency is the perception of identity. We
talk with accomplished persons who appear to
be strangers in nature. The cloud, the tree, the
turf, the bird, are not theirs, have nothing of
them ; the world is only their lodging and table.
But the poet, whose verses are to be spheral and

complete, is one whom Nature cannot deceive,
whatsoever face of strangeness she may put on.
He feels a strict consanguinity, and detects more
likeness than variety in all her changes. We are
stung by the desire for new thought; but when
we receive a new thought it is only the old
thought with a new face, and though we make
it our own we instantly crave another; we are
not really enriched. For the truth was in us before it was reflected to us from natural objects;
and the profound genius will cast the likeness of
all creatures into every product of his wit.

But if the constructive powers are rare and it
is given to few men to be poets, yet every man
is a receiver of this descending holy ghost, and
may well study the laws of its influx. Exactly
parallel is the whole rule of intellectual duty to
the rule of moral duty. A self-denial no less
austere than the saint's is demanded of the
scholar. He must worship truth, and forego all
things for that, and choose defeat and pain, so
that his treasure in thought is thereby augmented.[1]

God offers to every mind its choice between
truth and repose. Take which you please, —
you can never have both. Between these, as a
pendulum, man oscillates. He in whom the love

of repose predominates will accept the first creed, the first philosophy, the first political party he meets,—most likely his father's. He gets rest, commodity and reputation ; but he shuts the door of truth. He in whom the love of truth predominates will keep himself aloof from all moorings, and afloat. He will abstain from dogmatism, and recognize all the opposite negations between which, as walls, his being is swung. He submits to the inconvenience of suspense and imperfect opinion, but he is a candidate for truth, as the other is not, and respects the highest law of his being.

The circle of the green earth he must measure with his shoes to find the man who can yield him truth. He shall then know that there is somewhat more blessed and great in hearing than in speaking. Happy is the hearing man ; unhappy the speaking man. As long as I hear truth I am bathed by a beautiful element and am not conscious of any limits to my nature. The suggestions are thousand-fold that I hear and see. The waters of the great deep have ingress and egress to the soul. But if I speak, I define, I confine and am less. When Socrates speaks, Lysis and Menexenus are afflicted by no shame that they do not speak. They also

are good. He likewise defers to them, loves
them, whilst he speaks. Because a true and
natural man contains and is the same truth
which an eloquent man articulates; but in the
eloquent man, because he can articulate it, it
seems something the less to reside, and he turns
to these silent beautiful with the more inclina-
tion and respect. The ancient sentence said,
Let us be silent, for so are the gods.[1] Silence
is a solvent that destroys personality, and gives
us leave to be great and universal. Every man's
progress is through a succession of teachers,
each of whom seems at the time to have a su-
perlative influence, but it at last gives place to
a new. Frankly let him accept it all. Jesus
says, Leave father, mother, house and lands,
and follow me. Who leaves all, receives more.
This is as true intellectually as morally. Each
new mind we approach seems to require an ab-
dication of all our past and present possessions.
A new doctrine seems at first a subversion of
all our opinions, tastes, and manner of living.
Such has Swedenborg, such has Kant, such has
Coleridge, such has Hegel or his interpreter
Cousin seemed to many young men in this
country. Take thankfully and heartily all they
can give. Exhaust them, wrestle with them, let

them not go until their blessing be won, and after a short season the dismay will be over-past, the excess of influence withdrawn, and they will be no longer an alarming meteor, but one more bright star shining serenely in your hea-ven and blending its light with all your day.

But whilst he gives himself up unreservedly to that which draws him, because that is his own, he is to refuse himself to that which draws him not, whatsoever fame and authority may attend it, because it is not his own.[1] Entire self-reliance belongs to the intellect. One soul is a counterpoise of all souls, as a capillary col-umn of water is a balance for the sea. It must treat things and books and sovereign genius as itself also a sovereign. If Æschylus be that man he is taken for, he has not yet done his office when he has educated the learned of Europe for a thousand years. He is now to approve himself a master of delight to me also. If he cannot do that, all his fame shall avail him nothing with me. I were a fool not to sacrifice a thousand Æschyluses to my intellec-tual integrity. Especially take the same ground in regard to abstract truth, the science of the mind. The Bacon, the Spinoza, the Hume, Schelling, Kant, or whosoever propounds to

you a philosophy of the mind, is only a more
or less awkward translator of things in your
consciousness which you have also your way of
seeing, perhaps of denominating. Say then, instead of too timidly poring into his obscure
sense, that he has not succeeded in rendering
back to you your consciousness. He has not
succeeded ; now let another try. If Plato cannot, perhaps Spinoza will. If Spinoza cannot,
then perhaps Kant. Anyhow, when at last it
is done, you will find it is no recondite, but a
simple, natural, common state which the writer
restores to you.

But let us end these didactics. I will not,
though the subject might provoke it, speak to
the open question between Truth and Love.
I shall not presume to interfere in the old politics of the skies ; — " The cherubim know
most ; the seraphim love most." The gods
shall settle their own quarrels. But I cannot
recite, even thus rudely, laws of the intellect, ·
without remembering that lofty and sequestered
class who have been its prophets and oracles,
the high-priesthood of the pure reason, the
Trismegisti,[1] the expounders of the principles
of thought from age to age. When at long intervals we turn over their abstruse pages, won-

derful seems the calm and grand air of these
few, these great spiritual lords who have walked
in the world, — these of the old religion, —
dwelling in a worship which makes the sanctities of Christianity look *parvenues* and popular;
for " persuasion is in soul, but necessity is in
intellect." [1] This band of grandées, Hermes,
Heraclitus, Empedocles, Plato, Plotinus, Olym-
piodorus, Proclus, Synesius and the rest, have
somewhat so vast in their logic, so primary in
their thinking, that it seems antecedent to all
the ordinary distinctions of rhetoric and literature, and to be at once poetry and music and
dancing and astronomy and mathematics. I am
present at the sowing of the seed of the world.
With a geometry of sunbeams the soul lays the
foundations of nature. The truth and grandeur
of their thought is proved by its scope and ap-
plicability, for it commands the entire schedule
and inventory of things for its illustration. But
what marks its elevation and has even a comic
look to us, is the innocent serenity with which
these babe-like Jupiters sit in their clouds, and
from age to age prattle to each other and to no
contemporary. Well assured that their speech
is intelligible and the most natural thing in the
world, they add thesis to thesis, without a mo-

ment's heed of the universal astonishment of
the human race below, who do not comprehend
their plainest argument ; nor do they ever re-
lent so much as to insert a popular or explain-
ing sentence, nor testify the least displeasure or
petulance at the dulness of their amazed audi-
tory. The angels are so enamored of the language that is spoken in heaven that they will
not distort their lips with the hissing and un-
musical dialects of men, but speak their own,
whether there be any who understand it or not.

XII

ART

GIVE to barrows, trays and pans
Grace and glimmer of romance,
Bring the moonlight into noon
Hid in gleaming piles of stone;
On the city's pavéd street
Plant gardens lined with lilac sweet,
Let spouting fountains cool the air,
Singing in the sun-baked square.
Let statue, picture, park and hall,
Ballad, flag and festival,
The past restore, the day adorn
And make each morrow a new morn.
So shall the drudge in dusty frock
Spy behind the city clock
Retinues of airy kings,
Skirts of angels, starry wings,
His fathers shining in bright fables,
His children fed at heavenly tables.
'T is the privilege of Art
Thus to play its cheerful part,
Man in Earth to acclimate
And bend the exile to his fate,
And, moulded of one element
With the days and firmament,
Teach him on these as stairs to climb
And live on even terms with Time;
Whilst upper life the slender rill
Of human sense doth overfill.

ART

BECAUSE the soul is progressive, it never quite repeats itself, but in every act attempts the production of a new and fairer whole. This appears in works both of the useful and fine arts, if we employ the popular distinction of works according to their aim either at use or beauty. Thus in our fine arts, not imitation but creation is the aim. In landscapes the painter should give the suggestion of a fairer creation than we know. The details, the prose of nature he should omit and give us only the spirit and splendor. He should know that the landscape has beauty for his eye because it expresses a thought which is to him good; and this because the same power which sees through his eyes is seen in that spectacle; and he will come to value the expression of nature and not nature itself, and so exalt in his copy the features that please him. He will give the gloom of gloom and the sunshine of sunshine. In a portrait he must inscribe the character and not the features, and must esteem the man who sits to him as himself only an imperfect picture or likeness of the aspiring original within.[1]

What is that abridgment and selection we observe in all spiritual activity, but itself the creative impulse? for it is the inlet of that higher illumination which teaches to convey a larger sense by simpler symbols. What is a man but nature's finer success in self-explication? What is a man but a finer and compacter landscape than the horizon figures,— nature's eclecticism? and what is his speech, his love of painting, love of nature, but a still finer success, — all the weary miles and tons of space and bulk left out, and the spirit or moral of it contracted into a musical word, or the most cunning stroke of the pencil?

But the artist must employ the symbols in use in his day and nation to convey his enlarged sense to his fellow-men. Thus the new in art is always formed out of the old. The Genius of the Hour sets his ineffaceable seal on the work and gives it an inexpressible charm for the imagination. As far as the spiritual character of the period overpowers the artist and finds expression in his work, so far it will retain a certain grandeur, and will represent to future beholders the Unknown, the Inevitable, the Divine.[1] No man can quite exclude this element of Necessity from his labor. No man can quite emancipate himself from his age and country, or produce a model in which the education, the religion, the politics, usages and arts of his times shall have no share. Though he were never so original, never so wilful and fantastic, he cannot wipe out of his work every trace of the thoughts amidst which it grew. The very avoidance betrays the usage he avoids. Above his will and out of his sight he is necessitated by the air he breathes and the idea on which he and his contemporaries live and toil, to share the manner of his times, without knowing what that manner is. Now that which is inevitable in the work has a higher charm than individual talent can ever give, inasmuch as the artist's pen or chisel seems to have been held and guided by a gigantic hand to inscribe a line in the history of the human race. This circumstance gives a value to the Egyptian hieroglyphics, to the Indian, Chinese and Mexican idols, however gross and shapeless. They denote the height of the human soul in that hour, and were not fantastic, but sprung from a necessity as deep as the world.[1] Shall I now add that the whole extant product of the plastic arts has herein its highest value, *as history;* as a stroke drawn in the portrait of that fate, perfect and

II

beautiful, according to whose ordinations all beings advance to their beatitude?

Thus, historically viewed, it has been the office of art to educate the perception of beauty. We are immersed in beauty, but our eyes have no clear vision. It needs, by the exhibition of single traits, to assist and lead the dormant taste. We carve and paint, or we behold what is carved and painted, as students of the mystery of Form. The virtue of art lies in detachment, in sequestering one object from the embarrassing variety. Until one thing comes out from the connection of things, there can be enjoyment, contemplation, but no thought. Our happiness and unhappiness are unproductive. The infant lies in a pleasing trance, but his individual character and his practical power depend on his daily progress in the separation of things, and dealing with one at a time. Love and all the passions concentrate all existence around a single form. It is the habit of certain minds to give an all-excluding fulness to the object, the thought, the word they alight upon, and to make that for the time the deputy of the world. These are the artists, the orators, the leaders of society. The power to detach and to magnify by detaching is the essence of

rhetoric in the hands of the orator and the poet.
This rhetoric, or power to fix the momentary
eminency of an object, — so remarkable in
Burke, in Byron, in Carlyle, — the painter and
sculptor exhibit in color and in stone. The
power depends on the depth of the artist's insight of that object he contemplates. For every
object has its roots in central nature, and may
of course be so exhibited to us as to represent
the world.¹ Therefore each work of genius is
the tyrant of the hour and concentrates attention on itself. For the time, it is the only thing
worth naming to do that, — be it a sonnet, an
opera, a landscape, a statue, an oration, the plan
of a temple, of a campaign, or of a voyage of
discovery. Presently we pass to some other
object, which rounds itself into a whole as did
the first ; for example a well-laid garden ; and
nothing seems worth doing but the laying out
of gardens. I should think fire the best thing
in the world, if I were not acquainted with air,
and water, and earth. For it is the right and
property of all natural objects, of all genuine
talents, of all native properties whatsoever, to
be for their moment the top of the world. A
squirrel leaping from bough to bough and making the wood but one wide tree for his pleasure,

fills the eye not less than a lion, — is beautiful, self-sufficing, and stands then and there for nature.[1] A good ballad draws my ear and heart whilst I listen, as much as an epic has done before. A dog, drawn by a master, or a litter of pigs, satisfies and is a reality not less than the frescoes of Angelo. From this succession of excellent objects we learn at last the immensity of the world, the opulence of human nature, which can run out to infinitude in any direction. But I also learn that what astonished and fascinated me in the first work, astonished me in the second work also; that excellence of all things is one.

The office of painting and sculpture seems to be merely initial. The best pictures can easily tell us their last secret. The best pictures are rude draughts of a few of the miraculous dots and lines and dyes which make up the ever-changing "landscape with figures" amidst which we dwell. Painting seems to be to the eye what dancing is to the limbs. When that has educated the frame to self-possession, to nimbleness, to grace, the steps of the dancing-master are better forgotten; so painting teaches me the splendor of color and the expression of form, and as I see many pictures and higher genius

in the art, I see the boundless opulence of the
pencil, the indifferency in which the artist stands
free to choose out of the possible forms. If he
can draw every thing, why draw any thing? and
then is my eye opened to the eternal picture
which nature paints in the street, with moving men and children, beggars and fine ladies,
draped in red and green and blue and gray;
long-haired, grizzled, white-faced, black-faced,
wrinkled, giant, dwarf, expanded, elfish, —
capped and based by heaven, earth and sea.[1]

A gallery of sculpture teaches more austerely
the same lesson. As picture teaches the coloring, so sculpture the anatomy of form. When
I have seen fine statues and afterwards enter
a public assembly, I understand well what he
meant who said, "When I have been reading
Homer, all men look like giants." I too see
that painting and sculpture are gymnastics of
the eye, its training to the niceties and curiosi-
ties of its function. There is no statue like this
living man, with his infinite advantage over all
ideal sculpture, of perpetual variety. What a
gallery of art have I here! No mannerist made
these varied groups and diverse original single
figures. Here is the artist himself improvising,
grim and glad, at his block. Now one thought

strikes him, now another, and with each moment he alters the whole air, attitude and expression of his clay. Away with your nonsense
of oil and easels, of marble and chisels ; except
to open your eyes to the masteries of eternal
art, they are hypocritical rubbish.

The reference of all production at last to an
aboriginal Power explains the traits common to
all works of the highest art, — that they are uni-
versally intelligible; that they restore to us the
simplest states of mind, and are religious. Since
what skill is therein shown is the reappearance
of the original soul, a jet of pure light, it should
produce a similar impression to that made by
natural objects. In happy hours, nature appears to us one with art; art perfected, — the
work of genius. And the individual in whom
simple tastes and susceptibility to all the great
human influences overpower the accidents of a
local and special culture, is the best critic of art.
Though we travel the world over to find the
beautiful, we must carry it with us, or we find
it not.[1] The best of beauty is a finer charm
than skill in surfaces, in outlines, or rules of art
can ever teach, namely a radiation from the work
of art, of human character, — a wonderful expression through stone, or canvas, or musical

sound, of the deepest and simplest attributes of
our nature, and therefore most intelligible at last
to those souls which have these attributes. In
the sculptures of the Greeks, in the masonry of
the Romans, and in the pictures of the Tuscan
and Venetian masters, the highest charm is the
universal language they speak. A confession of
moral nature, of purity, love, and hope, breathes
from them all. That which we carry to them,
the same we bring back more fairly illustrated
in the memory. The traveller who visits the
Vatican and passes from chamber to chamber   ·
through galleries of statues, vases, sarcophagi
and candelabra, through all forms of beauty cut
in the richest materials, is in danger of forget-
ting the simplicity of the principles out of which
they all sprung, and that they had their origin
from thoughts and laws in his own breast. He
studies the technical rules on these wonderful
remains, but forgets that these works were not
always thus constellated; [1] that they are the con-
tributions of many ages and many countries;
that each came out of the solitary workshop of
one artist, who toiled perhaps in ignorance of the
existence of other sculpture, created his work
without other model save life, household life,
and the sweet and smart of personal relations,

of beating hearts, and meeting eyes ; of poverty
and necessity and hope and fear. These were
his inspirations, and these are the effects he carries home to your heart and mind. In proportion to his force, the artist will find in his work
an outlet for his proper character. He must not
be in any manner pinched or hindered by his
material, but through his necessity of imparting
himself the adamant will be wax in his hands,
and will allow an adequate communication of
himself, in his full stature and proportion. He
need not cumber himself with a conventional
nature and culture, nor ask what is the mode in
Rome or in Paris, but that house and weather
and manner of living which poverty and the fate
of birth have made at once so odious and so
dear, in the gray unpainted wood cabin, on the
corner of a New Hampshire farm, or in the log-
hut of the backwoods, or in the narrow lodging
where he has endured the constraints and seeming of a city poverty, will serve as well as any
other condition as the symbol of a thought which
pours itself indifferently through all.

I remember when in my younger days I had
heard of the wonders of Italian painting, I fancied the great pictures would be great strangers ;
some surprising combination of color and form ;

a foreign wonder, barbaric pearl and gold, like
the spontoons and standards of the militia, which
play such pranks in the eyes and imaginations
of school-boys. I was to see and acquire I knew
not what. When I came at last to Rome and
saw with eyes the pictures, I found that genius
left to novices the gay and fantastic and osten-
tatious, and itself pierced directly to the simple
and true; that it was familiar and sincere; that
it was the old, eternal fact I had met already in
so many forms, — unto which I lived; that it
was the plain *you and me* I knew so well, — had
left at home in so many conversations. I had
had the same experience already in a church at
Naples. There I saw that nothing was changed
with me but the place, and said to myself —
'Thou foolish child, hast thou come out hither,
over four thousand miles of salt water, to find
that which was perfect to thee there at home?''
That fact I saw again in the Academmia at Naples, in the chambers of sculpture, and yet again
when I came to Rome and to the paintings of
Raphael, Angelo, Sacchi, Titian, and Leonardo
da Vinci. "What, old mole! workest thou in
the earth so fast?"² It had travelled by my
side; that which I fancied I had left in Boston
was here in the Vatican, and again at Milan and

at Paris, and made all travelling ridiculous as a treadmill.¹ I now require this of all pictures, that they domesticate me, not that they dazzle me. Pictures must not be too picturesque. Nothing astonishes men so much as common-sense and plain dealing. All great actions have been simple,² and all great pictures are.

The Transfiguration, by Raphael, is an eminent example of this peculiar merit. · A calm benignant beauty shines over all this picture, and goes directly to the heart. It seems almost to call you by name. The sweet and sublime face of Jesus is beyond praise, yet how it disappoints all florid expectations! This familiar, simple, home-speaking countenance is as if one should meet a friend. The knowledge of picture dealers has its value, but listen not to their criticism when your heart is touched by genius. It was not painted for them, it was painted for you; for such as had eyes capable of being touched by simplicity and lofty emotions.

Yet when we have said all our fine things about the arts, we must end with a frank confession that the arts, as we know them, are but initial. Our best praise is given to what they aimed and promised, not to the actual result. He has conceived meanly of the resources of

man, who believes that the best age of production is past. The real value of the Iliad or the
Transfiguration is as signs of power; billows
or ripples they are of the stream of tendency;
tokens of the everlasting effort to produce, which
even in its worst estate the soul betrays.[1] Art
has not yet come to its maturity if it do not put
itself abreast with the most potent influences of
the world, if it is not practical and moral, if it
do not stand in connection with the conscience,
if it do not make the poor and uncultivated feel
that it addresses them with a voice of lofty cheer.
There is higher work for Art than the arts.
They are abortive births of an imperfect or vitiated instinct. Art is the need to create; but
in its essence, immense and universal, it is impatient of working with lame or tied hands, and of
making cripples and monsters, such as all pictures and statues are. Nothing less than the creation of man and nature is its end. A man should
find in it an outlet for his whole energy. He
may paint and carve only as long as he can do
that. Art should exhilarate, and throw down the
walls of circumstance on every side, awakening
in the beholder the same sense of universal relation and power which the work evinced in the artist, and its highest effect is to make new artists.[2]

Already History is old enough to witness the old age and disappearance of particular arts. The art of sculpture is long ago perished to any real effect. It was originally a useful art, a mode of writing, a savage's record of gratitude or devotion, and among a people possessed of a wonderful perception of form this childish carving was refined to the utmost splendor of effect. But it is the game of a rude and youthful people, and not the manly labor of a wise and spiritual nation. Under an oak-tree loaded with leaves and nuts, under a sky full of eternal eyes, I stand in a thoroughfare; but in the works of our plastic arts and especially of sculpture, creation is driven into a corner. I cannot hide from myself that there is a certain appearance of paltriness, as of toys and the trumpery of a theatre, in sculpture. Nature transcends all our moods of thought, and its secret we do not yet find. But the gallery stands at the mercy of our moods, and there is a moment when it becomes frivolous. I do not wonder that Newton, with an attention habitually engaged on the paths of planets and suns, should have wondered what the Earl of Pembroke found to admire in "stone dolls." [1] Sculpture may serve to teach the pupil how deep is the secret of form, how purely the

spirit can translate its meanings into that eloquent dialect. But the statue will look cold and
false before that new activity which needs to roll
through all things, and is impatient of counter-
feits and things not alive. Picture and sculpture
are the celebrations and festivities of form. But
true art is never fixed, but always flowing. The
sweetest music is not in the oratorio, but in the
human voice when it speaks from its instant
life tones of tenderness, truth, or courage. The
oratorio has already lost its relation to the morning, to the sun, and the earth, but that persuad-
ing voice is in tune with these. All works of art
should not be detached, but extempore performances. A great man is a new statue in every
attitude and action. A beautiful woman is a picture which drives all beholders nobly mad. Life
may be lyric or epic, as well as a poem or a
romance.

A true announcement of the law of creation,
if a man were found worthy to declare it, would
carry art up into the kingdom of nature, and
destroy its separate and contrasted existence.
The fountains of invention and beauty in modern
society are all but dried up. A popular novel, a
theatre, or a ball-room makes us feel that we are
all paupers in the almshouse of this world, with-

out dignity, without skill or industry. Art is as
poor and low. The old tragic Necessity, which
lowers on the brows even of the Venuses and
the Cupids of the antique, and furnishes the sole
apology for the intrusion of such anomalous figures into nature, — namely that they were inevitable ; that the artist was drunk with a passion
for form which he could not resist, and which
vented itself in these fine extravagances, — no
longer dignifies the chisel or the pencil. But the
artist and the connoisseur now seek in art the
exhibition of their talent, or an asylum from
the evils of life. Men are not well pleased with
the figure they make in their own imaginations,
and they flee to art, and convey their better sense
in an oratorio, a statue, or a picture. Art makes
the same effort which a sensual prosperity makes ;
namely to detach the beautiful from the useful,
to do up the work as unavoidable, and, hating
it, pass on to enjoyment. These solaces and
compensations, this division of beauty from use,
the laws of nature do not permit. As soon as
beauty is sought, not from religion and love but
for pleasure, it degrades the seeker. High beauty
is no longer attainable by him in canvas or in
stone, in sound, or in lyrical construction ; an
effeminate, prudent, sickly beauty, which is not

beauty, is all that can be formed ; for the hand
can never execute any thing higher than the
character can inspire.'

The art that thus separates is itself first separated. Art must not be a superficial talent, but
must begin farther back in man. Now men do
not see nature to be beautiful, and they go to
make a statue which shall be. They abhor men
as tasteless, dull, and inconvertible, and console
themselves with color-bags and blocks of marble. They reject life as prosaic, and create a
death which they call poetic. They despatch
the day's weary chores, and fly to voluptuous
reveries. They eat and drink, that they may
afterwards execute the ideal. Thus is art vili-
fied ; the name conveys to the mind its secondary and bad senses ; it stands in the imagination
as somewhat contrary to nature, and struck with
death from the first. Would it not be better to
begin higher up, — to serve the ideal before
they eat and drink ; to serve the ideal in eating
and drinking, in drawing the breath, and in the
functions of life? Beauty must come back to
the useful arts, and the distinction between the
fine and the useful arts be forgotten. If history were truly told, if life were nobly spent, it
would be no longer easy or possible to distin-

guish the one from the other. In nature, all is
useful, all is beautiful. It is therefore beautiful
because it is alive, moving, reproductive ; it is
therefore useful because it is symmetrical and
fair. Beauty will not come at the call of a legis-
lature, nor will it repeat in England or America
its history in Greece. It will come, as always,
unannounced, and spring up between the feet
of brave and earnest men. It is in vain that we
look for genius to reiterate its miracles in the
old arts ; it is its instinct to find beauty and
holiness in new and necessary facts, in the field
and road-side, in the shop and mill. Proceeding from a religious heart it will raise to a divine
use the railroad, the insurance office, the joint-
stock company ; our law, our primary assem-.
blies, our commerce, the galvanic battery, the
electric jar, the prism, and the chemist's retort ;
in which we seek now only an economical use.
Is not the selfish and even cruel aspect which
belongs to our great mechanical works, to mills,
railways, and machinery, the effect of the mer-
cenary impulses which these works obey ? When
its errands are noble and adequate, a steamboat
bridging the Atlantic between Old and New
England and arriving at its ports with the punc-
tuality of a planet, is a step of man into har-

mony with nature. The boat at St. Petersburg, which plies along the Lena by magnetism, needs little to make it sublime. When science is learned in love, and its powers are wielded by love, they will appear the supplements and continuations of the material creation.[1]

II

NOTES

NOTES

AFTER the publication of *Nature*, the first hint that appears of the collection by Mr. Emerson of his writings into a second book, occurs in the end of a letter to Mr. Alcott, written April 16, 1839, which Mr. Sanborn gives in his *Memoir of Bronson Alcott:* "I have been writing a little, and arranging old papers more, and by and by I hope to get a shapely book of Genesis."

In a letter written in April, 1840, to Carlyle, Mr. Emerson thus alludes to the *Essays :* —

"I am here at work now for a fortnight to spin some single cord out of my thousand and one strands of every color and texture that lie ravelled around me in old snarls. We need to be possessed with a mountainous conviction of the value of our advice to our contemporaries, if we will take such pains to find what that is. But no, it is the pleasure of the spinning that betrays poor spinners into the loss of so much good time. I shall work with the more diligence on this book-to-be of mine, that you inform me again and again that my penny tracts[1] are still extant; nay, that beside friendly men, learned and poetic men read and even review them. I am like Scholasticus of the Greek Primer, who was ashamed to bring out so small a dead child before such grand people. Pygmalion shall try if he cannot fashion a better, — certainly a bigger." Four months later he tells of the problems at home, — "a good deal of movement and tendency emerging into sight every day in church and state, in social modes and in letters. You will natu-

[1] *Nature*, and the various addresses, published at first separately in pamphlet form.

rally ask me if I try my hand at the history of all this. . . . No, not in the near and practical way in which they seem to invite. I incline to write philosophy, poetry, possibility — anything but history. And yet this phantom of the next age limns himself sometimes so large and plain that every feature is apprehensible and challenges a painter. . . . I dot evermore in my endless journal, a line on every knowable in nature ; but the arrangement loiters long, and I get a brick-kiln instead of a house.''

Soon after the coming in of the new year he sends word : '' In a fortnight or three weeks my little raft will be afloat. Expect nothing more of my powers of construction, — no ship-building, no clipper, smack, nor skiff even, only boards and logs tied together.''

In his Journal he wrote, in January, 1841 : '' All my thoughts are foresters. I have scarce a day-dream on which the breath of the pines has not blown and their shadows waved. Shall I not therefore call my little book *Forest Essays* ? ''

The book was published in March, 1841, in Boston, by James Munroe and Company.

Soon after *Nature* had appeared, Carlyle had written to his friend : '' There is a man here called John Sterling, . . . whom I love better than any one I have met with, since a certain sky-messenger alighted to me at Craigenputtock and vanished in the Blue again.[1] . . . Well, and what then, cry you ? Why then, this John Sterling has fallen overhead in love with a certain Waldo Emerson ; that is all. He saw the little book *Nature* lying here ; and, across a whole *silva silvarum* of prejudices, discerned what was in it, took it to his

---

[1] Alluding to Emerson's first visit to him among the moors of Nithsdale in 1833.

heart, — and indeed into his pocket. . . . This is the small piece of pleasant news, that two sky-messengers (such they were, both of them, to me) have met and recognized each other, and by God's blessing there shall one day be a trio of us ; call you that nothing ? " Sterling wrote to Emerson and a noble friendship resulted. Although they never met in the body, these friends had more in common with each other in their hope, their courage, and their desire for expression in poetry than either had with Carlyle. Sterling died in 1844.

Emerson sent Sterling his *Essays*, saying, " They are not yet a fortnight old. I have written your name in a copy and sent it to Carlyle by the same steamer. . . . I wish, but scarce dare hope, you may find in it any thing of the pristine sacredness of thought. All thoughts are holy when they come floating up to us in magical newness from the hidden Life, and 't is no wonder we are enamoured with these Muses and Graces, until, in our devotion to particular beauties and in our efforts at artificial disposition, we lose somewhat of our universal sense and the sovereign eye of Proportion. All sins, literary and æsthetic and scientific, as well as moral, grow out of unbelief at last. We must needs meddle ambitiously, and cannot quite trust that there is life, self-evolving and indestructible, but which cannot be hastened, at the heart of every physical and metaphysical fact. Yet how we thank and greet, almost adore the person who has once or twice in a lifetime treated any thing sublimely, and certified us that he beheld the Law. The silence and obscurity in which he acted are of no account, for every thing is equally related to the soul.

" I certainly did not mean, when I took up this paper, to write an essay on Faith, and yet I am always willing to declare how indigent I think our poetry and all literature is become for want of that. My thought had only this scope, no more : that though I had long ago grown extremely discontented with my little book, yet were the thoughts in it honest in their first rising and honestly reported, but that I am very sensible how much in this, as in very much greater matters, interference, or what we miscall art, will spoil true things." [1]

Carlyle now had opportunity to return his friend's kindness in introducing him to American readers. In a letter written to Emerson on June 25, 1841, he said : "My second piece of news . . . is that Emerson's *Essays*, the book so called, is to be reprinted here ; nay, I think, is even now at press. . . . Fraser undertakes it on 'half profits ;' T. Carlyle writing a preface, which accordingly he did. . . . The edition is of Seven Hundred and Fifty. . . . With what joy shall I sack up the small Ten Pounds Sterling perhaps of 'Half Profits,' and remit them to the man Emerson ; saying: 'There, Man ! tit for tat, the reciprocity *not* all on one side !' I ought to say, moreover, that this was a volunteer scheme of Fraser's ; the risk is all his, the origin of it was with him: I advised him to have it reviewed, as being a really noteworthy Book. 'Write you a Preface,' said he, and 'I will reprint it;' to which, after due delay and meditation, I consented."

In a curious and characteristic preface, among other things, Carlyle said: —

"The name of Ralph Waldo Emerson is not entirely new, in England ; distinguished travellers bring us tidings of such a man ; fractions of his writings have found their way into the hands of the curious here ; fitful hints that there is in New England some spiritual notability called Emerson glide through the reviews and magazines.

"Emerson's writings and speakings amount to something ;

[1] *A Correspondence between John Sterling and Ralph Waldo Emerson.*

and yet, hitherto, as it seems to me, this Emerson is far less
notable for what he has spoken or done than for the many
things he has not spoken and has forborne to do. . . .

" For myself, I have looked over with no common feeling
to this brave Emerson, seated by his rustic hearth on the other
side of the ocean (yet not altogether parted from me either),
silently communing with his own soul and with the God's
World it finds itself alive in yonder. Pleasures of Virtue,
Progress of the Species, Black Emancipation, New Tariff,
Eclecticism, Locofocoism, Ghost of Improved Socinianism, —
these, with many other Ghosts and substances, are squeaking,
jabbering according to their capabilities round this man. To
one man among the sixteen millions their jabber is all unmusi-
cal. The silent voices of the stars above and of the green earth
beneath are profitable to him — tell him gradually that these
others are but ghosts which will shortly have to vanish ; that
the life-fountain these proceed out of does not vanish. . . .

" Emerson, I understand, was bred to theology ; of which
primary bent his latest way of thought still bears traces. In a
very enigmatic way, we hear much of the ' Universal Soul of
the,' etc., flickering like bright bodiless northern streamers.
Notions and half-notions of a metaphysic, theosophic kind are
seldom long wanting in these *Essays*. I do not advise the
British public to trouble itself much with all that : still less to
take offence at it. . . . That this little book has no system,
and points or stretches far beyond all systems, is one of its
merits. We will call it the soliloquy of a true soul alone under
the stars, in this day."

Mr. George W. Cooke, in his careful study of the life of
Mr. Emerson,[1] relates that five years later the Countess

1 *Ralph Waldo Emerson, his Life, Writings, and Philosophy.* Boston:
J. R Osgood & Co. 1887.

d'Agoult, who wrote under the *nom de plume* of " Daniel Stern," told in the *Revue Indépendante* (July) how having read a mention of the *Essays* by Philarète Chasles in an article on literary tendencies in America, and later heard a quotation from them in a lecture by a foreign poet, Mickiewicz, she tried to obtain the book in Paris, but had to send to London for it. She was greatly pleased, and in her article expressed surprise at the general ignorance concerning the writer. " The singular charm of the *Essays*," she said, " is that we hold him accountable for nothing, because he pretends to nothing. He draws you after him with irresistible *bonhomie*. There is no difficulty in following him, for we breathe a salubrious atmosphere in his work. Nothing offends, not even the discords, because all is resolved and harmonized in the sentiment of a superior truth."

In Berlin, Herman Grimm (who later wrote the lives of Michelangelo and Raphael), while waiting his turn in the parlor of the American dentist, chanced to pick up the *Essays* from the table ; " read a page, and was startled to find that I had understood nothing, though tolerably well acquainted with English. I inquired as to the author. In reply I was told that he was the first writer in America, an eminently gifted man, but somewhat crazed at times, and often unable to explain his own words. Notwithstanding, no one was held in such esteem for his character and for his prose writings. In short, the opinion fell upon my ears as so strange that I reopened the book. Some sentences, upon a second reading, shot like a beam of light into my very soul, and I was moved to put the book in my pocket, that I might read it more attentively at home. . . . I took Webster's Dictionary and began to read. The construction of the sentences struck me as very extraordinary. I soon discovered the secret : they were real thoughts, an individual language, a sincere man that I had be-

fore me ; naught superficial, second-hand. Enough ! I bought
the book ! From that time I have never ceased to read Emerson's works, and whenever I take up a volume anew it seems
to me as if I were reading it for the first time.''

But at home the book was not well received in all quarters.

Mr. Cooke, in his biography, quotes an author in the
Princeton Review who had found the *Essays* '' more devoid of
real meaning than any other book which ever fell into his
hands, and thought such essays could be produced through a
lifetime as rapidly as a human pen could be made to move.''

Another critic, a distinguished classical scholar connected
with one of the universities, seems to have recognized Mr.
Emerson's debt to the Greek and, through these, the Oriental
philosophers, seeing in the ideas set forth '' ancient errors,
mistaken for new truths and disguised in the drapery of a
misty rhetoric.''

HISTORY

The first essay in the volume, '' History,'' was not delivered
as a single lecture, but in writing it Mr. Emerson made use
of passages from lectures in three distinct courses ; namely,
that on '' English Literature '' (1835–36), on '' The Philosophy of History '' (1836–37), and on '' Human Life ''
(1837–38), as is shown by Mr. Cabot in the chronological
list of lectures and addresses in the Appendix (F) to his
Memoir.

The essay is a fit gateway to those that lie behind, for on its
threshold is the doctrine of the Universal Mind, and beyond
will be found those depending on and illustrating this, the
Unity underlying the Flowing of Nature through endless cycles
of Protean disguises, the Symbolism of Nature, the beauty

of Law, working forward and upward alike in Nature, in races, and in the individual and his works.

The course on " The Philosophy of History " (1836-37) had the following lectures, many of which appear as such or in their matter in the *Essays*.

I. Introduction (History has been ill written ; its meaning and future, etc.)	VI. Religion.
	VII. Society.
	VIII. Trades and Professions.
II. Humanity of Science.	IX. Manners.
III. Art.	X. Ethics.
IV. Literature.	XI. Present Age.
V. ·Politics.	XII. Individualism.

In his Journal, Mr. Emerson thus lays out the course in advance, with the belief in the Over-Soul as the foundation of all. ·

There is one soul.

It is related to the world.

Art is its action thereon.

Science finds its methods.

Literature is its record.

Religion is the emotion of reverence that it inspires.

Ethics is the soul illustrated in human life.

Society is the finding of this soul by individuals in each other.

Trades are the learning the soul in nature by labor.

Politics is the activity of the soul illustrated in power.

Manners are silent and mediate expressions of soul.

Page 2, note 1. Both of these mottoes appear in the first edition : in both is the thought of the Over-Soul, which later appeared in Oriental form in Brahma. The desire to express himself in verse, which Mr. Emerson felt so strongly, had so far overcome his humility that during the months in which he was preparing this essay he had contributed to the first number of the *Dial* "The Problem," and "The Sphinx" appeared in the third.

Page 4, note 1. It will be remembered that the Sphinx's fatal riddle, which Œdipus solved, related to Man in his infancy, his prime and his decline.

In the end of *Nature* (vol. i.), man as a microcosm had been considered, and Herbert brought to testify in his beautiful poem "Man."

Page 5, note 1. In this passage, and one in " Self-Reliance," — " An institution is the lengthened shadow of one man," with the work of St. Anthony, Luther, Fox, Wesley and Clarkson as instances, — came out Mr. Emerson's belief in the duty and the power of the man of thought, a messenger of the Eternal Mind.

Page 6, note 1. In the affectionate sympathy for reading boys, which crops out so often in his books, memories of his boyhood and of his brothers and some near friends, like Dr. William H. Furness, come to light.

Page 7, note 1.

> Methought the sky looked scornful down
> On all was base in man.

" Walden," Poems, Appendix.

Page 8, note 1. Mr. Emerson often used to speak of the pitiful figure that certain scholars and statesmen presented, uttering elevated sentiments about Liberty and Justice in 1776, and being dumb on the subject of the flagrant violation of these principles in their own day.

Page 9, note 1. That a man was principally of value for his "atmosphere," and an event for the soul of it which survived for an example or in a poem, was a favorite idea with Mr. Emerson. He praised Sterling's line in *Alfred the Harper,* —

> Still lives the song, though Regnar dies!

With Swedenborg he valued Nature as a symbol.

Page 10, note 1. I am indebted to Professor Charles Eliot Norton for calling my attention to the probable compounding of the name Marmaduke Robinson, through a slip of Mr. Emerson's memory, out of the names of the two Quakers hung on Boston Common in 1659, Marmaduke Stevenson and William Robinson.

Page 12, note 1. In "The Problem" he describes the evolution of the grand architecture, the temples and cathedrals, "out of Thought's interior sphere," and Nature's ready adoption of them as her own.

Page 15, note 1. Mr. Emerson was much more alive to the beauty of form than of color. Sculpture appealed to him more than painting.

Page 15, note 2. The doctrine of the pervading unity which appears in the poem "Xenophanes," written in 1834, hence one of the earliest of the published poems.

Page 16, note 1. In the month of April, 1839, Carlyle sent Raphael Morghen's engraving of the Aurora, by Guido in the Rospigliosi palace in Rome, to Mr. Emerson, saying, "It is my wife's memorial to your wife. . . . Two houses divided by wide seas are to understand always that they are united nevertheless." The picture still hangs in the parlor of Mr. Emerson's home, with the inscription which accompanied it : "Will the lady of Concord hang up this

Italian sun-chariot somewhere in her Drawing Room, and, looking at it, think sometimes of a household here which has good cause never to forget hers.   T. Carlyle.''

Mr. Emerson used to point out to his children how the varied repetition of the manes, heads and prancing forefeet of the horses were imitations of the curved folds of a great cumulus cloud.

Page 17, note 1. Here, as in the two essays on Art, in this volume and in *Society and Solitude,* the same thought appears, embodied also in " The Problem " in the lines beginning, —

The hand that rounded Peter's dome, etc.

Page 19, note 1.

Come see the north wind's masonry, etc.
" The Snow-Storm," *Poems.*

Page 21, note 1. The works of Heeren and others on Egypt, and the architectural handbooks of Fergusson and Garbett, with some of Ruskin's writings, were read with interest by Mr. Emerson. The idea of Evolution, whether in the works of Nature or of man, early and always appealed to him.

Perhaps the first suggestion of the ideas on this page came to him in his boyhood, in the welcome form of Scott's description of Melrose Abbey in the *Lay of the Last Minstrel :* —
The moon on the east oriel shone
Through slender shafts of shapely stone,
By foliaged tracery combined ;
Thou wouldst have thought some fairy's hand
'Twixt poplars straight the osier wand
In many a freakish knot had twined,

Then framed a spell when the work was done,
And changed the willow wreaths to stone.

Page 22, note 1. Astaboras was a river of Æthiopia mentioned by Strabo.

Page 22, note 2. The following is the version of the re-
mainder of this paragraph in the first edition of the *Essays :* —

" The difference between men in this respect is the faculty
of rapid domestication, the power to find his chair and bed
everywhere which one man has, and another has not. Some
men have so much of the Indian left, have constitutionally
such habits of accommodation, that at sea, or in the forest, or
in the snow, they sleep as warm and dine with as good appetite and associate as happily as in their own house. And, to
push this old fact one degree nearer, we may find it a representative of a permanent fact in human nature. The intellectual nomadism is the faculty of objectiveness, or of eyes which
everywhere feed themselves. Who hath such eyes everywhere falls into easy relation with his fellow-men. Every
man, every thing, is a prize, a study, a property to him, and
this love smooths his brow, joins him to men, and makes him
beautiful and beloved in their sight. His house is a wagon :
he roams through all latitudes as easily as a Calmuc."

Page 22, note 3.

And well he loved to quit his home
And Calmuc in his wagon roam
To read new landscapes and old skies.
                    "The Poet," *Poems*, Appendix.

Page 23, note 1. In the balancing of the claims on the
scholar of society and solitude, so frequent in his writings,
Mr. Emerson always gives most weight to solitude, yet admitting the necessity, for his sanity, his character, and his supply

of raw material to work on, of mingling with the world and sharing the common exposures and experiences.

In his journal of his first trip to Europe, it is remarkable how little he found to detain him and how anxious he was to return to his proper field of action and work. The same feeling was very marked during his visit to Europe and Egypt in his old age.

Page 25, note 1. The freedom, the dignity and profit of self-help was a rule of practice, not a mere theory, with Mr. Emerson.

Page 28, note 1. Many strange pilgrims were on the road in those days, ridiculous enough to the eye of the average New Englander, and these were attracted to Concord by the report that there hospitality to thought could be found. Their host ministered to their physical wants, and to their hunger to be heard. He took them by " their best handle," — and, as he wrote of his ideal man, " The madness which he harbored he did not share."

Page 29, note 1. The respect for the old religion that made New England, remained deeply ingrained in Mr. Emerson, though he had left that phase of belief and spiritual growth behind. Yet it was always before him in the fiery faith of his Aunt Mary, and in his own household in the devoted Christianity of his mother and his wife. He was aware of the losses that might well accompany too extreme reaction from early faith, and the Luther anecdote might well have had something akin to it in his domestic experience.

Page 30, note 1. Compare Byron's *Prometheus.*

> Titan, to whose immortal eye
> The sufferings of mortality,
> Seen in their sad reality,
> Were not as things that gods despise, etc.

II

Page 31, note 1. The power of true vision to unsettle and move and elevate everything, indeed the old doctrine of "The Flowing" of Heracleitus, the dance of the trees and the very mountains that Orpheus led, occurs in the prose, but especially in Mr. Emerson's "Poet" in the Appendix to the *Poems.*

Page 32, note 1.

> I drank at thy fountains
> False waters of thirst.
> "Ode to Beauty," *Poems.*

Page 32, note 2. "We probably perceive the influence of these latent inheritances" [dormant tendencies to suppressed bestial parts or traits] "when, in the battle of existence, species undergo retrograde changes, or, as naturalists phrase it, revert to a lower state of being. . . . In the moral as well as the physical world, we·may see these hidden seeds of ancestral impulse, when no longer overshadowed by the newer and therefore stronger motives, spring into activity and win the creature back to a lower estate."— *The Interpretation of Nature,* by Professor N. S. Shaler. Boston, 1893.

Page 33, note 1. See the opening paragraphs of "The Poet," *Essays, Second Series,* and "Poetry and Imagination," *Letters and Social Aims,* for the true use of facts.

Mr. Emerson eagerly sought facts, not for themselves, but as oracles from which he was to draw the hidden but universal meaning. In his Journal in 1847, he speaks of the avarice with which he looks at the Insurance Office, and his longing to be admitted to hear the gossip of the notables of the village there: "For an hour to be invisible and hear the best informed men retail their information he would pay great prices, but every company dissolves at his approach. He so eager and they so coy. . . ."

"We want society on our own terms. Each man has facts that I want, and, though I talk with him, I cannot get at them for want of the clue. He does not know what to do with his facts: I know. . . . Here is all Boston, — all railroads, all manufactures and trade, in the head of this well-informed merchant at my side. . . . Here is Agassiz with his theory of anatomy and nature; I am in his chamber and I do not know what question to put. . . . Here is all Fourier in Brisbane's head; all language in Kraitser's; all Swedenborg in Reed's; all the Revolution in old Adams's head; all modern Europe and America in John Quincy Adams's, and I cannot appropriate a fragment of all their experience. . . . Now if I could cast a spell on this man at my side, and see his pictures without his intervention or organs, and having learned that lesson, turn the spell on another, lift up the cover of another hive, and see the cells and suck the honey . . . they were not the poorer and I the richer."

Page 34, note 1. When asked by one of his children whether some verse of Shakspeare, or perhaps it was a picture by Michelangelo, really was meant to carry with it the significance attributed to it, Mr. Emerson answered: "Every one has a right to be credited with whatever of good another can find in his work."

Page 35, note 1. Perceforest was a mediæval French historical romance, its scene being Britain in the pre-Arthurian period.

Amadis de Gaul, a romance written in the fourteenth century, by Vasco de Lobeira, in Portugal, but which became very popular in later versions in other tongues.

The Boy and the Mantle, an ancient English ballad. See *Percy's Reliques.*

Page 36, note 1. This passage with regard to man's faculties occurred in a lecture called "The Doctrine of the Hands" in the course on "Human Culture," 1837–38.

Page 37, note 1. See Shakspeare's *Henry VI.*, Part I., Act II., Scene iii.

Page 40, note 1. It was a characteristic of Mr. Emerson's writings to concentrate attention on some aspect of the matter on which he was speaking. He did not weaken a sentence, a paragraph, even, in some cases, a whole poem or lecture, by much qualification of his statement. He reserved the counter-statement, the other aspect, to present as neatly in another place. Hence, if but one essay be read, his position with reference to the church, or towards society, or reform, might be misunderstood.

Page 41, note 1. This passage appears in verse in "Limits," *Poems*, Appendix.

SELF-RELIANCE

During the period of Mr. Emerson's ministry in Boston he had written thus in his Journal : —

"CHARDON ST., OCT. 14TH, 1832.

" The great difficulty is that men do not think enough of themselves, do not consider what it is that they are sacrificing when they follow in a herd, or when they cater for their establishment. They know not how divine is a Man. I know you say such a man thinks too much of himself. Alas! he is wholly ignorant. He yet wanders in the outer darkness, in the skirts and shadows of himself, and has not seen his inner light.

" Would it not be a text of a useful discourse to young men, *that every man must learn in a different way?* How much is lost by imitation. Our best friends may be our worst enemies. A man should learn to detect and foster that gleam of light which flashes across his mind from within far more than the lustre of the whole firmament without. Yet he dismisses without notice his peculiar thought *because* it is peculiar. The time will come when he will postpone all acquired knowledge to this spontaneous wisdom, and will watch for this illumination more than those who watch for the morning. For this is the principle by which the other is to be arranged. This thinking would go to show the significance of self-education, that in reality there is no other, for all other is nought without this.''

This entry is continued by the passage now appearing in the latter part of '' Self-Reliance '' beginning, '' That which each can do best, none but his Maker can teach him,'' ending with the sentence about '' the Scipionism of Scipio.'' After several more jottings as to what might be said on the subject, he writes: —

'' Landor knows many things — treats of the continual appeal that is made from the facts to the feelings, from the world to the high, inward, infallible Judge, ever suggesting a grander creation,'' etc.

In the entry of the preceding day he transcribes various sentences from Landor's *Imaginary Conversations* (mostly from the talk of Epicurus with his friends), among them this: '' Since all transcendent, all true and genuine greatness must be of a man's own raising, and only on the foundation that the hand of God has laid, do not let any touch it: keep them off civilly, but keep them off.''

Thus it appears that the writings of Landor, read the year before Mr. Emerson sought him out in Rome, may have given the original push towards the writing of this essay on '' Self-Reliance.'' A small portion of the essay came from the lecture

"Individualism," the last in the course on "The Philosophy of History" in 1836–37, and other passages from the lectures "School," "Genius," and "Duty" in the course on "Human Life," 1838–39.

In reading this essay, it is well to call to mind, 1st, Mr. Emerson's fear of weakening the effect of his presentation of a subject by qualification ; 2d, That the Self he refers to is the higher self, man's share of divinity. Hence "The Over-Soul" should be read after "Self-Reliance."

Journal, Oct. 23, 1840. "And must I go and do somewhat if I would learn new secrets of self-reliance ? for my chapter is not finished. But self-reliance is precisely that secret to make your supposed deficiency redundancy. If I am true, the theory is, the very want of action, my very impotency, shall become a greater excelling than all skill and toil."

Page 45, note 1. Perhaps these were the poems of Washington Allston. His "Paint-King" is quoted in the chapter on Plato in *Representative Men.* If not these, it is probable that William Blake's remarkable poems are alluded to.

Page 46, note 1. This image recalls the departure of the Day in his poem, when the thoughtless poet from among her proffered gifts chose —

> A few herbs and apples . . .
> . . . I, too late,
> Under her solemn fillet saw the scorn.

Page 47, note 1. The doctrine of "The Over-Soul."

Page 48, note 1. Sympathy for children, loving reverence for unspoiled boys and girls, was part of Mr. Emerson's character, and appears throughout his writings, especially in "Domestic Life" and "Education."

Page 49, note 1. An annoyance at the notoriety which followed his action with regard to the rite of the Last Supper in his church, and later, on his simple statement to the Divinity students of the message that came to him with regard to the torpor of the church of that day, and their resulting duties, shows in Mr. Emerson's letters and journals at these times rather than any deeper trouble. It is that "sad self-knowledge" of Uriel.

Page 52, note 1. A characteristic case of his presentation of aspects. "But it is the fault of our rhetoric that we cannot strongly state one fact without seeming to belie some other." — "History."

Page 52, note 2. Of his "own poor" and his own causes, Mr. Emerson was mindful, and his hand was free.

Page 54, note 1. It need hardly be said that Mr. Emerson was an independent in politics, as in social or ecclesiastical movements. He writes in his Journal : "The relation of men of thought to society is always the same; they refuse that necessity of mediocre men, to take sides. They keep their own equilibrium. The sun's path is never parallel to the equator."

Page 57, note 1. Mr. Emerson said, "I deny personality to God because it is too little — not too much."

Page 58, note 1. It may be interesting to reproduce here the version of the first edition with a ruder vigor, more adapted to delivery in the Lyceum.

"With consistency a great soul has simply nothing to do. He may as well concern himself with his shadow on the wall. Out upon your guarded lips! Sew them up with pack-thread, do! else, if you would be a man, speak what you think to-day in words as hard as cannon-balls, and to-morrow speak what to-morrow thinks in hard words again, though it contradict

everything you said to-day. Ah, then, exclaim the aged
ladies, you shall be sure to be misunderstood! Misunderstood!
It is a right fool's word. Is it so bad then to be misunderstood ? Pythagoras was misunderstood, and Socrates, and
Jesus, and Luther, and Copernicus, and Galileo, and Newton,
and every pure and wise spirit that ever took flesh. To be
great is to be misunderstood.''

Page 58, note 2.

As sunbeams stream through liberal space
And nothing jostle or displace,
So waved the pine-tree through my thought
And fanned the dreams it never brought.
                    ''Woodnotes,'' II., *Poems.*

Page 61, note 1. Mr. Emerson's reading was largely in
biographies. For novels and romances he cared little, but the
human, the heroic, the individual in historic characters, he was
keen to find out, and equally so the natural speech, the independent action and native refinement in persons whom he met,
whether high or low. From his childhood he copied anecdotes of persons, and he read them to his scholars. Plutarch
was his delight. Dr. Holmes interested himself in making a
list of the persons most often referred to by Mr. Emerson,
and found that after Shakspeare, Napoleon, and Plato came
Plutarch, and there were seventy references to him.

Page 62, note 1. A version of this story is the Induction
of *The Taming of the Shrew.*

Page 64, note 1. This paragraph furnishes two instances
of the nicety of Mr. Emerson's choice of words in closest
accordance with their derivation to make clear his thought.
His doctrine, — that there was one great source of all special
manifestation of spirit, which was from the beginning [*ab*

origine — "In the Beginning was the Word"] ; that this spirit was self-renewed in each one who would listen, by teachings from within [in-tuitions], and could go out from the receiver to help the world [tuitions], — made clearer by exactly fitting words, shows the real Self on which men shall rely.

Page 65, note 1. He went alone to the woods to *listen.* Perhaps his early friends among the Quakers at New Bedford had confirmed this tendency in him to wait until the Spirit spoke. He felt himself the mere ambassador charged to faithfully deliver the message committed to him. This must be its own evidence and it was not for him to argue about it.

Page 67, note 1. Compare the seventh stanza of "The Sphinx."

Page 69, note 1. Though Mr. Emerson's is by no means a Latin style, the training of his youth shows often in the use of words of Latin origin, not as adjectives but as present participles; as "man, agent and patient," and here "power not confident but agent."

Page 71, note 1.

> Hold of the Maker, not the Made ;
> Sit with the Cause, or grim or glad.
> "Fragments on The Poet," *Poems,* Appendix.

Page 72, note 1. "Respect the child, respect him to the end, but also respect yourself. Be the companion of his thought, the friend of his friendship, the lover of his virtue, — but no kinsman of his sin. Let him find you so true to yourself that you are the irreconcilable hater of his vice and the imperturbable slighter of his trifling." — "Education," *Lectures and Biographical Sketches.*

Page 74, note 1. After the somewhat startling and radical

counsels of the last paragraph, it is well that some mitigation of their drastic quality should follow. Dr. Holmes does well in calling attention to what follows to show how Mr. Emerson "guarded his proclamation of self-reliance as the guide of mankind."

Page 76, note 1. In the first half of the nineteenth century, many a New England boy thus acquired experience and laid the foundations of his fortune, pecuniary or intellectual. Mr. Alcott went on foot with his pack more than once through Virginia and the Carolinas, furnishing Connecticut wares or teaching, at the option of the owners of the plantations.

Page 78, note 1. While studying divinity, Mr. Emerson one day, as he worked in his uncle's hayfield beside a Methodist farm-hand, fell into talk with him. This man maintained that men are always praying, and that all prayers are answered. This statement interested Mr. Emerson, and on this theme he wrote his first sermon, adding for a third point that it behooves men to well consider these acted prayers. After his "approbation to preach," he read this sermon in the pulpit of his kind uncle, Rev. Mr. Samuel Ripley, of Waltham, and the next day a stranger addressed him in the stage-coach, saying, "Young man, you'll never preach a better sermon than that."

A short paper, "Prayers," originally printed in the *Dial*, is included in the volume *Natural History of Intellect.*

Page 80, note 1.

>The inevitable morning
>Finds them who in cellars be.
>>"The World-Soul," *Poems.*

Page 82, note 1. Mr. Emerson, when he first went abroad in 1833, was sick and sad, with prospects all unsettled,

and he was little engaged by the novelty and beauty of the
sights which met his eye when, after a short stay in Malta, he
landed at Naples. This paragraph reflects the tone of his
journals, and in them he wrote verses recording his feeling
at Naples and at Rome. Both of these are printed in the
Appendix to the *Poems*.

But his call to his appointed work made him through life a
bad visitor, and also traveller, except in the line of his duty,
when his lines in " Woodnotes " were true for him : —

> Go where he will, the wise man is at home, . . .
> Where his clear spirit leads him, there 's his road,
> By God's own light illumined and foreshowed.

Page 83, note 1. Most of the paragraph up to this point
was from the entry in the Journal in 1832, mentioned in the
introduction to this essay, when the thought of writing on
this theme first came to him.

Page 85, note 1. The checks in development, later much
emphasized by the Evolutionists, seem to have been early
apprehended by him.

Page 88, note 1. This saying of Ali is rendered in the last
lines of the second motto of " Compensation."

COMPENSATION

When in 1865 Mr. Emerson met by invitation many of
the ladies who, as girls, had attended the finishing school for
young ladies kept in Boston by his brother William and himself, when hardly more than boys, he told them that he felt
certain regrets with regard to his teaching. " I was at that
very time already writing every night in my chamber my first

thoughts on morals and the beautiful laws of Compensation and of individual genius, which to observe and illustrate have given sweetness to my life. I am afraid no hint of this ever came into the school, where we clung to the safe and cold details of languages, geography, arithmetic and chemistry. Now I believe that each should serve the other by his or her strength, not by their weakness, and that if I could have had one hour of deep thought at that time, I could have engaged you in thoughts that would have given reality, depth and joy to the school, and raised all these details to the highest pleasure and nobleness."

During the days of his ministry, he wrote thus in his Journal: —

CHARDON ST., JUNE 29, 1831.

Is not the law of Compensation perfect ? It holds, as far as we can see, different gifts to different individuals, but with a mortgage of responsibility on every one. " The gods sell all things." — Well, old man, hast got no farther ? Why, this was taught thee months and years ago. It was writ on the autumn leaves at Roxbury in keep-school days — it sounded in the blind man's ear at Cambridge.[1] And all the joy and all the sorrow since have added nothing to thy wooden book. I can't help it. Heraclitus, grown old, complains that all resolved itself into identity. . . . And I have nothing charactered in my brain that outlives this word Compensation.

Three years later, in 1834, he wrote the verses entitled " Compensation " which are printed in the *Poems*.

It does not appear that the essay " Compensation," as it stands, was ever delivered as a lecture. No doubt portions

[1] Referring to a time when trouble with the eyes deprived him for a time of their use.

of it appeared in many sermons, and several pages of it came from the lecture " Duty " in the course on " Human Life," given in 1838–39.

In the first motto the image of " The lonely Earth amid the balls " is one among many instances of the charm which astronomical phenomena had for Mr. Emerson. Evidences of his reading treatises on the heavenly bodies, and of walks for the purpose of gazing on them, occur frequently in journals and writings.

Page 93, note 1. Mr. Emerson, having left the pulpit, was striving the harder to awaken real religion among those to whom he spoke, to make them feel, not only on Sundays, but through the week, day and night, a beautiful, present Deity working surely through law.

Page 94, note 1. Dr. Holmes ekes out the forlorn view of the preacher whose representations of the Christian's aims and spirit had stirred Mr. Emerson to write this discourse, by the statement of the unhappy John Bunyan : —

> A Christian man is never long at ease;
> When one fright 's gone, another doth him seize.

Page 96, note 1. This is a keynote of many of the essays.
" The soul is superior to its knowledge, wiser than its works." — *The Over-Soul.* " Heroism is an obedience to a secret impulse of an individual's character."— *Heroism.*

> Himself from God he could not free ;
> He builded better than he knew.
> > " The Problem," *Poems.*

Page 96, note 2. " In this and the following chapter."

Compensation is not so obviously treated of in "Spiritual Laws" as might be expected from this expression. Yet the doctrine is there in "A man passes for what he is worth," and other statements of the great laws of balance and return.

Page 97, note 1. Every scientific fact and law had its charm for Mr. Emerson, and he sought its spiritual correspondent. Again and again he uses polarity as a parable. It may be found in the third stanza of "The Sphinx" and in "Merlin."

The reconciliation in the very definition of Polarity [1] of the apparently contradictory notions held by the early philosophers and priests, viz., of the One, and of the Duality that is more obvious in the world, delighted him.

Page 99, note 1. One day Mr. Emerson saw the little child of a neighbor, whom he had always thought to be a sulky churl, playing with a pretty painted cart. He asked the child who made it. "My Papa," answered he, and this fortified Mr. Emerson in the optimism from which he had temporarily lapsed.

Page 101, note 1.

> *or better yet,*
> *as well, "upon a Drop*
> *Dew", of which this*
> *poor paraphrase...*

No ray is dimmed, no atom worn,
My oldest force is good as new,
And the fresh rose on yonder thorn
Gives back the bending heavens in dew.
                    "Song of Nature," *Poems.*

[1] "Polarity (Physics). A term used to designate opposite or dissimilar properties or powers simultaneously developed by a common cause in opposite or contrasted parts, as in the extremities of a magnet, or in the sides of a polarized ray of light, situated respectively in the plane of polarization and the plane perpendicular to it." — *Worcester's Dictionary.*

Page 102, note 1. A fragment from a lost play of Sophocles.

Page 103, note 1. In the poem " Voluntaries," after the
national crime of the long tolerance by our people of African
slavery has been told, these lines follow: —

> Destiny sat by, and said,
> " Pang for pang your seed shall pay,
> Hide in false peace your coward head,
> I bring round the harvest day."

And this Nemesis, denied the name of Fate, because justice
is a beneficent force, appears as " Worship " in the poem
which serves as motto to the essay so named.

Page 105, note 1.

> Naturam expellas furca, tamen usque recurret,
> Et mala perrumpet furtim fastidia victrix.
>   Horace, *Epistles*, i. 10.

Page 106, note 1.   *Confessions* of St. Augustine, Book I.
Page 106, note 2.   From the *Prometheus* of Æschylus.
Page 108, note 1.   The same thought that is more fully
expressed in the extract from the letter to Sterling given in the
Introduction to the notes on the essays of this volume. It also
appears in " The Problem."

Page 110, note 1. Mr. Emerson, after his return from
Europe in 1833, preached often at New Bedford, and later
gave a course of lectures at Nantucket, remaining for some time
on the island. Those were the great days of the whaling industry of both those towns, and Mr. Emerson used to repeat
the anecdotes of peril and accident in hunting the monster
which had been told him by his hosts.

Page 112, note 1. Herodotus tells that Fortune had so favored Polycrates, the tyrant of Samos, that his friend Amasis, king of Egypt, sent him word that to ward off the fate sure to follow unbroken prosperity, he ought to sacrifice whatever he valued most. Struck by this counsel, Polycrates cast into the sea his emerald ring. Next day it returned to him in the stomach of a fish sent as a present. Amasis at once broke off the alliance, foreseeing in this event the impending doom of Polycrates. Revolt of his subjects, and civil and foreign wars followed, and not long after the tyrant was lured out of his domain by the satrap of Sardis and crucified.

Page 113, note 1. This maxim was a household word with Mr. Emerson. He was loath to place himself under obligation. He wrote: —

> Wilt thou seal up the avenues of ill ?
> Pay every debt as if God wrote the bill.

See also in the *Poems,* the "Translation from Ibn Jemin."

Page 115, note 1. These thoughts find expression in the arguments used by educators in the last few years to show the mental and moral advantage of manual training schools.

Page 116, note 1. Wordsworth's *Sonnets to Liberty,* "September, 1802."

Page 117, note 1. This passage, expanded from an entry made in Mr. Emerson's Journal of Oct. 18, 1832, was distinctly personal in its origin, and shows his habitual humility and courage. It continues: "The stammering tongue and awkward and formal manners which hinder your success in social circles keep you true to the mark which is your own — to that particular power which God has given you for your own and others' benefit."

Page 118, note 1. This and the next two sentences are

the entry made by Mr. Emerson in his Journal, Sept. 29, 1838, two months after he had delivered his earnest message to the young divines on the eve of their entry into the ministry, and the ensuing disclaimers and attacks on his address had been made by professors and clergymen, vigorously answered by Mr. George Ripley, Mr. Brownson, Professor Parsons, and Rev. James Freeman Clarke.

Page 119, note 1.

> If the Law should thee forget,
> More enamoured serve it yet ;
> Though it hate thee, suffer long ;
> Put the Spirit in the wrong.
>> "The Poet," *Poems*, Appendix.

Page 120, note 1. This was well said in Boston, where, within a few years, Mr. Garrison, for attempting to address an anti-slavery meeting, had been hustled up State Street with a rope around his body, by the solid men of business and of the professions ; and the mayor, to save his life, had him committed to the jail as a " disturber of the peace." His statue stands now at the head of the handsomest avenue in Boston.

Page 121, note 1. The translation of " Being " in the next word into its pleasing Latin form, and immediately making it the same as God, is a striking and condensed statement of the creed Each in All, the Universal Mind.

Page 123, note 1. This passage, as written in the Journal, March 19, 1839, is perhaps more fresh and vigorous: —

" Such is my confidence in the compensations of nature, that I no longer wish to find silver dollars in the road, nor to have the best of the bargain in my dealings with people, nor that my property should be increased, knowing that all such

II

gains are apparent and not real ; for they pay their sure tax. But the perception that it is not desirable to find the dollar I enjoy without any alloy. This is an abiding good : this is so much accession of Godhead.''

The description of the growth and liberation of the ideal man, which follows, written forty years before Mr. Emerson's death, is strangely autobiographical.

Page 125, note 1. Compare the last stanza of '' Give All to Love,'' *Poems.*

SPIRITUAL LAWS

This essay does not appear to have been given in its present form as a lecture; it may have been so used in Concord or some neighboring town just before the *Essays* were published, but was not in the Boston courses. Certain passages of the essay, however, are found in the lectures '' Religion '' and '' Manners '' in the course on '' The Philosophy of History '' (1836–37), in '' Being and Seeming '' in the course on '' Human Culture '' (1837–38), and in '' School '' and '' Duty '' in the course on '' Human Life '' (1838–39).

There was no motto to '' Spiritual Laws '' in the first edition.

The verses that he placed before the new edition in 1847 show the fear which he felt, especially at that period, of weakening the poetic thought by what, in the letter to Sterling which has been already quoted, he calls '' meddling ambitiously.'' Here, in twelve strong lines presenting the great Laws of the Universal Mind, Self-Reliance, Compensation, and Good out of Evil, he followed the counsel to the bard that he puts in the lips of Merlin in his poem: —

Great is the art,
Great be the manners of the bard.
He shall not his brain encumber
With the coil of rhythm and number;
But, leaving rule and pale forethought,
He shall aye climb
For his rhyme.
" Pass in, pass in," the angels say,
" In to the upper doors,
Nor count compartments of the floors,   .
But mount to paradise
By the stairway of surprise."

Page 131, note 1. In the year of the publication of this essay, his honored friend, the Rev. Doctor Ripley, the minister of Concord for more than half a century, died. He had married the widow of William Emerson, his predecessor, a chaplain in the army at Ticonderoga. Dr. Ripley had been a true friend to his wife's grandchildren. Mr. Emerson tells in his Journal of his visit to the Old Manse at the time of his death : —

" His body is a handsome and noble spectacle. My mother was moved just now to call it ' the beauty of the dead.' He looks like a sachem fallen in the forest, or rather ' like a warrior taking his rest with his martial cloak around him.' I carried Waldo to see him and he testified neither repulsion nor surprise, but only the quietest curiosity. He was ninety years old. . . . Yet this face has the tension and resolution of vigorous manhood. . . . A man is but a little thing in the midst of these great objects of nature, . . . yet a man by moral quality may abolish all thoughts of magnitude, and in his manners equal the majesty of the world."

Page 131, note 2. This passage calls to mind the " morning thought," the " Matutina Cognitio " of St. Augustine. See Notes to *Nature* (" Prospects ").

Page 132, note 1. He would have liked the answer which William Morris gave.to one who asked if he were subject to the extreme despondency which so often accompanies the highly poetic temperament. " I dare say I am," said he, " but I 've never had the time to think of it, so I really can't say."

Page 132, note 2. From Wordsworth's Sonnet XII. in *Poems dedicated to National Independence,* part ii.

Page 133, note 1. The relative value of his imposed and his chosen studies came up often in Mr. Emerson's mind to the advantage of the latter. Always an eager and delighted reader of the books (or a few passages in books) that he knew as " written for him," he found little in the text-books at school or college, besides the classics, that interested him. In " Heroism " he tells of the power for good of a romance " over a boy who grasps the forbidden book under the bench at school; our delight in the hero is the main fact to our purpose. . . . If we dilate in beholding the Greek energy, the Roman pride, it is that we are already domesticating the same sentiment."

Page 134, note 1. Purified mankind as transmitters of divine thought are described in the poetical note-books as —

Pipes through which the breath of God doth blow
A universal music.

Page 135, note 1. The image of Mother Nature calming her flustered little son is repeated, still with a little humor, in the poem " Experience," which serves as motto to the essay of that name in *Essays, Second Series.*

Page 138, note 1. Pyrrho of Elis (360–270 B. C.), a

Greek painter, poet and philosopher, who joined the expedition of Alexander to conquer the East, but returned to Elis and became a priest. "He held that the only condition worthy of a philosopher was that of suspended judgment. Virtuous imperturbability was the highest aim of life, but truth was unattainable."—Appleton's *Encyclopædia*.

Page 140, note 1. During his stay in New Bedford, in 1834, while officiating for his friend the Rev. Dr. Dewey, Mr. Emerson heard the doctrine of Obedience as adopted by the Friends,—renunciation of all will, and awaiting the divine motion in the breast.

Journal. "The sublime religion of Miss Rotch yesterday. She was very much disciplined, she said, in the years of Quaker dissensions, and driven inward, drawn home to find an anchor, until she learned to have no choice, to acquiesce without understanding the reason when she found an obstruction to any particular course of acting. She objected to having this spiritual direction called an impression, or an intimation, or an oracle. It was none of them. It was so simple it could hardly be spoken of."

This statement of faith interested him, but he had already learned to yield himself to the divine stream sweeping away the distinctions of forms.

Page 141, note 1. The boast of Glendower to Hotspur, *Henry IV.*, Part I., Act III., Scene i.

Page 142, note 1. Mr. Emerson thus celebrates the dignity of the farmer's work:—

> He planted where the deluge ploughed,
> His hired hands were wind and cloud;
> His eye detects the Gods concealed
> In the hummocks of the field.

> "Fragments," *Poems*, Appendix.

Page 143, note 1. This image was suggested by a passage in Scott's *Old Mortality* which Mr. Emerson often repeated with something of the pleasure it had given him in his boyhood. The fierce fanatic, Balfour of Burley, speaks of the possibility of influencing some opponents of the Covenanters by prospects of worldly gain, but thus tells in his wrath of the incorruptibility of the young nobleman who opposes them: " But Lord Evandale is a malignant of heart like flint and brow like adamant; the goods of this world fall on him like the leaves on the frost-bound earth, and unmoved he will see them whirled off by the first wind. The heathen virtues of such as he are more dangerous to us than the sordid cupidity of those who . . . may be compelled to work in the vineyard, were it but to earn the wages of sin."

Page 147, note 1.

Earth fills her lap with pleasures of her own.

Wordsworth, *Intimations of Immortality.*

Page 148, note 1. In the essay " Demonology," in *Lectures and Biographical Sketches,* dreams are treated of. See also the quatrain " Memory " in the *Poems.*

Page 151, note 1. When somewhat importunately urged to be presented to a person for whom he felt no affinity, Mr. Emerson said, " Whom God hath put asunder, let no man put together."

Page 153, note 1. It was the sentence more than the paragraph in the essay that he valued, hence he strove to make every syllable tell.

Page 156, note 1. This was the remark of his honored friend, Samuel Hoar, Esq. See the notice of him in *Lectures and Biographical Sketches,* and the sonnet by Mr. F. B. Sanborn prefixed to it. Also Mr. Emerson's quatrain " S. H." in *Poems.*

Page 164, note 1.

> Jack was embarrassed, — never hero more,
> And, as he knew not what to say, he swore.

> > Byron's *Island*, Canto III., 5.

It was, however, Jack Skyscrape and not Ben Bunting.

Page 165, note 1. Another name for the British queen Boadicea. Mr. Emerson valued certain passages in Beaumont and Fletcher's "Tragedy of Bonduca," especially the speeches of Caratach in the first scene.

Page 166, note 1. Dr. Holmes in his Life of Emerson quotes the passage, and thus comments: "This is not any the worse for being the flowering out of a poetical bud of George Herbert's." He alludes to "The Elixer," beginning —

> Teach me, my God and King,
> In all things thee to see ;

and especially to the verse —

> A servant with this clause
> Makes drudgerie divine ;
> Who sweeps a room as for thy laws,
> Makes that and th' action fine.

LOVE

This essay is almost identical with the fourth lecture in the course on "Human Life," given in Boston by Mr. Emerson in the winter of 1838–39. He made a few verbal changes and unimportant omissions in the later editions from the earlier form. Because the love that Emerson treats of here is not considered from the point of view of young lovers alone, but as life-long, and unfolding to "a love which knows not sex, nor

person, nor partiality, but which seeks virtue and wisdom everywhere," his poem " Eros " might have served for its motto:—

> The sense of the world is short, —
> Long and various the report, —
> To love and be beloved ;
> Men and gods have not outlearned it;
> And, how oft soe'er they 've turned it,
> Not to be improved.

In a letter written to a friend in the year of the publication
of this essay, this passage occurs : —

" The same Goodness in which we believe, or rather which
alway believes on itself, as soon as we cease to consider duties
and consider persons, becomes Love, imperious Love, that
great Prophet and Poet, that Comforter, that Omnipotency
in the heart. Its eye falls on some mortal form, but it rests
not a moment there ; but, as every leaf represents to us all
vegetable nature, so Love looks through that spotted, blighted
form to the vast spiritual element of which it was created and
which it represents. We demand of those we love that they
shall be excellent in countenance, in speech, in behavior, in
power, in will. They are not so ; we are grieved, but we
were in the right to ask it. If they do not share the Deity
that dictated to our thought this immense wish, they will
quickly pass away, but the demand will not die, but will go
on accumulating as the supply accumulates, and the virtues of
the soul in the remotest ages will only begin to fulfil the first
craving of our poor heart."

Page 167, note 1. In a note-book Mr. Emerson gives
the quotation from the Koran thus : —

" I was as a treasure concealed: then I loved that I might
be known."

And below it his own rendering —
> I was as a gem concealed;
> I burned with love and was revealed.

And then the second line altered thus : —
> Me my burning love revealed.

Page 171, note 1. Although Mr. Emerson did not allow his mind to revert, looking ever to the brightness before, yet when, of a sudden, a memory came over him of his young wife, his brothers, his mother, gone from this life, he would, for the moment, start and moan, wrung by "infinite compunctions," due to his own tenderness and humble rating of himself, not thinking how they had prized him.

Page 172, note 1. Once a young school-teacher was invited to tea at his house. He was, as ever, courteous and kind, but after she had gone, he mentioned that, perhaps a dozen years before, he had found on the way to Walden a childish love-letter, open and weather-stained, addressed to her, and, though he did not know the schoolgirl, he had remembered her name and the little romance.

Page 175, note 1. From the *Epithalamium* of John Donne.

Page 176, note 1. This was a favorite line of Mr. Emerson's, perhaps written by one of his friends; but I have never been able to find whence it came.

Page 177, note 1. From *A Nice Valour*, by John Fletcher, III., 3.

Page 177, note 2.
> He looketh seldom in their face,
> His eyes explore the ground, —
> The green grass is a looking-glass
> Whereon their traits are found.
>> "Manners," *Poems.*

Page 179, note 1. " 'The end of all liberal training should be the love of beauty'' — Socrates having previously described proper education as a training in virtue. (Plato's *Republic*, Book III.)

Page 181, note 1. This passage recalls the one from Plutarch, already quoted, to the effect that the Sun is the cause why all men are ignorant of Apollo, by sense withdrawing the mind from that which is to that which seems.

Professor Wright, of Harvard University, says of this paragraph of Mr. Emerson's, " It is distinctly Platonic, and seems to be an echo of the *Phædrus*, where the entombment of the soul is referred to, and the necessity that it must see true being before it can take human form is stated. The thought that it is ' stupefied by the light of the natural sun and unable to see any other object but those of this world, which are but shadows of real things,' is perhaps supported by the opening of the seventh book of the *Republic*, where appears the famous ' image of the cave.' "

Page 182, note 1. I think that the word " base'' is used in its primary sense, to signify the humble foundation on the earth.

> Thou shalt not scale Love's height divine
> By burrowing at its earthly base ;
> Nor call the priceless treasure thine
> Who car'st but to affront the case.
> " The Angel in the House,'' Coventry Patmore.

Page 184, note 1. From Donne's " Elegy on Mistress Drury.''

Page 185, note 1. Compare Emerson's early poem, "Thine Eyes Still Shined.''

Page 186, note 1. From Abraham Cowley's " Resolved

to be Beloved,'' in *The Mistress; or, Several Copies of Love Letters.*

FRIENDSHIP

This essay was not given as a lecture under this title and as a whole in any of the Boston courses, although very probably it served in that capacity in some of the Lyceums. As is shown in Mr. Cabot's Memoir (Appendix F), portions of it were taken from the lecture on '' Society,'' in the course on '' The Philosophy of History '' (1836–37), and others from '' The Heart '' in the course on '' Human Culture,'' given in Boston the following year. Several paragraphs come from ''Private Life,'' in the course on '' The Present Age '' (1839–40).

Friendship, as Mr. Emerson said in the essay, seemed '' too good to be believed,'' and he earnestly desired it, yet so high was his standard that he felt that he had not his share of this blessing and cast the blame on himself.

> Friends to me are frozen wine ;
> I wait the sun on them should shine.

He had many, in the usual sense of the word, and their number increased with the years ; many also unknown to him ; but he had few close friends in all his life. This lack he recognized as temperamental and deplored. But here too was '' good out of evil '' for him. At a little distance he could take the greatest pleasure in his friends, could see them in their proper atmosphere. The treatment that he asked for himself he gave in some tempered degree to them : —

> You shall not love me for what daily spends ;
> You shall not know me in the crowded street,

Where I, as others, follow petty ends ;
Nor when in fair saloons we chance to meet.
Nor when I 'm jaded, sick, anxious or mean.
But love me then and only, when you know
Me for the channel of the rivers of God
From deep, ideal, fontal heavens that flow.

In practice he was loyal and serviceable to his friends, yet preferred to see them sparingly, to find in them what they were meant to be, and " take each by his best handle."

In writing to one of his nearest friends through life, a gentleman of great charm and culture, Mr. Emerson said, probably about the new essay on " Love " or on " Friendship," a year before its publication : —

" I send you . . . [a paper] of last winter's composition, a piece which I wrote with good heart, and trust you may find some sparks still alive in the cinders. The argument were fitter for rhyme, but that comes only by the special favor of the skies. . . . Certainly we discover our friends by the very highest tokens, and these not describable, often not even intelligible, but not the less sure to that augury which is within the intellect, and therefore higher. This is to me the most attractive of all topics, and, I doubt not, whenever I get your full confession of faith, we shall be at one on the matter. Because the subject is so high and sacred, we cannot walk straight up to it; we must saunter if we would find the secret. Nature's roads are not turnpikes, but circles, and the instincts are the only sure guides." [1]

While lecturing in Philadelphia, in January, 1843, he wrote to the same friend as follows : —

" I must thank the Quaker City, however, for a new conviction, that this whim called friendship was the brightest

[1] *Letters from Ralph Waldo Emerson to a Friend.* Houghton, Mifflin & Co., 1899.

thought in what Eden or Olympus it first occurred. I think the two first friends must have been travellers. — I doubt you think my practice of the *finest art* to be bad enough, but friendship does not ever seem to me quite real in the world, but always prophetic; and if I wrote on the Immortality of the Soul, this would be my first topic. Yet is nothing more right than that men should think to address each other with truth and the highest poetry at certain moments, far as their ordinary intercourse is therefrom and buried in trifles. I will try if a man is a man. I will know if he feels that star as I feel it : among trees, does he know them and they him ? Is he at the same time both flowing and fixed ? Does he feel that Nature proceeds from him, yet can he carry himself as if he were the meanest particle ? All and nothing ? These things I would know of him, yet without catechism : he shall tell me them in all manner of unexpected ways, in his behavior and in his repose.''

Page 191, note 1. Journal, 1838. " At church I saw that beautiful child —— and my fine, natural, manly neighbor, who bore the bread and wine to the communicants with so clear an eye and excellent face and manners.

   .   .   .   .

" The softness and peace, the benignant humanity that hovers over our assembly when it sits down at the morning service in church.''

Page 192, note 1.

      The tongue is prone to lose the way ;
      Not so the pen, for in a letter
      We have not better things to say,
      But surely say them better.
                " Fragments on Life,'' *Poems.*

Page 194, note 1. The high sidewalk under the warm sandy southern slope of hills opposite Mr. Emerson's house, on the " Great Road " to Boston, has a different climate from the rest of Concord, and so used to be a favorite walk in the cold half of the year. Mr. Alcott and Mr. Hawthorne lived on this road, and it was the venerable Squire Hoar's favorite walk. Not only these friends, but the farmers and laborers, the schoolgirls and the schoolboys would have been surprised if they had known with what respectful or admiring eyes Mr. Emerson looked on them from his study windows, and had heard his comments on them.

Page 195, note 1. Milton, *Comus.*

Page 196, note 1. Compare with this paragraph " The Park " in the *Poems.*

Page 197, note 1. Journal, 1833. " My entire success, such as it is, is composed wholly of particular failures."

Page 197, note 2.

> When half-gods go
> The gods arrive.
>> " Give All to Love," *Poems.*

Page 199, note 1.

> If love his moment overstay,
> Hatred's swift repulsions play.
>> " The Visit," *Poems.*

Page 200, note 1. Shakspeare, *Sonnet xxv.*

Page 202, note 1. In his first letter to John Sterling, May 29, 1840, a few months before the publication of this essay, Mr. Emerson wrote : " I am a worshipper of Friendship, and cannot find any other good equal to it. As soon as any man pronounces the words which approve him fit for that great office, I make no haste : he is holy; let me be holy also;

our relations are eternal; why should we count days and weeks? I had this feeling in reading your paper on Carlyle, in which I admired the rare behavior, with far less heed the things said; these were opinions, but the tone was the man."[1]

Page 203, note 1. The allusion is to Jones Very, of Salem, a mystic and ascetic, of whom an interesting account is given in Mr. Cabot's *Memoir of Emerson*, vol. i., chapter x., and a fuller one by Mr. W. P. Andrews, in his introduction to *Essays and Poems by Jones Very*. In a letter to Miss Margaret Fuller, written in November, 1838, Mr. Emerson wrote: "Very has been here lately and stayed a few days, confounding us all with the question whether he was insane. At first sight and speech you would certainly pronounce him so. Talk with him a few hours, and you will think all insane but he. Monomania or monosania, he is a very remarkable person; and though his mind is not in a natural, and probably not in a permanent state, he is a treasure of a companion, and I had with him most memorable conversations."

He records that Very said to him : " I always felt, when I heard you read or speak your writings, that you saw the truth better than others, yet I felt that your spirit was not quite right. It was as if a vein of colder air blew across me."

Page 204, note 1. This quotation is from Montaigne, Book I., chapter xxxix., "A Consideration upon Cicero."

Page 207, note 1. In converse with Nature he felt that the same rule held. "Nature says to man, 'One to one, my dear.'"— *Journal.*

Page 208, note 1. Compare with this paragraph his poem "Étienne de la Boéce."

Page 209, note 1. From the recent notice of the death of a business man of integrity in Chicago, who was also a lover

---

[1] *Correspondence of Sterling and Emerson.*

of good books and a loyal friend of Mr. Emerson, I copy this anecdote showing Mr. Emerson's conscience, and that of his friend also, in the matter of rashly endeavoring to come near to those whom we admire by letters of introduction. "Mr. —— wanted to know Mr. Longfellow and desired Mr. Emerson to introduce him. The cautious philosopher replied that he would do so if his young friend could truthfully say that he stood in such relation to the genius of the poet as made it fitting. This the youth decided that he could not do. There seems to me something charming in Mr. Emerson's reliance on the integral delicacy of the boy to guard him against a possible false position."

Page 212, note 1. Here followed in the first edition these two sentences : " The only money of God is God. He pays never with anything less or anything else."

Page 213, note 1. See the poem " Rubies."

Page 214, note 1. This paragraph closes in the first edition with the sentence, " It is the property of the divine to be reproductive."

Page 215, note 1. Carrying out the comparison of friends and books in the chapter " Nominalist and Realist " in the second series of *Essays,* Mr. Emerson writes: " I find most pleasure in reading a book in a manner least flattering to the author. . . . I read for the lustres, as if one should use a fine picture in a chromatic experiment for its rich colors."

Page 216, note 1. " The astronomers are very eager to know whether the moon has an atmosphere ; I am only concerned that every man have one. I observe however that it takes two to make an atmosphere. I am acquainted with persons who go attended with this ambient cloud."— " Aristocracy," *Lectures and Biographical Sketches.*

Page 217, note 1. This trait may be found in all Mr.

Emerson's letters to his friends, especially those to Carlyle, wherein all his friend's petulances and faults are ignored.

PRUDENCE

The greater part of this essay was probably given as a lecture in Boston, the seventh in the course on "Human Culture" in the winter of 1837–38. Mr. Emerson was by education and temperament prudent, but in no petty way. Knowing his want of practical faculty, and the idea of debt or of dependence on others being abhorrent to him, he strove to practise honorable economies. But every humblest fact was valuable to him as a symbol, and he loved to detect the workings of the great laws in small things. Recalling in one of his note-books two or three of his experiences as a young Boston minister, he wrote, "One day when I read a sermon of which the text might have been ' Don't mind trifles,' old William Little said to me at the door that, ' if he were to make the sermon, he should have taken the other side.' "

In the chapter on "Swedenborg" in *Representative Men*, he said, "Malpighi, following the high doctrines of Hippocrates, Leucippus and Lucretius, had given emphasis to the dogma that nature works in leasts, — ' tota in minimis existat natura.' " So accepting Plato's word that the macrocosm may be known by the microcosm, in spite of poetic traditions, yet, as a poet, and still young, he found pleasure in a

> Theme no poet gladly sung,
> Fair to old and foul to young,—

as he calls it in the motto which he wrote for the second edi-

II

tion. An example of the fitness and seeming originality of his English, by steadily holding its classic foundations in mind, occurs in the diminutive in the fourth line, where the little arts of which great arts are built find due recognition.

Page 221, note 1. The other Garden is described in his poem of that name. Although in the early years of his house-keeping, for economy's sake and health's, he hoed and weeded, he soon found that a higher prudence required his spending the time hitherto given to the home garden in that by Walden's shores, whence he brought home better and more lasting fruit.

Page 221, note 2. This is a good illustration of the pleasure Mr. Emerson took in "Aspects"; in coming to firm, homely ground after a high flight.

Page 222, note 1. The influence of his reading of the old philosophers, and also of Swedenborg, shows in this paragraph.

Mr. Emerson loved to look for what his friend Whittier called —

The unsung beauty hid life's common things below.

Page 223, note 1. "Nature is too thin a screen; the glory of the one breaks in everywhere." — "The Preacher," *Lectures and Biographical Sketches.*

Page 223, note 2. A less complimentary estimate of proverbs than that given in the essay on "Compensation." It recalls Stevenson's essay "Crabbed Age and Youth" in *Virginibus Puerisque,* in which, among other strictures on cowardly and prudential proverbs, he says that, according to them, "never to forget your umbrella through a long life would seem to be a higher and wiser flight of achievement than to go smiling to the stake; and so long as you are a bit of a coward, and inflexible in money matters, you fulfil the whole duty of man."

Page 226, note 1. The necessary interruptions of his study and writing that befell Mr. Emerson as a householder he bore with philosophy. He never allowed himself to complain of mischances in the house or abroad, unless later to serve up his misfortune in an amusing manner. Of one thing he was sure, — that there was some modest share of benefit in it, and that was his business to find.

Page 226, note 2. The austere benefits which the North gives to her children are celebrated in the *Poems* in the lesson which the hardy Titmouse gives to the wanderer in the woods, in "Voluntaries," a war poem, and in the lines in "May-Day:" —

> Titan-born, to hardy natures
> Cold is genial and dear.
> As Southern wrath to Northern right
> Is but straw to anthracite ;
> As in the day of sacrifice,
> When heroes piled the pyre,
> The dismal Massachusetts ice
> Burned more than others' fire,
> So Spring guards with surface cold
> The garnered heat of ages old.

Of course the constant consideration of the effect of Slavery and Free Labor on our people before the Civil War emphasized these distinctions.

Page 230, note 1. Amidst the stream of visionaries flowing by him, often without visible means of support, it was important that some one should stand firm, with feet planted on the ground.

Page 231, note 1. Compare his poem " Limits," *Poems,* Appendix.

Page 232, note 1. Mr. Emerson could never hear with patience of the divorce of Morals from Intellect. There was always abatement of his enjoyment of Goethe because of his shortcomings in morals, and hence in insight.

Page 233, note 1. In scattered verses on " The Poet " or " The Discontented Poet," written in the same years with these *Essays,* and only gathered after Mr. Emerson's death in the Appendix to the *Poems,* he describes these floods and ebbs in the passage beginning —

> Ah! happy if a sun or star
> Could chain the wheel of Fortune's car.

Page 235, note 1. Again the ancient doctrine of " The Flowing," shown in the hurrying life of the Yankee of the nineteenth century.

Page 237, note 1. " In prœliis oculi primi vincuntur " (Tacitus); a quotation often used by Mr. Emerson, but without giving the source.

Page 239, note 1. " He who taketh the sword shall perish by the sword " was a rule that Mr. Emerson held to with regard to argument, whether as a weapon offensive or defensive. His feeling on this subject is shown in his second letter to his friend, Rev. Henry Ware, after the Divinity School Address, printed by Mr. Cabot in his *Memoir of Emerson,* vol. ii., p. 689.

Page 239, note 2. By adhering to this simple rule and faith in " The Universal Mind," Mr. Emerson, as Dr. Holmes said, " could go anywhere and find willing listeners among those farthest in their belief from the views he held. · Such was his simplicity of speech and manner, such his transparent sincerity, that it was next to impossible to quarrel with the gentle image-breaker." Suggesting George Herbert's teaching in his "Church Porch:"—

> Scorn no man's love, though of a mean degree;
> (Love is a present for a mightie king.)
> Much lesse make any one thine enemie.
> As gunnes destroy, so may a little sling.

HEROISM

This essay is probably the lecture of that name essentially as delivered in the course on "Human Culture" in Boston, in the winter of 1837–38.

The homage which Mr. Emerson felt bound to render to the lowly virtues of Prudence, after dealing with "the fine lyric words of Love and Friendship," made an interesting contrast for his hearers, the more effective by his leading them up to the heights of Heroism in the succeeding lecture.

In a lecture called "The Present Age," delivered in the following year, this expression occurs, — his recognition of the awakening of those days to the need of individual, social, and political reform: — "Religion does not seem now to tend to a *cultus*, but to a heroic life. He who would undertake it is to front a corrupt society and speak rude truth, and he must be ready to meet collision and suffering."

The saying of Mahomet alone served for motto in the first edition.

Page 245, note 1. In this list of plays, all from Beaumont and Fletcher, Mr. Emerson evidently trusted to his memory, and gave to one the name from a leading character. There is no play by the name of "Sophocles," but the extract given is from

a piece called " Four Plays in One," the special play being
" The Triumph of Honor." This is founded on a story of
Boccaccio's in the *Decameron*, the tenth day and the fifth
novel.

Page 247, note 1. Burley's description of the incorruptibility of the young nobleman in *Old Mortality*, chapter xlii.,
— a passage often repeated by Mr. Emerson to his children.

Page 248, note 1. From youth to age he took delight in
Plutarch, the *Lives* and the *Morals*. This passage from Mr.
Emerson's Introduction to Professor William Watson Good-
win's translations of the *Morals* (printed also in *Lectures
and Biographical Sketches*) shows what attracted him to Plutarch. " His extreme interest in every trait of character and
his broad humanity lead him constantly to Morals, to the
study of the Beautiful and Good. Hence his love of heroes,
his rule of life, and his clear convictions of the high destiny
of the Soul."

Page 250, note 1. This paragraph is suggestive of much
that is written in " Aristocracy," in *Lectures and Biographical Sketches*.

Page 251, note 1. ·

> So nigh is grandeur to our dust,
> So near is God to man,
> When Duty whispers low, *Thou must,*
> The youth replies, *I can.*
>
> .   .   .   .   .   .
>
> Best befriended of the God
> He who, in evil times,
> Warned by an inward voice,
> Heeds not the darkness and the dread,
> Biding by his rule and choice,
> Feeling only the fiery thread

Leading over heroic ground,
Walled with mortal terror round,
To the aim which him allures,
And the sweet heaven his deed secures.
                    "Voluntaries," *Poems*.

Page 253, note 1. From Shakspeare's *Henry IV.*, Part II., Act II., Scene ii.

Page 253, note 2. In the translation of the Oriental Geography of Ibn (or Ebn) Haukal, by Sir George Ouseley, published in London in 1800, this anecdote may be found with somewhat different wording.

Page 254, note 1. One of the most remarkable instances of Mr. Emerson's applied philosophy is the absence in his journals of complaint of untimely, exacting, and wearisome visitors, towards whose bodies and souls he had to exercise hospitality. Once or twice nature asserts herself by a half-humorous explosion of protest.

The subjects that inspired the poem "The Visit" were probably unaware that they outstayed their welcome.

Page 256, note 1. Another version of this story is told by Plutarch in his "Apothegms of Kings and Great Commanders," in the *Morals*, "When Pætilius and Quintus accused him of many crimes before the people; 'On this very day,' he said, 'I conquered Hannibal and Carthage; I for my part am going with my crown on to the capitol to sacrifice; and let him that pleaseth stay and pass his vote upon me.' Having thus said, he went his way; and the people followed him, leaving his accusers declaiming to themselves."

Page 257, note 1. An allusion to the charm of "the novel, hardly smuggled into the tolerance of father and mother" by the schoolboy, occurs again in "Domestic Life" in the passage which describes the home life of the Emerson brothers in childhood.

Page 258, note 1.

> Because I was content with these poor fields,
> Low, open meads, slender and sluggish streams,
> And found a home in haunts which others scorned,
> The partial wood-gods overpaid my love
> And granted me the freedom of their state.
>
> " Musketaquid," *Poems.*

Page 260, note 1. "Scorn trifles, lift your aims ; do what you are afraid to do : sublimity of character must come from sublimity of motive." These were the teachings which the Emerson boys received in their youth from their brilliant, loving, and eccentric aunt, Miss Mary Moody Emerson. Her nephew has left an account of her in *Lectures and Biographical Sketches.* His words concerning her are carved upon her gravestone in Concord Cemetery : " She gave high counsels. It was the privilege of certain boys to have this immeasurably high standard indicated to their childhood, a blessing which nothing else in education could supply."

Page 262, note 1. The Rev. Elijah P. Lovejoy, a Presbyterian minister of intelligence, courage and blameless character, devoted himself to the cause of awakening public sentiment in the Southern and Border States to the wrong of Slavery and its evil results, and became editor of the St. Louis *Observer.* His press was destroyed by a mob, and he and his family were driven from the city. He then settled in Alton, Illinois, and established his paper, maintaining anti-slavery views. Riots resulted, and three presses, furnished in succession by friends of the cause, were destroyed. Mr. Lovejoy sent for another press. A public meeting of citizens was called because of the excited state of public opinion in the city. Resolutions were passed requiring Lovejoy to retire from the charge of his paper. He stood upon his rights under the Constitution to publish his beliefs freely. To the demand that in deference to mob law he should yield up his post, he said: " This I *never* will do. God in his providence — so say all my brethren, and so I think — has devolved upon me the responsibility of maintaining my ground here; and, Mr. Chairman, I am determined to do it. A voice comes to me from Maine, from Massachusetts, from Connecticut, from New York, from Pennsylvania, — yea, from Kentucky, from Mississippi, from Missouri, calling upon me in the name of all that is dear in heaven or earth to stand fast, and by the help of God *I will stand*. I know I am but one and you are many. My strength will avail but little against you all. You can crush me if you will, but I shall die at my post, for I cannot and will not forsake it." The press arrived and was lodged by his friends in a stone warehouse belonging to one of a gallant little company who undertook to defend the right of free speech. On the night of November 7, 1837, the mob demanded the press. The city authorities gave no protection. Mr. Lovejoy's friends refused to surrender and were attacked. They resisted, and when the building was set on fire, Lovejoy coming out to prevent it was shot dead.

Mr. George P. Bradford, one of Mr. Emerson's nearest friends, described to me the occasion when he delivered this discourse in Boston. Towards the end of the lecture, while carrying his audience — the cultivated people of Boston — with him, in full sympathy with devoted courage in other times and lands, suddenly, looking his hearers in the eyes, he brought before them the instance in their own day and country, and told of the martyrdom of Lovejoy for the right of free speech. Mr. Bradford said that a cold shudder seemed to run through the audience at this calm braving of public opinion twenty years before its ripening in the great war for freedom. Of course Lovejoy had other defenders in Boston, notably Wendell Phillips, who first entered the lists as an anti-slavery champion at the time of his slaying.

Page 262, note 2.

> Freedom's secret wilt thou know ?
> Counsel not with flesh and blood ;
> Loiter not for cloak or food ;
> Right thou feelest such to do.

Page 263, note 1. These lines were evidently quoted from memory from "A Dirge," one of Tennyson's early poems. The burden, "Let them rave," runs through all the verses. The following one comes as near the lines as quoted as any of them : —

> Thou wilt not turn upon thy bed ;
> Chaunteth not the brooding bee
> Sweeter tones than calumny ?
>   Let them rave.
> Thou wilt never raise thine head
> From the green that folds thy grave —
>   Let them rave.

THE OVER-SOUL

This essay was not given as a lecture in the Boston courses. Portions of it came from "Religion" in that on the "Philosophy of History" (1836–37), from "Holiness" in that on "Human Culture" (1837–38); much was taken from the "Doctrine of the Soul," the first lecture in the course on

"Human Life," and a little from " School " in the same course.

Mr. George Willis Cooke in his Life of Emerson speaks of the influence first exerted by German thought in this country about the year 1830, received mainly through Coleridge as a medium, in opposition to the utilitarian views held by English moralists. I quote from his interesting chapter on " The Era of Transcendentalism: " " The new thought was everywhere a reaction against it [the philosophy of Locke and Bentham, and of many English Unitarians]. . . . It declared that man has innate ideas, and a faculty transcending the senses and the understanding. It identified morality and religion, and made intuition their source. Coleridge calls this transcendent faculty Reason, and regarded it as the immediate beholding of supersensual things. He says it cannot be called a faculty, and much less a personal property of the human mind. We do not possess it, but partake of it. It is identical with the Universal Reason, a spark from which enters the human mind. He says there is but one reason, which all intelligent beings share in, and it is identical in them all. This idea became most fruitful in Emerson's mind, the source of his doctrine of the Over-Soul."

It is certain that Mr. Emerson set a high value on Coleridge's teachings, through which he first came in contact with German ideas, but his eager readings of Plato, beginning in college, led him later to Plotinus, Porphyry, Synesius, Proclus, and the other Neo-platonists influenced by Oriental thought. These " great spiritual lords who have walked in the world," " the high priesthood of the pure reason," [1] had given him a broader conception than contemporary preachers entertained of " Him in whom we live and move and have our being."

[1] In the last pages of the essay on "Intellect."

Dr. Holmes, in commenting on "The Over-Soul," says: "It is a curious amusement to trace many of these thoughts and expressions to Plato, or Plotinus, or Proclus, or Porphyry, to Spinoza or Schelling, but the same tune is a different thing according to the instrument on which it is played. There are songs without words, and there are states in which, in place of the trains of thought moving in endless procession with ever-varying figures along the highway of Consciousness, the soul is possessed by a single all-absorbing idea, which, in the highest state of spiritual exaltation, becomes a vision."

The only motto which was prefixed to the essay in the first edition was that from the *Psychozoia, or Life of the Soul,* Canto II., 19, by Henry More, printed in 1620. This verse was included by Mr. Emerson in his collection of poems, *Parnassus,* where he gave it the title "Euthanasia."

Page 267, note 1. Hardly anywhere in his writings has Mr. Emerson stated his belief in the sure triumph of beneficent law more compactly than in this sentence, suggesting that the leaven of conscience would work to the salvation of the race.

Page 268, note 1. This expression recalls the line in which Mr. Emerson took great pleasure in a poem sent to him by Mr. George E. Tufts, of New York : —

Life is a flame whose splendor hides its base.

Page 268, note 2. Again the doctrine of "The Flowing" :

Far seen the river glides below,
Tossing one sparkle to the eyes.
I catch thy meaning, wizard wave ;
The River of my Life replies.

"Peter's Field," *Poems*, Appendix.

Page 270, note 1. Dr. Holmes said that "In the 'Over-

Soul' Emerson attempted the impossible. He is as fully conscious of this fact as the reader of his rhapsody, — nay, he is more profoundly penetrated with it than any of his readers. . . . The 'Over-Soul' might almost be called the Over-*flow* of a spiritual imagination.''

Page 270, note 2. Compare the essay on '' Demonology '' in *Lectures and Biographical Sketches.*

Page 270, note 3. This suggests the expressions of Coleridge as rendered by Mr. Cooke in the note at the beginning of this chapter.

Page 271, note 1. This, as Mr. Emerson says elsewhere, is the weakness of talent as compared with genius.

Page 271, note 2. Found in a list of Spanish proverbs given in one of his early journals.

Page 272, note 1.

> Olympian bards who sung
> Divine ideas below,
> Which always find us young,
> And always keep us so.

Lines from the ''Ode to Beauty,'' *Poems;* used also as motto to '' The Poet,'' in *Essays, Second Series.*

Page 274, note 1. In the first edition this last clause is thus given : '' All else is idle weeds for her wearing.''

Page 275, note 1. The doctrine of Each in All, the ἕν καὶ πᾶν of Xenophanes, and '' the venerable and awful Parmenides,'' is also a familiar thought of Plato.

Page 275, note 2. Through his preaching, and increasingly through his lecturing experiences, Emerson honored his hearers, however humble, by not '' coming down to them,'' but reached them by his assuming their virtue, and speaking to the '' common soul '' in them.

Page 276, note 1. A favorite image with him, drawn from

the Copernican astronomy, which, by considering the system from the central sun, did away with the perturbations apparent in the Ptolemaic system. This is spiritualized in the poem " Uriel."

Page 278, note 1. John Murray Forbes, a great and silent power for good in the State and Country during and after the Civil War, and one of Mr. Emerson's valued friends, used to tell his children : " So *the thing is done*, it is of no consequence who does it."

Page 278, note 2. " We know better than we do," and " We are wiser than we know," recur in Emerson's teachings. The line in " The Problem," —

> He builded better than he knew, —

has passed into a proverb.

Page 278, note 3. In the end of the poem " Worship " this image is rendered in verse.

Page 279, note 1. With this may be compared a paragraph in the essay " Education " in *Lectures and Biographical Sketches.*

Page 281, note 1. Here, as also some three pages earlier in this essay, recurs the favorite image —

> Being's tide
> Swells hitherward, and myriads of forms
> Live, robed with beauty, painted by the sun;
> Their dust, pervaded by the nerves of God,
> Throbs with an overmastering energy
> Knowing and doing.
>
> " Pan," *Poems*, Appendix.

Page 281, note 2. He quotes Bacon elsewhere as saying, " Nature is commanded by obeying her."

Page 282, note 1.

> Blasted with excess of light.
>
> Gray, *Progress of Poesy.*

Page 282, note 2. It was Emerson's custom to answer the crude inquiries on great subjects of his young visitors courteously, not directly, but in a way to show the great proportions of the subject, and set them really thinking. "The gods like indirect names and dislike to be named directly."

Page 283, note 1. This is like a passage in "Demonology," in *Lectures and Biographical Sketches.*

Page 284, note 1. Believing in the indestructibility of spirit and of matter, and regarding the latter as a method of instruction, he never disquieted himself, but, assured that he and all men shared in the universal existence, did not care to peep beyond the curtain. He said, "I am. .The whole fact is here or nowhere."

Page 285, note 1. The Spirit lodged in man has spurred him to seeking light, and works out the answer in his life.

> They reckon ill who leave me out;
> When me they fly, I am the wings;
> I am the doubter and the doubt,
> And I the hymn the Brahmin sings.
>
> "Brahma," *Poems.*

Page 286, note 1.

> Thou art the unanswered question.
>
> "The Sphinx," *Poems.*

God enters by a private door into every individual. — "Intellect," *Essays, Second Series.*

Page 286, note 2. In his first letter to John Sterling Emerson said, speaking of Sterling's paper on Carlyle, "In it I admired the rare behavior, with far less heed the things said ; these were opinions, but the tone was the man.''

Page 288, note 1. Journal, 1851. '' There is something — our brothers over the sea do not know it or own it ; Scott, Southey, Hallam, and Dickens would deny and blaspheme it — which is setting them all aside, and the whole world also, and planting itself forever and ever.''

Page 289, note 1.

> Himself from God he could not free.
>
> '' The Problem,'' *Poems.*

Page 289, note 2. This image is used in some lines on the transient character of grief, printed among the '' Fragments on Life '' in the Appendix to the *Poems.*

Page 292, note 1. Emerson believed that in saying '' I and the Father are one '' Jesus meant to teach that all men could become channels of deity, instancing himself.

Page 292, note 2. Dr. Holmes spoke of him as '' an iconoclast without a hammer, who took down our idols from their pedestals so tenderly that it seemed like an act of worship.'' In quoting this passage, Mr. Cabot adds : '' That is well said. But I am not sure that he took them down, or ever thought it worth while that they should come down so long as they were really objects of worship. What he wished to disturb was formalism, . . . the gazing after past revelations until we are blind to the present.''

Page 293, note 1. This thought is found in the second motto of '' Compensation,'' '' And all that Nature made thine own,'' etc.

Page 293, note 2. This sentence was first an entry made by Mr. Emerson in his Journal on the eve of going to deliver his Divinity School Address in 1838. The sentence and the

entire paragraph were a portion of a sermon preached, probably in the following winter, in East Lexington. Mrs. Emerson cared so much for this passage that she gave it to her
children to read while they were very young.

Page 297, note 1.

> No ray is dimmed, no atom worn,
> My oldest force is good as new,
> And the fresh rose on yonder thorn
> Gives back the bending heavens in dew.
>
>   "Song of Nature," *Poems.*

CIRCLES

No part of this essay appears to have been taken from earlier papers, and no lecture of that name is recorded. On the
12th of September, 1840, in a letter to Miss Elizabeth Hoar,
Mr. Emerson wrote : "My chapter on 'Circles' begins to
prosper, and when it is October I shall write like a Latin
Father."

His friend, William Ellery Channing, thus spoke of the range
of Emerson's mind : —

> The circles of thy thought shine vast as stars,
> No glass shall round them,
> No plummet sound them,
> They hem the observer like bright steel wrought bars,
> And limpid as the sun,
> Or as bright waters run
> From the cold fountain of the Alpine springs,
> Or diamonds richly set in the king's rings.

Dr. Richard Garnett [1] writes: "The object of this fine essay

[1] *Life of Ralph Waldo Emerson*, by Richard Garnett, LL. D., London,
Walter Scott, 1888.

II

quaintly entitled 'Circles' is to reconcile this rigidity of unalterable law with the fact of human progress. Compensation illustrates one property of a circle, which always returns to the point where it began, but it is no less true that around every circle another can be drawn. . . . Hence there is no security but in infinite progress. . . . Emerson followed his own counsel ; he always keeps a reserve of power. His theory of 'Circles' reappears without the least verbal indebtedness to himself in the splendid essay on 'Love.'"

The poem " Uriel " should be read in connection with this essay.

Page 301, note 1.

> Line in Nature is not found,
> Unit and Universe are round.
>
> " Uriel," *Poems.*

Page 301, note 2.

> Another morn has risen on mid-noon.
>
> Milton, *Paradise Lost*, V., 310.

The last clause in the sentence suggests one by Mr. Emerson's neighbor poet, William Ellery Channing, in " The Poet's Hope," —

> If my bark sinks, 't is to another sea.

Page 302, note 1. The old doctrine of Heracleitus again, brought to the modern use of progress by evolution. The prophecies of 1841 made in the later portion of this paragraph have been strangely fulfilled in sixty years.

Page 303, note 1.

> Giddy with motion, Nature reels,
> Sun, moon, man, undulate and stream,
> The mountains flow, the solids seem,

Change acts, reacts ; back, forward hurled,
And pause were palsy to the world.
"The Poet," *Poems*, Appendix.

Page 304, note 1. "Throw a stone into the stream, and the circles that propagate themselves are the beautiful type of all influence." — *Nature*, chapter iv.

The ripples in rhymes the oar forsake.
"Woodnotes," II., *Poems*.

Page 304, note 2. It was a curious superstition in the Middle Ages that evil spirits could not get out of a circle drawn around them. Some American Indians leave a slight break in the colored circles that decorate their baskets for the Devil to get out.

Page 307, note 1.

Unless above himself he can
Erect himself, how poor a thing is man.
Samuel Daniels "To the Countess of Cumberland." (Quoted in "Civilization," *Society and Solitude*.)

Page 307, note 2. The ideas expressed in this paragraph may also be found in the *Poems*.

Have I a lover
Who is noble and free ? —
I would he were nobler
Than to love me.
"The Sphinx," *Poems*.

Heartily know,
When half-gods go
The gods arrive."
"Give All to Love," *Poems*.

See also "The Park."

Page 308, note 1. It was Mr. Emerson's own habit in his lectures, after presenting strongly one side of his theme, suddenly to show the other aspect of it, almost ignored before. This might be done in another lecture of the course, but often in the same one.

> In vain produced, all rays return.
> Evil will bless, and ice will burn.
>
> " Uriel," *Poems.*

Page 311, note 1. In "The Poet," I. (Appendix), and in "Woodnotes," II., in the passage beginning, "Hearken once more," he tells of the instability of apparent permanencies.

Page 312, note 1. The necessary alternation from books to nature, from society to solitude, was always urged by Mr. Emerson, the latter in each case ranking the former. See the passage in "The American Scholar" beginning "Undoubtedly there is a right way of reading, so it be sternly subordinated."

> See thou bring not to field or stone
> The fancies found in books ;
> Leave authors' eyes, and fetch your own,
> To brave the landscape's looks.
>
> "Waldeinsamkeit," *Poems.*

Page 313, note 1. The need of direct relation of the soul with God is dwelt upon at length in the latter part of the "Address to the Senior Class of the Divinity School" in *Nature, Addresses, and Lectures:* "Let me admonish you, first of all, to go alone . . . and dare to love God without mediator or veil," etc.

Page 314, note 1. The welcome idea of the symbolism of Nature he received first from Plato, and it was this which gave him pleasure in Swedenborg's teachings. "The noblest ministry of Nature is to stand as an apparition of God." — *Nature*, chapter vii.

Page 314, note 2. Compare the second motto of "Compensation" in this volume.

Page 317, note 1. From Young's *Night Thoughts*.

Page 317, note 2. Pyrrho of Elis (360–270 B. C.) taught that truth was unattainable, and that men should be indifferent to all external circumstances.

Page 318, note 1. This consoling idea of Good out of Evil is taught in the motto for "Spiritual Laws" in this volume and in "Uriel" in the *Poems*.

> The balance-beam of Fate was bent,
> The bounds of good and ill were rent,
> Strong Hades could not keep his own,
> But all slid to confusion.

Page 318, note 2. Dr. Holmes, referring to this paragraph, says : "But Emerson states his own position so frankly in his essay entitled 'Circles,' that the reader cannot take issue with him as against utterances which he will not defend."

Page 319, note 1. His poem "Terminus" shows how Emerson met advancing old age.

INTELLECT

This lecture was not given in any of the Boston courses. Passages of no great length were taken from the lectures on "Literature" in the course on "The Philosophy of History" (1836–37), and from "The Doctrine of the Soul" and "Genius" in that on "Human Life" (1838–39).

Mr. Emerson never took any pleasure in systems of metaphysics. He even once said in a lecture, "Who has not looked into a metaphysical book? And what sensible man ever looked twice?" "Yet," as Mr. Cabot says in his Memoir, "the repulsiveness lay not in the subject, but in the way in which it is treated." He wished to "state the laws and powers of the mind as simply and as attractively as the physical laws are stated by Owen and Faraday." He welcomed all the scientific discoveries of his day for their symbolic value, assured that the same laws ruled mind and matter. Hence for years he planned a work on the Natural History of Intellect. He gave three lectures on that subject in England in 1848, and later others in America, especially two courses at Harvard College. But he was prevented by failing strength from completing the work he designed. After his death Mr. Cabot collected what matter was available from the manuscripts, and this gives the title to the volume *Natural History of Intellect*.

The motto of this chapter appears in one of Mr. Emerson's note-books as the third verse of a short poem which is included in the Appendix to the *Poems*, among the "Fragments on the Poet." The introductory verses run thus : —

> Pale genius roves alone,
> 　No scout can track his way,
> None credits him till he have shown
> 　His diamonds to the day.
>
> Not his the feaster's wine,
> 　Nor land, nor gold, nor power,
> By want and pain God screeneth him
> 　Till his elected hour.

Page 325, note 1. Mr. Emerson at the age of nineteen was associated with his brother William, who taught a private school for young ladies in Boston. In this capacity he taught chemistry from some elementary text-book, possibly showing a few of the simpler experiments. Later he heard with great interest of the discoveries in that science from his wife's brother, Dr. Charles T. Jackson, an accomplished chemist and geologist. Each new fact he viewed as a symbol awaiting interpretation.

Page 327, note 1. Journal, "Of the most romantic fact the memory is more romantic."

Page 327, note 2. "Thoughts come into our minds by avenues which we never left open."

Page 328, note 1. In the early part of "Natural History of Intellect" in the volume thus named, Intellect is considered "as an ethereal sea, which ebbs and flows, which surges and washes hither and thither, carrying its whole virtue into every creek and inlet which it bathes. To this sea every human house has a water front. But this force, creating nature, visiting whom it will and withdrawing from whom it will, making day where it comes and leaving night when it departs, is no fee or property of man or angel. It is as the light, public and entire to each, and on the same terms."

Page 329, note 1. Mr. Emerson himself strove to render the thought that came to him truly, not to "meddle ambitiously" and spoil it by "what we miscall Art," as he said in his letter to Sterling.[1] He brought kindred thoughts together, but purposely did not elaborate the argument, and left to the reader the pleasure of letting the electric spark pass and show the connection.

[1] Letters of Emerson and Sterling, No. IV.

Page 332, note 1. "It is a little seed," found in the first edition, is here omitted.

Page 333, note 1. "Day creeps after day, each full of facts, dull, strange despised things. . . . And presently the aroused intellect finds gold and gems in one of these scorned facts, — then finds that a day of facts is a rock of diamonds ; that a fact is an Epiphany of God." — "Education," *Lectures and Biographical Sketches.*

Page 335, note 1. The seeming contradiction by this sentence of what has gone before, as to the reception rather than the originating of ideas, is done away with by the author's strictly classic use of the word *produce,* — to *bring forward* the ideas received, joined perhaps with others that shed light on them.

Page 336, note 1.

> Unless to thought be added will,
> Apollo is an imbecile.
> > Lines from one of the Note-books.

Page 339, note 1. "Excess of individualism, when it is not corrected or subordinated to the Supreme Reason, makes that vice which we stigmatize as monotones, . . . or, as the French say, *enfant perdu d'une conviction isolée,* which give such a comic tinge to all society." — *Natural History of Intellect.*

Page 340, note 1.

> For thought, and not praise,
> Thought is the wages
> For which I sell days,
> Will gladly sell ages,
> And willing grow old,
> Deaf and dumb and blind and cold,

> Melting matter into dreams,
> Panoramas which I saw,
> And whatever glows or seems
> Into substance, into law.
>   " Fragments on the Poet," *Poems*, Appendix.

Page 341, note 1. The duties and sacrifice required of the scholar are dwelt on in " The American Scholar " in *Nature, Addresses, and Lectures,* and in " The Man of Letters " and " The Scholar " in *Lectures and Biographical Sketches.*

Page 343, note 1. The Egyptian god Horus is represented with his finger on his lips.

Page 344, note 1. His counsel was always to " read a little proudly," and in life he urged that one should not mistake others' chivalries for one's own.

Page 345, note 1. A name given to a group of philosophers, mostly Neo-platonists, from the mythical Hermes Trismegistus (thrice great), a Greek name for the Egyptian god Thoth, to whom many of these writings were ascribed.

Page 346, note 1. This saying is quoted from Plotinus. It is evident from his mention of these masters of ancient thought and his markings on the fly-leaves of their books, that, following his custom, he rapidly found such things as were for him, and turning their abstruse pages " read for lustres." It was evidently the lofty tone that pleased him, and certain quotations and " Chaldean Oracles."

Mr. George Willis Cooke in his book on Emerson, chapter xix., gives an interesting brief abstract of the doctrines of the Neo-platonists.

ART

In the course on the " Philosophy of History " given in Boston in 1836–37, the third lecture was on " Art," following " The Humanity of Science," and preceding " Literature." Much from this lecture appears in this essay, but some pages come from " Eye and Ear," in the next year's course.

In Mr. Emerson's youth there were almost no works of art, except portraits, to be seen in New England. At a sad epoch of his life he landed in Italy and spent a few weeks there. He saw the statues in the museums of Naples and Rome. Looking for greatness of character through works of art, endowed with a good sense of form and fitness, but little for color, and none for technique, he evidently took great and lasting pleasure in the works of Michelangelo and Raphael in the Vatican. The temperance, simplicity and perfect taste of Greek art always charmed him. He saw the Elgin Marbles in London.

After his return he saw the paintings of Allston, enjoyed the drawings of Flaxman, and a friend, a connoisseur in art, lent him his collection of engravings and drawings, in which Mr. Emerson took great pleasure.[1] Among the artists he had few friends, but he read works on art, especially valuing them for the glimpses they gave of the artist at work, and his sayings.

Dr. Holmes, while praising the clothing by Emerson of the common aspects of life with the colors of his imagination, feels that the danger line was crossed when, in the motto to " Art," he would have us give even to

> Barrows, trays and pans
> Grace and glimmer of romance.

Yet he could do so, and see even planetary motion in a school-

[1] See *Letters of Emerson to a Friend.* Houghton, Mifflin & Co., 1899.

boy's play. Journal. " I saw a boy on the Concord Common pick up an old bruised tin milk pan that was rusting by the roadside, and, poising it on the top of a stick, . . . made it describe the most elegant imaginable curves."

Page 351, note 1. Thomas Couture, in his admirable little book, *Méthode et Entretiens d'Atelier,* speaks thus of the portrait painter's duty of giving the best that can be seen in his sitter : " Faites faire à toutes vos formes, à toutes vos lignes, un travail ascensionnel vers ce que constitue la beauté, tout en restent cependant dans les limites du vrai, et vous obtiendrez un portrait ressemblant qui, à l'étonnement de tous, excepté pourtant celui que vous aurez représenté, semblera beaucoup moins laid que le modèle."

Page 352, note 1. " The universal soul is the alone creator of the useful and the beautiful ; therefore to make anything useful or beautiful the individual must be submitted to the universal mind." — " Art," *Society and Solitude.*

Page 353, note 1. These thoughts are expressed in his poem " The Problem " and in the essay on " History " in this volume.

" Every genuine work of art has as much reason for being as earth and sun." — " Art," *Society and Solitude.*

Page 355, note 1. Selection, " the first office of art," and then what Ruskin calls " Principality," — the concentration of interest, or focussing in a picture, — are dwelt upon in this paragraph, and the old doctrine of the Macrocosm shown in the Microcosm.

Page 356, note 1. As stated by the squirrel to the mountain, in an early poem of Emerson's, —

> Talents differ,
> All is well and wisely put ;

If I cannot carry forests on my back,
Neither can you crack a nut.

Page 357, note 1.   Mr. Emerson found, and said of himself, that, though he did not have a musical ear, he had
" musical eyes."   In the physical and metaphysical sense
his eyes were opened.   Like his Seyd, —

Beauty chased he everywhere, —
and he found what he looked for.

Page 358, note 1.   Mr. Emerson knew well the truth
which the French artist insisted on to his pupils : " It is not
true that one knows what one sees.   One sees what one
knows."

This paragraph was taken from the lecture " Eye and
Ear " in the course on " Human Culture."

Page 359, note 1.   An instance of his happy use of his
classical studies in the choice of this best yet unusual word.

Page 361, note 1.

Coelum non animum mutant
Qui trans mare currunt.

Horace.

Page 361, note 2.   See *Hamlet*, Act I., Scene v.

Page 362, note 1.   In the " Fragments on the Poet," in
the *Poems*, he tells of a random word, overheard from the
Muse, —

I travelled and found it at Rome ;
Eastward it filled all Heathendom,
And it lay on my hearth when I came home.

Page 362, note 2.   " Newton did not exercise more
ingenuity, but less than another to see the world."

" Art," *Society and Solitude.*

Page 363, note 1. His application of the evolution doctrines of Hunter and Lamarck appears in the words *tendency* and *effort*.

Page 362, note 2. With " the negative," the dismal, or sceptical in painting or in writing he had no sympathy.

Page 364, note 1. This paragraph seems a strong instance of that quality of Mr. Emerson of stating aspects without qualification, against which he warns his readers in " Circles " : " When I obey my whims, let me remind the reader that I am only an experimenter. Do not set the least value on what I do, or the least discredit on what I do not, as if I pretended to settle any thing as true or false. . . . I simply experiment, an endless seeker, with no Past at my back." He valued painting, and sculpture more, and the motto, written long after the essay itself, shows his feeling of the necessity and blessing of art.

Page 367, note 1. The low state of art in his day and country should be remembered.

Page 369, note 1. Emerson's far sight and faith went beyond the materialism of his age and country, regarding these as a necessary stage in evolution.

The Riverside Press
Electrotyped and printed by H. O. Houghton & Co
Cambridge, Mass., U. S. A.

www.ingramcontent.com/pod-product-compliance
Lightning Source LLC
LaVergne TN
LVHW012207040326
832903LV00003B/176